D0624973

to a Better Horse

Jaki Bell

A DAVID & CHARLES BOOK

David & Charles is an F+W Publications Inc. company
4700 East Galbraith Road
Cincinnati, OH 45236

First published in the UK in 2006

A catalogue record for this book is available from the British Library.

ISBN-13: 978-0-7153-2371-7 hardback
ISBN-10: 0-7153-2371-7 hardback

Printed in Singapore by KHL
for David & Charles
Brunel House Newton Abbot Devon

Commissioning Editor Jane Trollope
Editor Jennifer Proverbs
Head of Design Prudence Rogers
Designer Jodie Lystor
Production Controller Beverley Richardson

Visit our website at www.davidandcharles.co.uk

David & Charles books are available from all good bookshops; alternatively you can contact our Orderline on 0870 9908222 or write to us at FREEPOST EX2 110, D&C Direct, Newton Abbot, TQ12 4ZZ (no stamp required UK only); US customers call 800-289-0963 and Canadian customers call 800-840-5220.

I've only got 30 minutes to spare!

How often have you said or heard that? However half an hour put to good use is as valuable as half a day spent drifting around the yard or an hour's aimless schooling.

And that's where this book comes in. It's packed full of 30-minute projects that can either be used on those occasions when your time is at a premium or be put together to ensure that you make the most of every minute you have with your horse.

Whether you own or loan, your goal, like that of every equestrian, is to build up the best possible relationship with your horse. This comes with time, but the good news is that the necessary time can be built up efficiently in well-planned 30-minute sessions.

Do you have schooling problems? Want to start jumping? Have issues with the handling of your horse? Breaking down any aspect of horsemanship into small achievable goals or targets makes the big picture – your ambitions – seem closer.

Is it possible to get a horse ready for competition, do a clip or beat your 'bogey' fences in 30 minutes? This book shows you how to tackle each of these challenges, and is packed full of tips that you're sure to find useful.

We all want to spend as much time as we can with our horses, but so often everyday life, whether it's work, the weather, partners, family or an accumulation of all these, has to come first. 30 Minutes a Day to a Better Horse *shows you how you can use even the smallest amount of time with your horse so you never have to say, 'I've only got 30 minutes' again.*

Jaki Bell

Contents

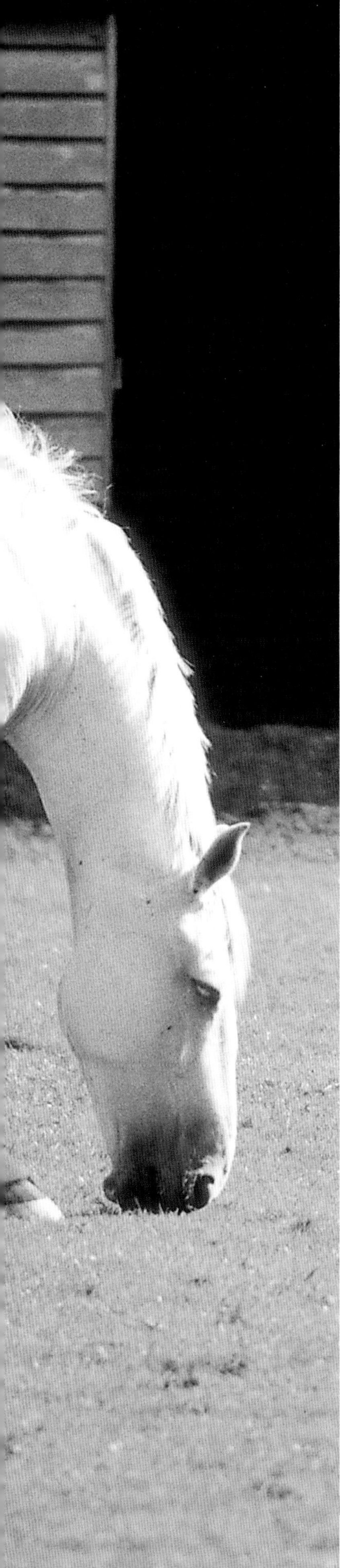

1 30 MINUTES TO A HEALTHIER HORSE

- *30 minutes checking your horse's home*
- *30 minutes analysing your horse's diet*
- *30 minutes to make a weekly health check*
- *30 minutes to give your horse a massage*

Whether you own your horse, have him on loan, share him with someone else, or ride regularly at a yard or school, it is important to be aware of the many things that make up the horse's lifestyle.

Just the slightest imbalance in the way he is cared for can cause all sorts of problems. For example, a horse kept in a stable from which he cannot see anything to keep him interested, let alone other horses, is likely to develop stable vices. By taking just 30 minutes to look around where your horse is kept, you can spot the weak areas and address any problems, hopefully before they begin to affect him either mentally or physically, or both.

Eating is the most important thing to any horse, whether he is used for recreational riding or for top competition. The subject of feed is a complex one, and an area that many riders are not interested in – until it affects the horse they are riding. There are several ways you can spend 30 minutes arming yourself with the knowledge needed to keep an eye on your horse's diet.

If you handle a horse regularly, you'll be the person who knows all his little idiosyncracies, and can spot when he's under the weather. Take 30 minutes out once a week to really get to know your horse's body so it's more than instinctive when you say something's wrong.

Have you ever had a massage? If so, you'll know how relaxed and well it made you feel. Horses are no different – in fact they're really tactile animals and appreciate time spent on the little details such as grooming or a 30-minute massage. Go on, spoil your horse!

30 minutes Checking Your Horse's Home

If you are responsible for the welfare of a horse, you are responsible for ensuring that all the parts of the jigsaw puzzle that combine to create a happy environment for him fit into place. Getting this right depends on you doing your homework, and then on a great deal of observation – horses are individuals, and what suits one may not be right for his neighbour. A good carer will subconsciously run regular checks on the various aspects of a horse's environment; a conscious review should be made at least every six months. It is amazing how small changes can creep into your day-to-day situation, become the norm, and upset a certain balance of things almost without your noticing.

What makes a healthy environment for your horse?

There are two sides to horse management:
• attention to the details that are important for your horse and his care; and
• attention to the details that optimize your time and safety.
Whilst caring for horses is our prime concern, a happy rider contributes towards a happy horse.

The things that are most important to your horse are safety, regular food, turn-out (because this represents freedom), companionship and routine. You will have read many times that a horse is a herd and flight animal, used to roaming rather than resting in one place, and eating almost constantly. The lifestyle that we impose on our horses, whilst dealing with issues such as where the next feed will come from and protection from natural predators contravenes many of these basic instincts, and so it is up to us to make it as suitable for him as possible. And once again, remember that all horses are individuals and it is the responsibility of the carer to recognize and institute a routine that is right for his or her horse.

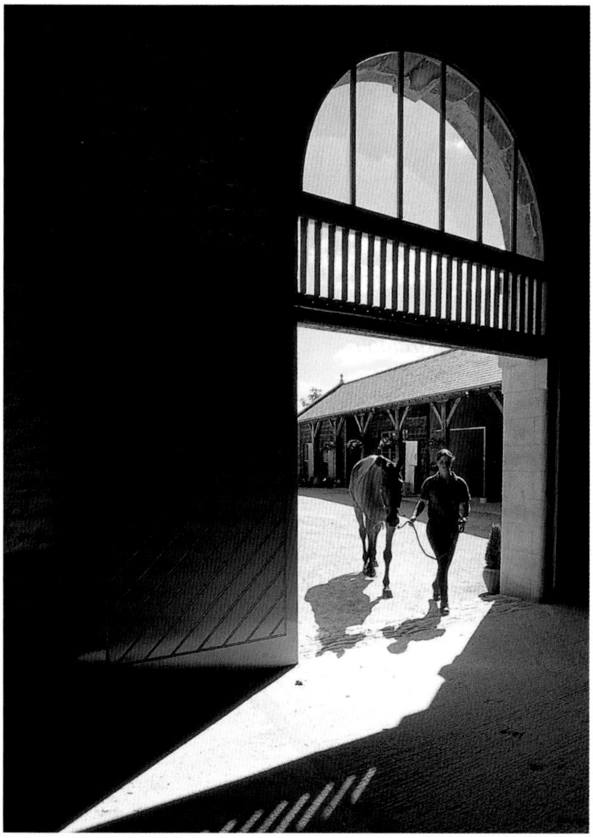

The yard

On the yard, your horse will need kind but firm handling: this is where bad habits are often creep in. For his and your own safety, he must respect your presence and do as asked (see Take 30 minutes to tackle your handling problems, page 60). Horses take security from knowing what is expected of them and when, so a regular routine for turning out, feeding and exercise is preferable. His safety and security, and that of your possessions, is important to both of you. Injuries and tack are expensive, and the loss of a horse either from theft or of injury is heart-breaking.

The stable

Within his stable or turn-out area, the horse should be comfortable – warm in the winter, cool in the summer, and dry. Wet or dirty beds bring trouble such as thrush and infections, especially if he has a cut or injury that is not spotted immediately. There should also be adequate ventilation and appropriate bedding to avoid illnesses such as RAO (recurrent airway obstruction). How much is he able to see when in his stable? Horses are inquisitive animals, even if nervous, and likely to become bored if stabled overlong. There is now a wide variety of stable toys available, but for the horse, nothing can replace being able to see his neighbours and yard activity. Once again, your horse's personality will be a deciding factor here, as some horses will prefer a slightly quieter corner of the yard and may become agitated by lots of activity. Watch out also for bullying, as this is possible between stables. A bored, stabled horse also invariably develops stable vices such as bed-walking, wind-sucking and weaving.

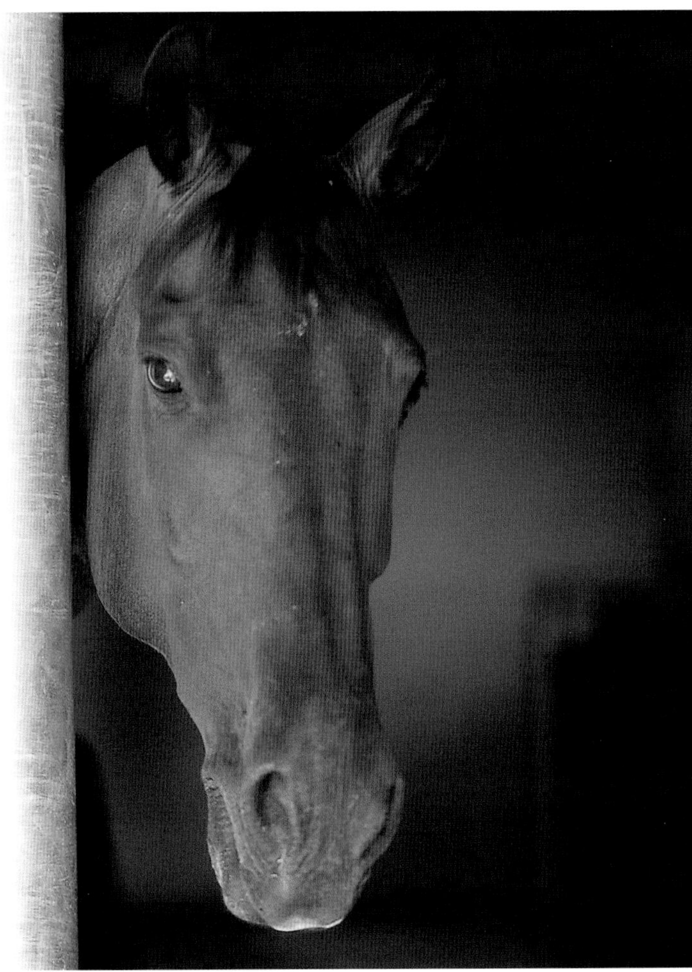

Feeding

If you are responsible for your horse's feed it is absolutely essential that you understand about the horse's nutritional requirements (see page 12). If your horse is at livery, the responsibility for regular feeding is with the yard manager, and you need to have confidence in his or her knowledge. Nevertheless, it is still important that you understand feed and the effect that it has on your horse's performance.

Turn-out

Horses need companionship, and regular turn-out is important to provide this. Your horse will find his place in the herd pecking order and establish natural relationships with his companions. Your paddocks are also an additional source of food, and the quality of the grazing is therefore important. Poisonous plants, including ragwort, and droppings must be removed regularly as they will damage this quality.

Likewise any paddock or turn-out area must be well fenced and secure. If your horse strays out on to the road and causes an accident, apart from the potential for him to be injured, you will be responsible. Post-and-rail

⇧ *Horses like to watch what is going on in the yard from the security and comfort of their stables.*

⇩ *Wire netting has the potential to trap a hoof and may therefore prove hazardous.*

fencing or natural hedges are preferable; barbed wire should be avoided as it is dangerous. Electric fences are a practical way of dealing with large areas economically, standing in as temporary fencing and sectioning off potential hazards such as ditches and farm machinery. Horses fast become aware of the effects of an electric fence, either by learning from the herd or from personal experience. It is therefore important that the voltage is regulated in accordance with the manufacturer's instructions.

Fitness

By imposing our requirements on the horse's lifestyle in terms of stabling and routine we affect his ability to keep fit naturally. It is therefore important that horses are worked regularly. Historically it is recommended that a horse is ridden or exercised six days a week, with one day off and in general for about one hour according to what he is doing (for example, 30 minutes is more than enough if you are lungeing). However, the quality of this work must be considered, as 10 minutes of effective and positive schooling will be far more useful and beneficial than one hour of monotonous exercise, which could even be harmful.

Your horse will appreciate a regular work schedule, for example, at a particular time of day – though quite often that is not possible; but not being able to arrive at the yard at a particular time should never be used as an excuse not to work your horse.

Your horse will also appreciate variety and challenge in his exercise programme. And don't forget to reward him with a pat or a kind word when he does as you ask.

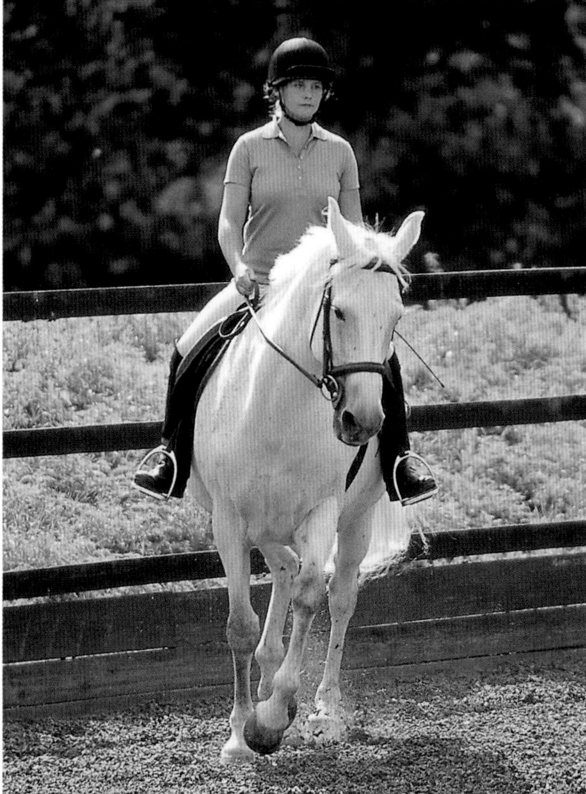

Tack and equipment

The number and type of rugs that your horse needs relates to his turn-out routine, the quality of the stabling used, what breed he is, and whether or not he is clipped. However, we all love to buy rugs and blankets! Today it is common for a horse to have lightweight, medium-weight and heavyweight stable and turn-out rugs.

⇧ *Proper storage for rugs and other equipment will help prolong its good condition.*

As his carer, it is up to you to ensure that your horse is warm and dry, and how you achieve this depends on your personal finances and preferences. Many yards still use old duvets or blankets beneath a top rug, secured with a surcingle, for example. As the weather changes, check on the condition of the rugs you have been using. Do they need cleaning or repair? Try to have this done before you put them away: it's amazing how quickly the winter season comes round again.

It cannot be said often enough that your horse must have a well fitting saddle and bridle. It is preferable for these to be fitted by a professional saddler. Try to keep tack to the minimum necessary: it is very easy to succumb to the temptation of buying all the latest gadgets, but always ask yourself first whether your horse really needs them.

Keeping your tack clean (see 30 Minutes for a Top Tack Clean, page 38) will prolong its life and enhance both your safety and your horse's comfort. Ensure that it is stored in an orderly and secure fashion.

⇦ *Vary your horse's training routine as much as possible, incorporating schooling, hacking, lungeing and competing, for example.*

30-minute checklist

The yard

- Is the atmosphere generally friendly? Do the horses appear happy and contented?
- Is it clean?
- Are the drains clear and do the taps work?
- Are the fire precautions adequate?
- Is there a list of important telephone numbers somewhere visible?
- Take a look at the muck heap. Is it practical and well positioned?
- What security arrangements exist?

The stable

- Are the door fittings working properly?
- Are there any hazards such as nails or splintered timbers protruding anywhere?
- Is the electrical wiring horse- and rodent-proof, and intact?
- Do you have rubber mats? Lift the edge of one: do they need removing and cleaning?
- Is your horse's bed dry? Put your hand into his bed beneath the banks at the point where the wall and the floor meet.
- Are you using the most suitable bedding for your horse, his health and lifestyle?
- How efficient is the ventilation?
- If you have automatic water troughs, are they clean and working properly?
- If you have a fixed manger, is it secure? Is it clean?

Feeding

- Is the feedroom clean?
- Is old feed left lying around?
- Could the storage be improved?

Turn-out

- Are your paddocks properly managed?
- What type of fencing is used? Is it regularly checked and repaired?
- Does your horse spend enough time in the field?
- Are the fields free of ragwort and poisonous plants?
- Do the horses have any shelter, either natural or man-made?

Fitness

- Do you get to ride your horse often enough?
- Is your routine consistent? Does it suit him? Are you happy with the way he is working?
- Could you benefit from some lessons?
- If you compete, have you managed to get out as much as you'd hoped to this season?
- Are there any other disciplines, training methods or schools of thought that you've wanted to investigate and not managed to get round to?
- Is your horse getting enough interaction with other horses?
- If you have a school, is the surface in good condition?
- Do you have jumps? Are they in a good state of repair?

ROUTINE HEALTHCARE

There are various routine aspects of healthcare that are essential to your horse's well-being:

- **SHOEING**
- **WORMING**
- **VACCINATIONS**
- **DENTIST**
- **SADDLE CHECKS**

These may be your responsibility or that of the yard manager. Whatever the case, keep a note of when your horse was last wormed, shod, vaccinated and saw the dentist and saddler, and put a reminder to arrange the next appointment in your diary or somewhere where you will not be able to miss it.

⇩ *Your horse should see the equine dentist every six months if possible.*

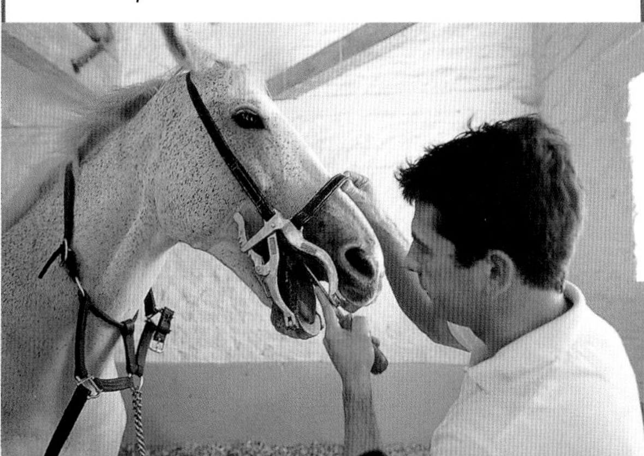

Tack and equipment

- Does your tack still fit your horse? When did you last have a saddle check?
- Is it clean and in good repair?
- Do you have any tack you could swop/sell/ that needs cleaning and storing?
- Is tack stored in an ordered manner? Do you have your own area? Do others regularly borrow your belongings? Would it be advisable to invest in a couple of containers in which to keep your tack?
- Is the tack room dry and secure?
- Are the rugs adequate and do they meet your needs?
- Do the rugs need cleaning or repairing? Can you do this yourself, or do you need to have them done professionally?

30-minute projects to improve your horse's home

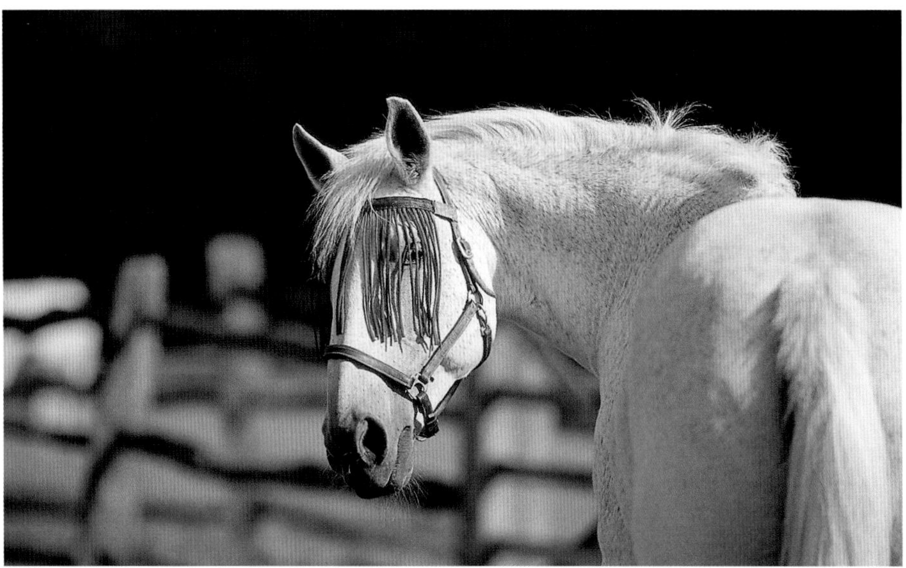

Next time you turn your horse out, spend half an hour watching him with his companions.

Watch your horse in the field with his companions for 30 minutes

Turn-out and interaction with other horses play an important role in the life of a horse. Whilst most horses would prefer to spend their days in the field in as natural an environment as possible, there are some that are just not suited for such a lifestyle, whether for psychological, practical or health reasons. It is important to know what is right for your horse and to be aware if his needs change. Is your horse a social horse, for instance? Does he have particular companions in the field, or is he a bit of a loner? Does he like to graze, play or even torment the others? Or do other horses bully him? A great deal can be learnt about your horse's character from observing him in this natural state.

The 30-minute feedroom clean-up

If you are on DIY or if you keep your horse at home, you will be responsible for your feed area. Take 30 minutes to give it a thorough clean:

- Remove all removable containers. Throw out any that contain food or supplements that are out of date and/or no longer in use.
- Have a good tidy up of anything else lying around in the feedroom. Remove anything that should not be there, and find it a proper home.
- Starting from the ceiling, sweep down the walls and the floor.
- Wash out any containers or feed buckets that are not in use. Wash out all your scoops and measures.
- Is your feed easily accessible and conveniently to hand when you are making up your feeds? Is there anything you can do to improve this? Would shelves, hooks or cupboards help?
- Do you have a noticeboard listing what your horse is being fed, and is it up to date?
- How soon are you going to need to re-order your feed? Can you afford to store feed, in both space and financial terms?

Spend 30 minutes planning your equestrian calendar

Do you find yourself never quite managing to fit in all your equestrian plans? If so, sit down and make a list of what you'd really like to do. Do you want to fit in more lessons? Compete regularly? Visit more equestrian events? Just see your horse more often?

Take 30 minutes to work out what it is you want to do, how often it is possible, and how you can make

Make time to plan your equestrian year, and you may find more time to spend with your horse.

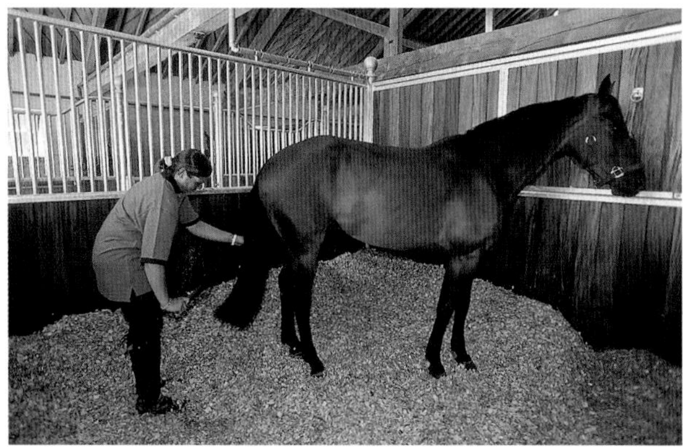

it happen. It may be that a bit of lateral thinking is necessary: perhaps you don't need to be quite so hard on yourself in your expectations or do something quite as regularly as has been suggested; or perhaps you can work something out with the help of others. If you make time to review what your aim is and investigate how it might be possible, then if you really want it to happen you'll probably find a way.

30 minutes to a cleaner stable

When did you last clean out your horse's stable? Ideally you should strip back the bedding and wash the floors at least quarterly, however that would take more than 30 minutes just to dry; but in half an hour you could:

- throw up the horse's bed and give the floor a thorough sweep;
- lift any mats and sweep beneath them;
- shake out and tidy up any rugs you keep in the stable;
- dust away all the cobwebs;
- wash out the manger and water buckets or trough;
- clean up all those awkward corners where bedding gets trapped;
- check the stable for loose kickboards, protruding nails, or anything else that could cause an injury.

Your stable should have a good clean-out at least quarterly.

Check the fencing around your horse's paddock.

The 30-minute paddock check

Make the following checks on the field that your horse is turned out in:

- Make sure that the fencing is secure and safe.
- Have a look round for anything that shouldn't really be there, such as empty cans, items of old farming equipment, rabbit holes, and remove them or fill them in.
- Pull up or destroy any poisonous plants, such as ragwort.
- Check that the water supply is working.
- Arrange to fence off or make safe any potholes or ditches that may have appeared.
- Test the gate to ensure that bolts and hinges are secure and working.

Take 30 minutes to make sure your trailer is safe

- Check the tyre pressures on your car and trailer using a pressure gauge. Your manual should tell you the correct pressure for towing a full load.
- On your trailer tyres, look for sidewall cracks, bulges and cuts, which are all indications of wear and damage.
- When you hitch up, check that the lights and indicators are working.
- Grease the towball and check it for wear.
- Check the ramps for damage and rot.
- Lift up the rubber matting and inspect the floors. If possible, also check floors from below. Prod suspect areas with a screwdriver.

Still short of ideas? Then spend 30 minutes:

- sorting out your rugs and organizing repairs;
- picking up droppings from your paddocks;
- pulling up ragwort;
- clearing weeds from the school;
- learning about poisonous plants;
- talking to the local fire prevention officer about safety.

30 minutes

Analysing Your Horse's Diet

When did you last review what you are feeding your horse? For many horse owners and carers, feed is one of the least interesting aspects of horse care, and we fall into the trap of just going along with what everyone else on the yard is feeding or feeding the horse exactly what he was being fed when we first bought him. Now, if your horse is in good condition, performing well and looking tip top, there's absolutely no reason to change that. However, it should be a periodic exercise to review all the elements that are a result of what you put in at the head end.

What changes?

As your horse ages, becomes fitter, or you change your work programme, his requirements can change. For example, if you ride your horse regularly and he is ageing, it may be that he will need a supplement, added to or included with his feed, to help with bodily repair and to delay the effects of ageing. He may seem a little less enthusiastic about life, or appear to feel the colder winter days just a little more. Adapting his diet to suit his changing needs may help.

Be aware

Whether you feed your horse yourself or leave it to the yard manager, as a conscientious person responsible for the welfare of a horse, in this area you should focus on three things:

1. Keeping up to date with developments in thought and products.
2. The fundamentals of feeding.
3. Your horse's condition.

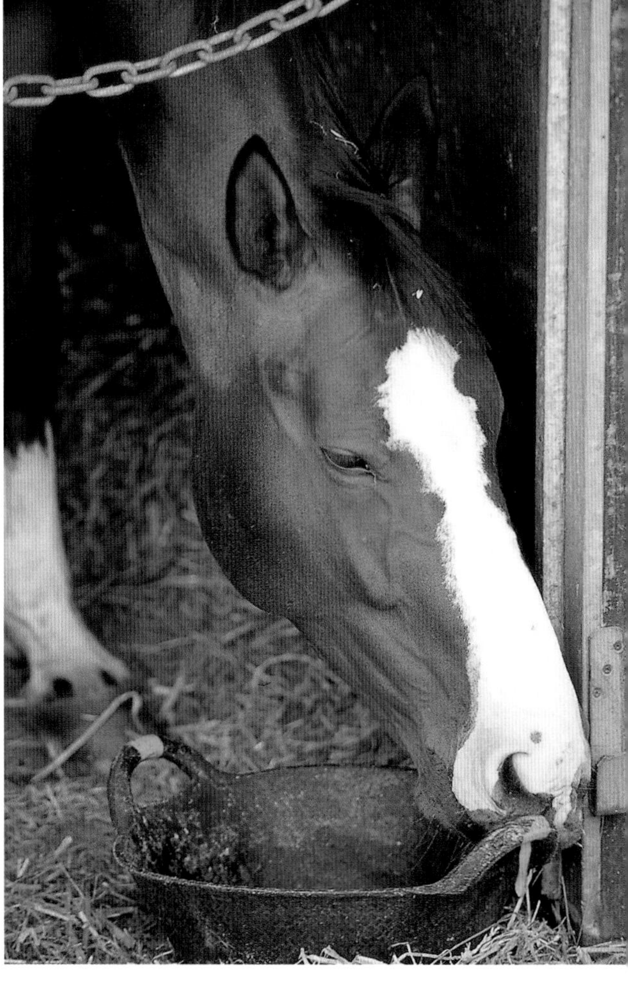

⇧ *You should review your horse's diet periodically.*

Take 30 minutes to keep up to date

This is not a difficult task. As feeding horses has turned into one of the most lucrative areas of the equestrian industry, developing almost on a daily basis, new products and theories are tried and tested and discussed regularly in the equestrian press, and most brand manufacturers have websites that offer useful information, access to their nutritionists, and news about new developments. If you have a particular issue about feeding your horse, put the question to at least two different brand nutritionists and compare their response before committing to a product. Remember, you should make changes to your horse's diet slowly, and if you choose the wrong product it will take a while to recover your original position.

Before making any changes, ensure you are as well informed as you can possibly be. There are also many books available on the subject of feeding that will help you to broaden your knowledge.

30 minutes to review your horse's current feed programme

THE TWELVE GOLDEN RULES OF FEEDING

Is this what you're doing?

1. Feed little and often

The horse's digestive system was designed to trickle feed for about 80 per cent of his day. He therefore finds small, regular meals easier to digest. For this reason, never leave a horse without forage or feed for more than three to four hours. Ignoring this can result in colic and difficulties with digestion.

2. Feed uniform quantities at the same time

This will aid digestion and deter bad behaviour that may result from irregular feeding times.

3. Always have water readily available

4. Always feed the best quality feeds possible

It is a false economy to feed poor quality feeds. Poor quality feed will equal poor condition and performance, and it will then be necessary to feed more, and probably to add supplements. Poor quality roughage can result in breathing disorders due to dust. If you are competitive it is recommended to buy feeds that are guaranteed to be free of illegal substances.

5. Remember that horses are individuals

What suits your neighbour or what suited your last horse, may not be right for this one.

6. Always feed plenty of roughage – hay, haylage and chaff

7. Never make sudden changes to your horse's diet

The bacteria in the horse's digestive system evolve so they are specific to what is being fed and sudden changes cause digestive disorders. If you are making changes, replace 0.5kg (1lb) daily, and watch for signs of colic or a change in droppings.

8. Always feed some form of succulents

This can be grass, vegetables, fruits or herbs.

9. Never exercise your horse immediately after feeding

Blood is diverted from the digestive process to major organs and muscles; furthermore a full stomach can restrict the lungs. Allow 1–1½ hours for digestion. Alternatively feed after exercise, but not until your horse has cooled down.

Make sure that your horse's manger and water buckets, if used, are scrubbed clean on a regular basis.

10. Practise good hygiene

11. Always measure quantities

12. Use clear and accurate feed-chart instructions

Pin these up where they can be seen. Keep them updated and easy to follow. Feed your horse by weight, not volume, and mark feed scoops to show weights. Use separate feed scoops for different feeds and label them accordingly.

The twelve golden rules give an overview of the basic principles of feeding, which will enable you to check your horse's current feed programme. There are four steps to planning or reviewing a feed programme:

1. Reviewing your horse's present condition and requirements.
2. Deciding on the quantity of feed required.
3. Deciding on the ratio of roughage to concentrate feed.
4. Deciding on the type of feed required.

Step 1: Review your horse's present condition and requirements

Before developing a feeding programme for a new horse, or reviewing your current horse's programme, you need to consider the following eight things:

a. His breed and type

Is he a pony or a horse? Breed and type can also have an effect on the condition of your horse. For example, thoroughbreds tend to be difficult to keep condition on, whereas a cob may be prone to becoming too fat. These are all generalizations, but should be borne in mind.

⇧ *A young horse may need extra carbohydrates and supplements to help him with his growth.*

b. Age
For example, youngsters need extra carbohydrates and protein, and older horses may need extra rations to help keep weight on through the winter and supplements to keep their joints moving.

c. Condition and health
Is he in good condition? Or does he need building up or to lose weight? Is he in good health or might he need a special diet if he has health issues?

d. Height and weight
Most of us know our horse's height, but weight is harder to establish. The most accurate way is via a weighbridge. This can be done at your vets or by the awkward process of weighing your lorry or trailer on a public weighbridge, and then returning with your horse loaded on board and subtracting one weight from the other. The simplest method is to use a weigh tape, available from most tack shops. Although not absolutely accurate, when it is used regularly and the results are recorded, it can provide a guide to whether your horse is gaining or losing weight.

e. Weather
Is he living out all year or in the summer only, or is he part stabled? How good is your grass throughout the year?

f. Temperament
Excitable horses need plenty of roughage and not too much concentrate, and lethargic ones may need a bit more energy. Your aim is to provide the correct nutrients for your horse's lifestyle without causing him to become fresh or difficult.

g. Work and circumstances
If your horse is living out, in good health and not in work or in light work, it is unlikely that he will need any additional feedstuffs, apart from hay or haylage. He may, however, need a supplement to help him keep his good condition in the winter, and restricted grazing in the summer. If he is living in part of the time, he may only need roughage during the period he is in his stable. However, if he is in hard competition, his diet will need to be planned accordingly (*see* chart, page 91).

h. Your ability
Keep in mind what you want from your horse. There is no point in feeding him for peak performance if he is then going to be so fresh or lively that he will scare you.

Step 2: Decide on the quantity of feed required

A horse should receive 2–2.5 per cent of his bodyweight as his total daily ration: 2 per cent maintains condition and is suitable for horses in moderate work, 2.5 per cent is suitable for horses in very hard training or to gain condition. Here are two examples:

500kg (1,100lb) horse on maintenance diet and moderate work:

$\frac{500}{100}$ = 5 x 2 = 10kg (22lb) feed daily

500kg horse building condition and in hard work:

$\frac{500}{100}$ = 5 x 2.5 = 12.5kg (26lb) feed daily

Step 3: Decide on the ratio of roughage to concentrate feed (see box below)

LEVEL	TYPE OF WORK	ROUGHAGE%	CONCENTRATE%
Maintenance	Box rest, retirement or hacking and occasional light schooling	100	0
Light work	Novice dressage and show-jumping competitions, hacking and light schooling	80-90	10-20
Light–medium work	Medium dressage, Foxhunter show jumping, pre-novice – novice eventer, endurance rider	70-80	20-30
Medium work	Hunting, advanced dressage, A & B show jumping, intermediate eventing, one star three-day eventing	50-60	40-50

Step 4: Decide on the type of feed required

Traditional feeding versus commercial feeding

Traditional feeding is a skill that used to be developed through years of working with horses and knowledge handed down from one generation to the next. Today most non-professional horse owners and yard managers will opt for the convenience and reliability of commercially produced mixes.

For the horse owner with limited time available it is recommended that you find the appropriate commercial cube or mix that will suit your requirements. Not only will this provide you with a documented menu of ingredients, but in most cases there will be a professional nutritionist available at the end of the brand's helpline should you have any queries.

If you are on a livery yard it may be that you have to fit in with the feed types available. It is therefore important that you understand as much as possible about their components in order to keep an eye on your horse's performance and condition; discuss these with the yard manager if necessary. Some yard managers will still use traditional feeding methods and for that reason a brief guide is included on these pages.

A basic breakdown of equine nutrition

There are four main food types: roughage, concentrates, succulents and supplements.

1. Roughage

This includes grass, hay, haylage, straw, chaff /chop.

Grass: the horse's natural food

- Grass is about 80 per cent water.
- The quality varies greatly.
- Monitor the horse's body condition regularly if he lives out.
- Additional hay or feed will be needed in the winter months.

Hay: the most important ingredient because it

- provides both fibre and protein;
- meets basic energy needs;
- reduces the risk of colic;
- keeps the stomach full;
- relieves boredom.

- Keep your hay in a cool, dry, well ventilated store. Good quality hay will be dry, dust free, pleasant smelling, and free from mould, thistles and weeds. Beware ragwort.
- If a horse is able to perform to your requirements and is maintaining an adequate body condition on pasture and hay alone, you don't have to feed concentrates. However, supplemental minerals and vitamins may be necessary.

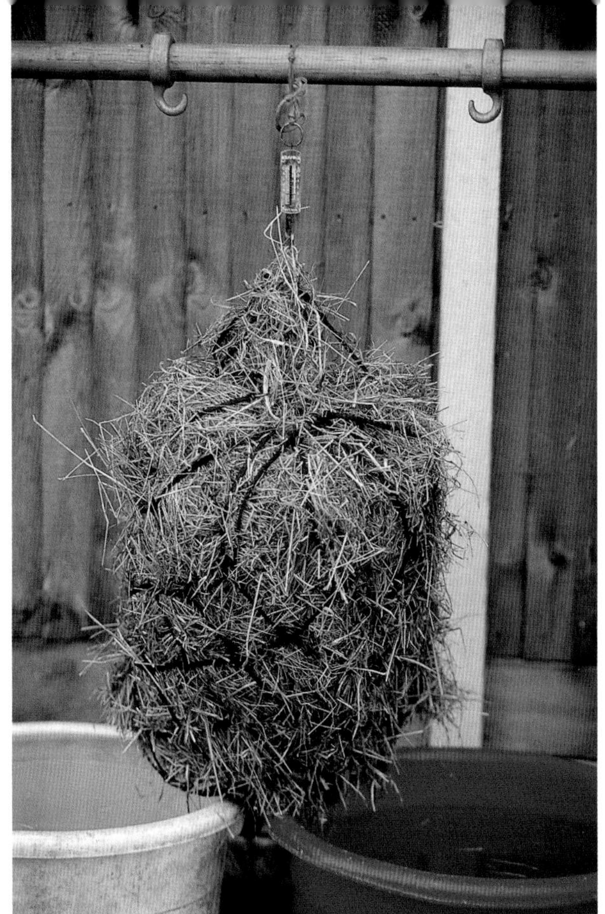

⇧ *Always try to weigh your hay to keep control on how much you are feeding to your horse.*

- Soaking hay helps to prevent mould spores invading your horse's respiratory tract and causing problems. Hay should be totally immersed in water for about 20 minutes, then allowed to drain before being given to the horse. Any longer than this and the nutritional value is reduced. However, if a horse is already suffering from RAD (respiratory airways disorder) it may be necessary to soak his hay overnight.
- The most natural way to feed hay is from the ground, although a net can be useful if a horse is greedy and eats very quickly.
- A mature horse would probably eat 9–11kg (20–25lb) of hay daily if it were available.
- It is possible to have the feed value of your hay analysed.

Don't forget: Your hay must be made at the right time – not too late in the summer season and in good weather (dry, sunny) – in order to preserve the nutrients it contains. Hay that has been harvested too late or during wet weather will be of poor quality.

Haylage: the airtight alternative

- Haylage is made from grass that is wilted, allowing the extraction of air and sealed in vacuum-packed wrapping, which reduces the amount of dust and fungal spores.
- If you are using home-grown haylage you should have it analysed for nutritional value. This will also tell you if it is safe to feed.
- Haylage is often higher in nutritional value than hay.
- By weight, it is necessary to feed more haylage than hay as it has a higher water content.

Straw

- Oat or barley straw is comparable to poor quality hay, and is usually fed as part of a controlled diet in order to add bulk.

Chaff/chop

- Chopped straw and hay, dried alfalfa or dried grass.
- Like concentrates, it is available in various mixes.
- Chaff is good for horses that rush their feed as it encourages chewing.
- It is high in fibre and used to add bulk.

2. Concentrates

This means 'straights', 'cubes' and 'mixes'. Straights are mostly cereals such as oats and barley and are a non-complete feed in that they are not nutritionally balanced. Most are a good source of carbohydrate and contain average protein, but are low in fibre, minerals and vitamins, and usually need to have a feed balancer or broad spectrum mineral and vitamin supplement added to correct any deficiencies that may affect performance. Avoid feeding more than 2.2kg (5lb) of concentrate at any time, and divide into as many small feeds as is practicable.

Straights:

- *Oats*: A good source of carbohydrate, oats contain 50 per cent starch, protein and fibre, and have been popular with traditional horsemen for years. Oats are now mostly used by racehorse owners and those who require fast work from their horses. If you are using oats, they must be of top quality. They do not have a high calcium-to-phosphorous ratio, and supplements are therefore required. They are not advisable for horses in light or irregular work.
- *Barley*: This needs to be processed – steamed, flaked, micronised or extruded – for ingestion by horses. It has a higher energy content than oats (60 per cent starch), but lower fibre content. The calcium-to-phosphorous ratio is low. Flaked barley is easier to digest, but more expensive.

⇧ *Commercial mixes are now available to suit all types of equine, from racehorse to laminitic, from foal to veteran.*

- *Maize*: This is fed steam flaked or micronized flaked. It has a higher digestible energy than oats, but a lower fibre content. Maize is high in starch (70 per cent) and can therefore cause digestive problems.
- *Bran*: Bran is a by-product of wheat and has a poor nutritional value. It can act as a laxative. It has a high fibre content but is low in protein and is difficult to digest. It also has a bad calcium-to-phosphorous ratio.
- *Linseed*: This must be cooked beforehand to deactivate poisonous hydrocyanic acid and soften it up before feeding. It should be weighed before cooking, and not more than 100g (3½oz) should be fed daily. Linseed is a good energy source and improves coat condition. It is high in poor quality protein and oil.
- *Sugar beet*: This root vegetable is processed to remove the sugar, and then developed into pulp or cubes. It must be soaked before feeding. It is a good energy provider and a source of digestible fibre. Sugar beet contains slow-release glucose and is rich in calcium, salt and potassium. It can therefore be used as a balancer to cereal feeds lacking in these nutrients. It encourages a horse to eat slowly and to chew thoroughly, and can be an appetizer.

Cubes and mixes:

These are commercially prepared and nutritionally balanced combinations of nutrients. They are available either in the form of cubes or as coarse mixes – tend to contain a higher level of cereals than cubes. Syrup and molasses are sometimes added to increase palatability. They come in four main forms; a. complete mixes; b. complete cubes; c. balancers to be fed with cereals; and d. a fibre mix to be added to other foods providing and alternative source of fibre to bran; chaff or sugar beet. Many varieties are available to suit all types of horse. Most brands provide support and advice to give you all the information you need.

3. Succulents

The following can all be included in your horse's diet to make up for any lack of natural succulents: carrots, apples, turnips, swede, cabbage leaves, pea pods, fresh herbs, garlic, comfrey, dandelions, nettles, seaweed. When chopping vegetables such as carrots, always cut them into sticks rather than rounds as horses may choke on the latter.

4. Supplements

Technology has provided us with many supplements that can now help our horses. The danger is in succumbing to too many of these. Remember that a supplement should be just that – something you feed your horse that is lacking in his diet. If you are feeding commercial mixes to your horse, always check what is already in the bag before adding any extras.

- If you are feeding a concentrate to a healthy adult horse in medium work or lower, providing it is fed at the levels recommended on the packaging, he should not need any supplements other than, perhaps, salt to encourage the consumption of water.
- If you are following traditional feeding methods, feed a broad spectrum multi-vitamin and mineral supplement to compensate for any deficiencies in cereal feeds.
- Some vitamins need to be considered in tandem as they need to be taken in certain combinations in order to be fully effective.
- During hard training a horse may need additional electrolytes and/or salt.
- Supplements may be needed following a bout of ill health.

- Salt can be added to your horse's diet via his daily feed, a rock of salt in his manger, a salt lick in the stable, or salt block in the field.
- Feed balancers usually come in the form of pellets and contain a combination of vitamins, minerals, probiotics and protein to redress the balance of the diet where necessary.

Broad spectrum multi-vitamin and mineral

When to feed?

- If your horse's diet is not meeting his nutritional requirements.
- If your horse is on a low concentrate diet.
- With traditional feeding regimes.
- To horses who don't finish their food.

Probiotics and prebiotics

When to feed?

- If your horse is in hard competition, competing and training regularly.
- If your horse is travelling long distances or is a bad traveller.
- If your horse's eating patterns have been disrupted, or he has had some digestive difficulties.

Probiotics help restore the micro flora, the bacteria that help with digestion in the gut, prebiotics increase their numbers. Probiotics therefore restore things to normal after a period of stress, whereas prebiotics can prepare the system for potential challenges. They improve the nutrient intake and vitamin production, and boost the immune system. And a prebiotic may also avoid any behavioural difficulties likely to arise as a result of dietary changes.

Joint supplements

When to feed:

- to older horses;
- to competition horses;
- to horses with joint problems.

Joint supplements have become increasingly popular over the last decade and are now available in a variety of forms and with various different active ingredients including glucosamine, chrondroitin and methyl-sulphonyl-methane (MSM). Devil's claw, an anti-inflammatory, is the natural herb alternative. They are generally found to work on the basis of prevention rather than cure, and each product has its fans.

⇦ *A horse that is living out on good grazing and in light work should not need any additional feed.*

FIVE ESSENTIAL NUTRIENTS

1. Protein
- essential for growth and repair;
- the mature horse requires 8–10 per cent protein in his diet;
- contained in soya bean (the best source, most commonly used in concentrates), peas and beans (in both to a lesser degree);
- cereals are low in protein;
- complete feeds contain the correct amount of protein according to the type of work;
- overfeeding can result in dehydration.

2. Carbohydrates (includes cellulose, sugars and starch)
- the main source of energy;
- starch provides rapid energy;
- can be heating;
- can cause digestive problems if fed in too large quantities.

3. Fibre
- aids digestion;
- a good source of slow-release energy;
- helps retain water throughout digestive process, acting as an electrolyte reserve and helping to replace fluids lost through sweating;
- helps prevent boredom;
- found in forage (hay, straw and grass);
- at least 30 per cent of the diet should be roughage.

4. Vitamins and minerals
- need to be considered to ensure the horse is receiving all nutritional requirements; but if the horse is being fed a correctly balanced diet and has a normal work regime, it will not need additional vitamins or minerals;
- most mixes provide the necessary vitamins and minerals.

5. Fats and oils
- an efficient source of slow-release energy;
- improve the skin and coat;
- help delay fatigue and thus improve performance;
- accelerate heart and respiration recovery during the first minutes of rest.

And don't forget water…
- clean, fresh water should be constantly available to a horse;
- the only time when his intake should be limited is immediately after heavy work, and before he has recovered;
- 50 per cent of a mature horse's body consists of water;
- without water a horse would not be able to survive for more than six days;
- water aids the digestive and circulatory systems, regulates body temperature and provides the basis of tears, mucus, joint fluid and milk;
- a healthy adult horse will drink between 23 and 68 litres (5 to 15 gallons) of water a day;
- using buckets in the stable enables you to monitor how much your horse is drinking, and when.

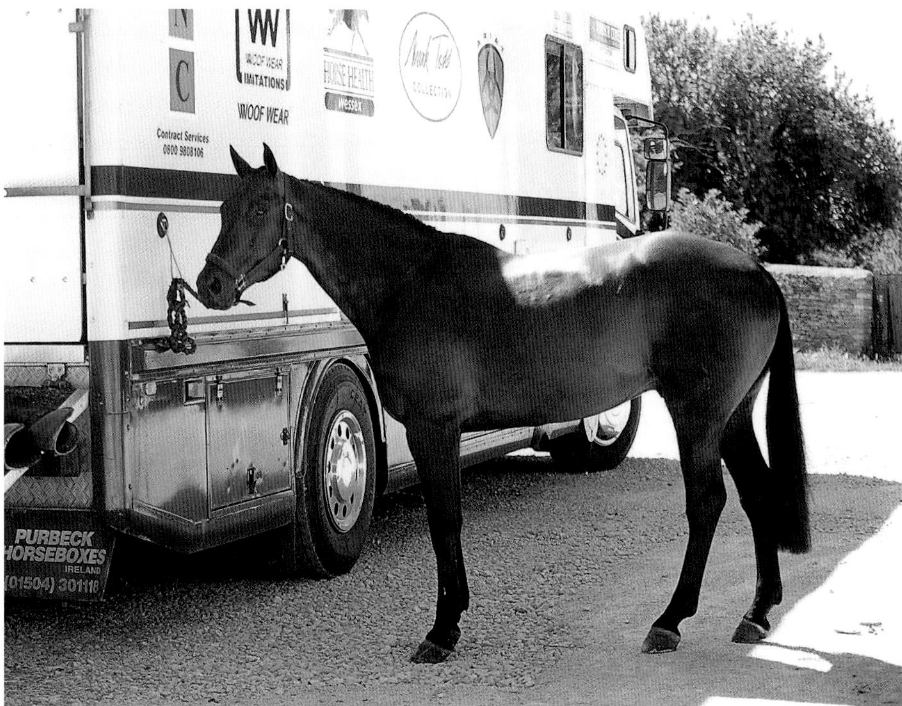

➪ *Study top competition horses to establish an eye for how a fit horse should look.*

Spend 30 minutes condition-scoring your horse

An important aspect of being on top of your horse's diet is to monitor his condition and spot potential problems before they become serious.

You need to have in your mind a picture of how you think your horse should look. A good way to do this is to study horses in the same area of activity. For example, if you aim to compete at eventing, dedicate some time to watching top class eventers to get an idea of how a fit, professional horse looks. Your own horse may not have the same breeding or abilities, but it will give you an idea of what you are trying to attain. Combine this ideal with what you think your horse can achieve and you should have a picture in your mind of what you are aiming for.

How to condition score

You will need to be able to look at your horse from the front, side and rear. He must not be cold, have just eaten, just come in from the field or just been exercised. If possible, take a photograph from all three perspectives, weekly is ideal. Judge his condition at the points listed below and mark him between 1 and 10. Your ideal is between 5 and 6. Make a note of the score: this will enable you to monitor his progress and to evaluate his feed and training programmes, and also to cross-reference this information from one year to the next.

1 POINT – POOR CONDITION
Croup, spinal processes, ribs and hip bones prominent. Hollow in front of the withers, and possible sunken eye. No fatty tissue visible.

2 POINTS – VERY THIN
Croup, spinal processes, ribs and hip bones still prominent, but slight fatty tissue over spinal processes, ribs visible but not prominent. Deep cavity either side of tail.

3 POINTS – THIN
Spinal processes and ribs still visible. Slight covering of fat over ribs. Withers, shoulders and neck muscles showing. Slight cavity under tail.

4 POINTS – MODERATELY THIN
Slight ridge along back, faint outline of ribs visible. Withers, shoulders and neck not particularly thin now.

5 POINTS – MODERATE
Back flatter. Withers, croup and hip rounded. Shoulders and neck blending into body. Ribs not distinguishable, but easily felt.

6 POINTS – MODERATELY FLESHY
Normal. May have slight crease down back. Ribs covered. Haunches, croup and buttocks covered. Neck firm and muscles obvious. Muscular development visible.

7 POINTS – FLESHY
Crest is developing, as is crease down back. Fat filling in between ribs, which can be still felt. Fat around pelvis and croup.

8 POINTS – FAT
Crease down back. No bones visible. Neck thickening. Fat appearing on inner thighs.

9 POINTS – EXTREMELY FAT
Ribs, quarters and back well covered with fat. Definite crease down back. Croup and hip bones difficult to feel.

10 POINTS – OBESE
Large fatty crest, wide neck, deep hollow down back. Pads of fat on shoulder and quarters. Skin distended.

Don't forget: Next time you're at a show spend 30 minutes condition-scoring the horses competing to help develop your eye.

Look at the horse from behind, and score the pelvis, then check the neck and back and adjust the score up and down by one grade if necessary.

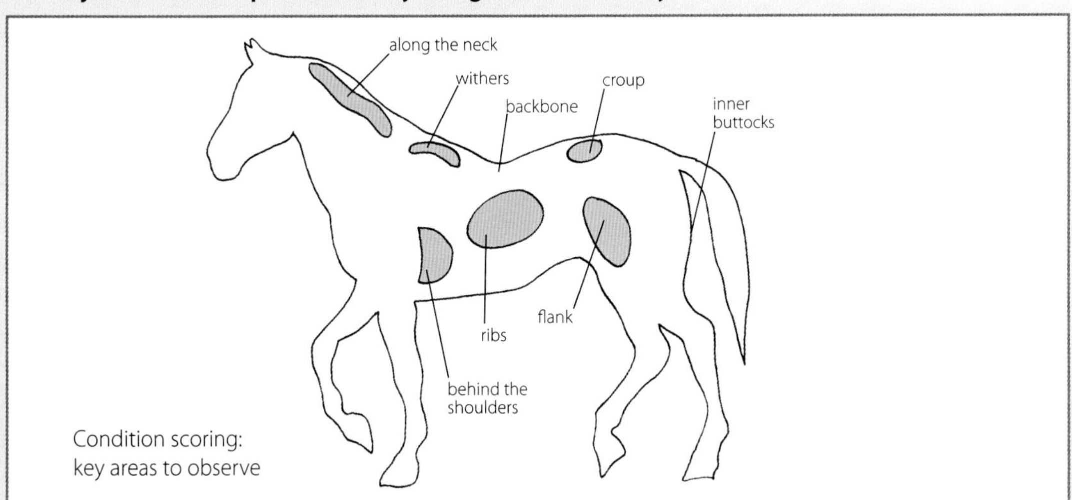

Condition scoring: key areas to observe

30 minutes to Make a Weekly Health Check

The better you know your horse, the more effortlessly you will register whether he looks 'normal' or under the weather. The ability to make an at-a-glance appraisal is essential, but a more thorough hands-on check should be carried out on a regular basis, and if you feel something is not quite right. Take 30 minutes once a week to run through this health check (details of each point are given on the following pages), and save yourself time and anguish by recognizing and dealing with any problems before they become major.

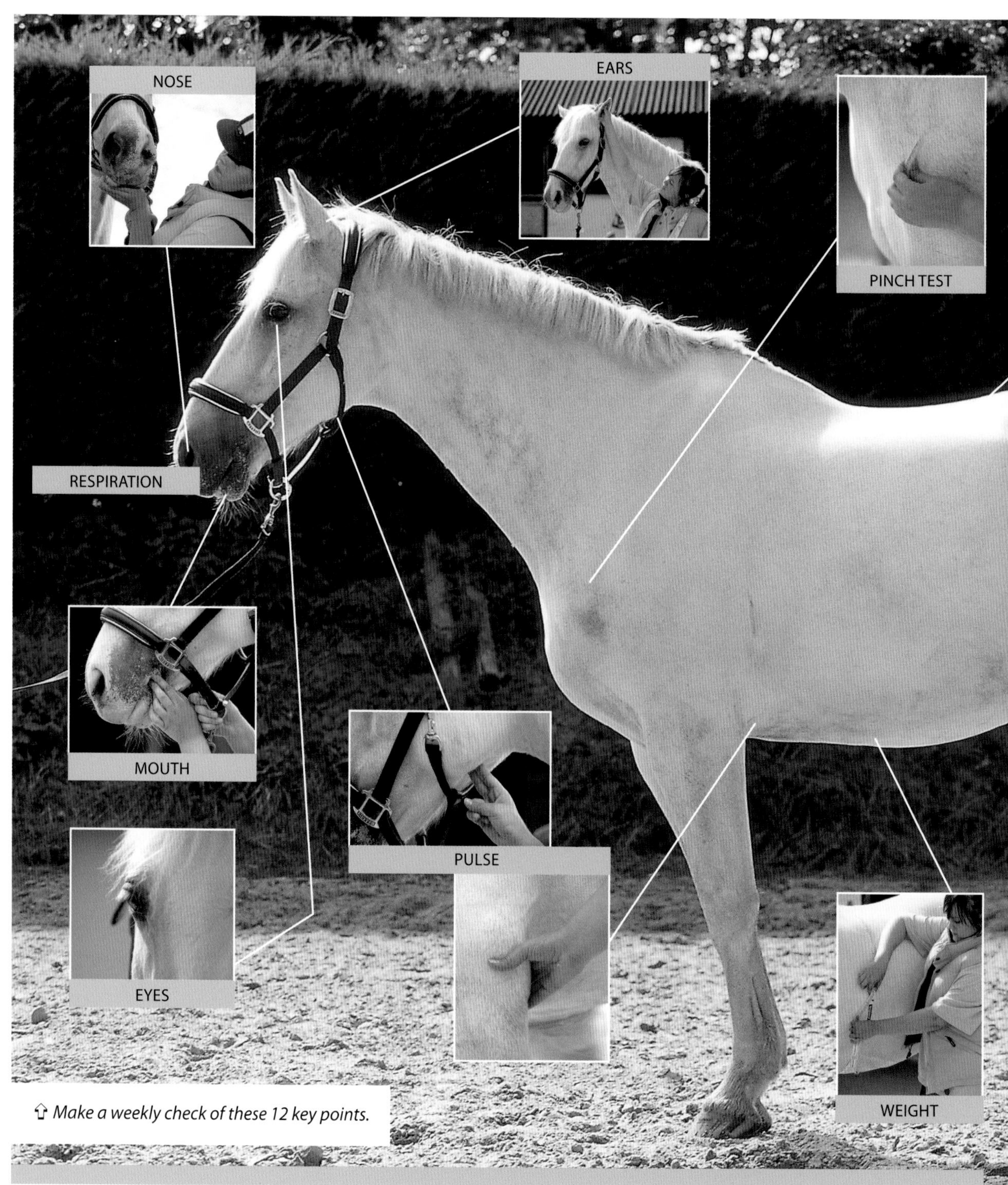

⇧ *Make a weekly check of these 12 key points.*

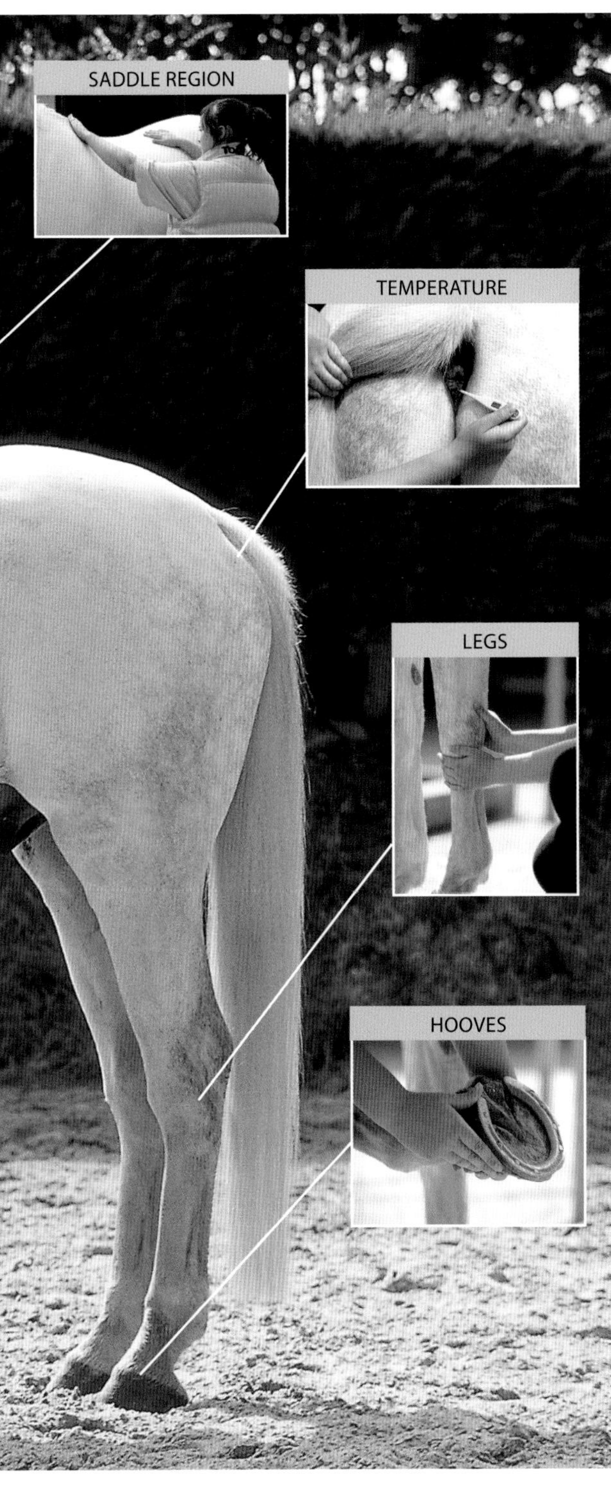

GENERAL CHECKS

First, check the ABS (Appearance, Behaviour, Stable). Tie your horse up safely.

- Step back and take a good look at him. The overall impression you receive should be of an alert, interested, healthy animal. He should be standing squarely, possibly resting a hind leg and dropping one hip, but definitely not resting a foreleg. Nor should he be shifting his weight from one foot to another. His coat should lie flat and have a bloom or shine to it; if he lives out this is quite difficult to perceive, but it should still be the case.

  Any of the following can be an indication that things are not quite right:

  - head hung
  - ears back
  - dull, staring coat
  - tail raised
  - any obvious swelling
  - runny eyes or nose
  - unusual posture
  - signs of tension or unexplained excitement

- Make a mental note of the horse's general behaviour, and register what is normal for your horse. A grumpy, argumentative horse showing signs of subservience is as much a cause for concern as a normally friendly horse suddenly being grumpy.
- Take a look around his stable: is he eating his feed, finishing off his hay and drinking all his water? (Difficult to measure if you don't use water buckets.) Are there little bits of food around the manger indicating that he is quidding (food is falling out of his mouth at one side or another due to an irregular bite or missing teeth) and has dental problems? Are there more, or fewer, droppings than usual? Try to watch your horse stale (urinate): the urine should be clear or slightly cloudy, but not thick, yellow or smelly. Does the stable look uncharacteristically messy?

⇧ *Keep an eye on how much water your horse drinks to ascertain what is normal for him.*

The 30-minute check in 12 steps

Now follow the 12 steps described here.

1. Ears

Run your hands over your horse's ears to gauge whether he is warm enough. (To find out what is normal for your horse, make a point of checking his ears in extremes of weather, both hot and cold.) His ears should be 'perky' and directed at you, or at anything else that might have drawn his attention.

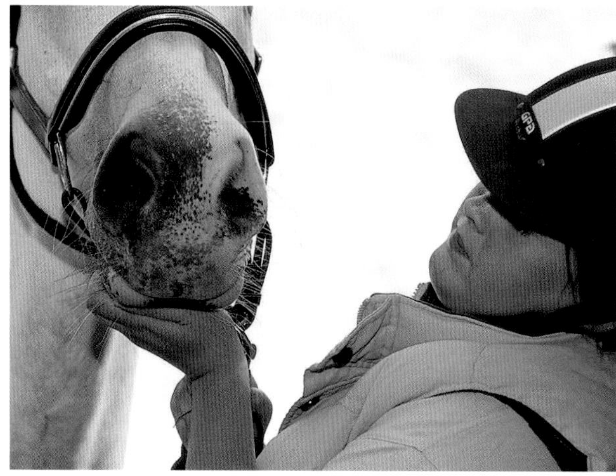

2. Nose

The membrane on the inside of the horse's nose should be a healthy red colour. A slight discharge, especially after exercise, is not abnormal, but anything else, such as blood or a thick yellow or green discharge (a sign of infection), is far from normal.

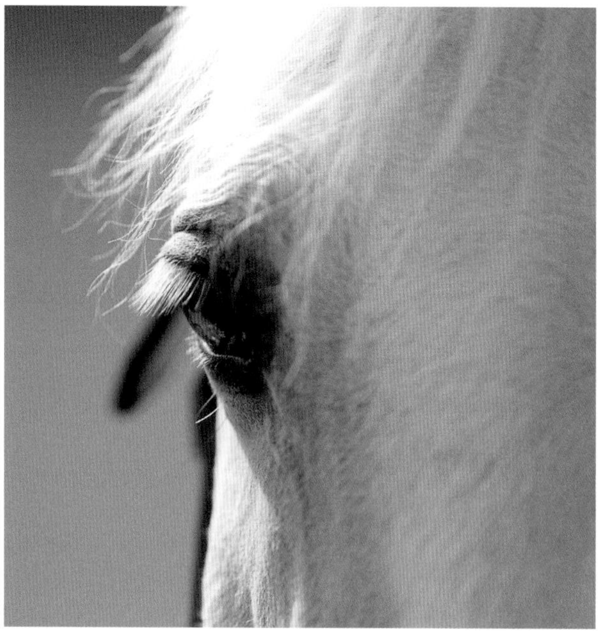

3. Eyes

Your horse's eyes should be bright and alert. There should be no discharge or unusual redness. If your horse is attempting to rub or close his eye, this could indicate that something is wrong.

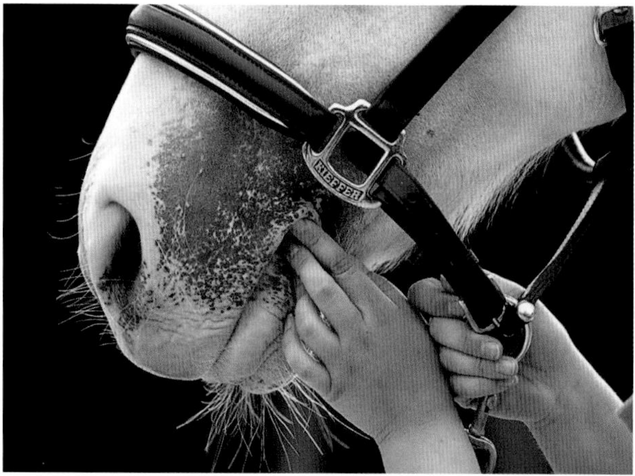

4. Mouth

Check the corners of his mouth to ensure that the bit is not rubbing here.

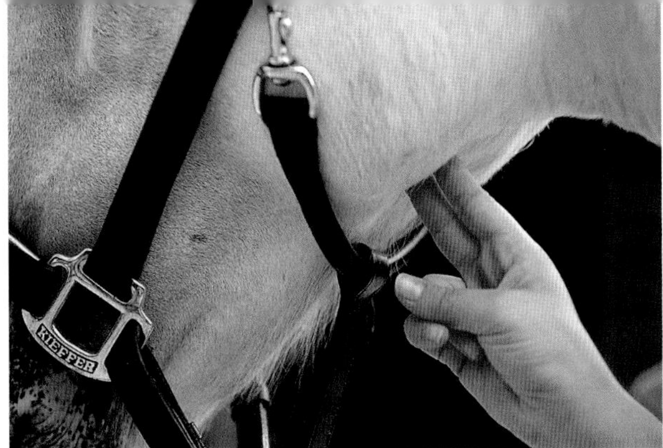

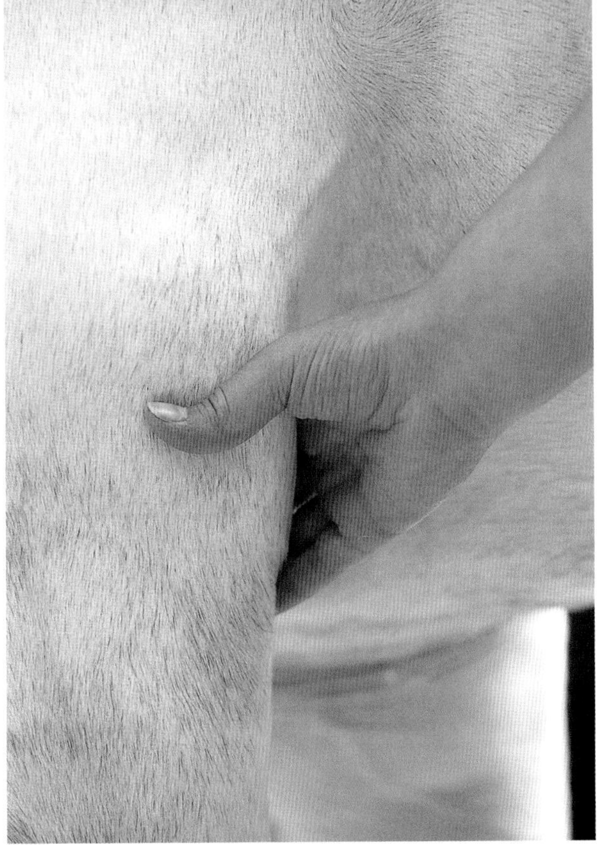

5. Pulse

The easiest places to feel a pulse is at one of the arteries either under the jawbone or inside the elbow. Make sure that the horse is relaxed and not eating, and after a few seconds you should feel the pulse. (It isn't easy to detect – be patient.) Count the beats for 30 seconds, and then double that figure to give the heart rate per minute. Remember that exercise, pain, a high temperature or excitement can all increase your horse's pulse rate. A resting horse should have a pulse of between 36–42 beats a minute.

(Note: An artery feels springy to the touch. A vein will flatten if you squash it.)

LOCATING THE PULSE OF THE DIGITAL ARTERY

It is a good idea to try to locate the pulse of the digital artery that runs through the fetlock. This pulse is a good indicator of more serious foot problems such as developing abscesses and laminitis.

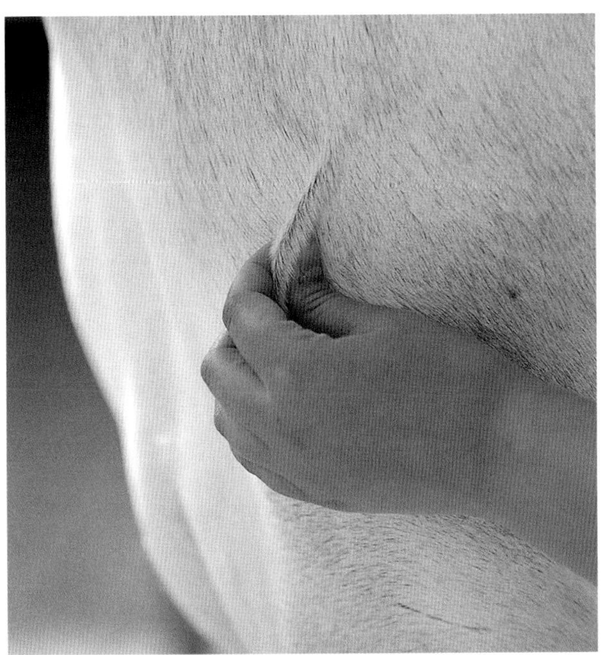

6. Pinch test

Is your horse dehydrated? Gently take a pinch of skin on the point of the shoulder: if your horse is not dehydrated, it will spring back into place immediately you let it go.

7. Legs

Run your hands over your horse's legs. You are checking for:

- heat
- swelling
- wounds

Check firstly for heat. If you can feel heat but are not sure whether it is 'normal', compare the heat of the problem spot to that of the same place in the opposite leg. Heat is an indication of a problem and should not be ignored.

You should treat any swelling that you may find in a like manner. At various stages in their lives and training horses may develop lumps and bumps such as windgalls and splints on their legs. It is important that you are familiar with these as they are permanent and unlikely to

TIP

Remember that a horse's legs may swell or become warm after exercise.

cause problems once established. However, swelling in more than one leg can be a sign of digestive problems, age, or lack of exercise. Swelling in one leg is more likely to be an injury and should be investigated. Locate your horse's tendons and familiarize yourself with how they feel. Any swelling or thickening here should be looked at by a vet immediately, because to work a horse with a damaged tendon can have long-term effects.

If you apply pressure to either a warm patch or a swelling and the horse reacts it is likely that he is in pain. If possible, trot him up carefully to establish whether or not he is lame before calling the vet.

Now check for any cuts, grazes or wounds. Look out for mud fever during wet weather.

8. Hooves

Check to ensure that the shoe is not loose and that the clenches – the nails attaching the shoe to the hoof wall – have not 'risen' (worked loose and moved too close to the sensitive laminae of the foot). The hooves should be evenly shaped with no cracks or missing chunks. The hind hoof should be slightly more upright than the fore. Take a look at the sole of the hoof: is the frog dry and clean? Does the foot smell clean and healthy? Any indication of decay could be thrush and will need treating immediately.

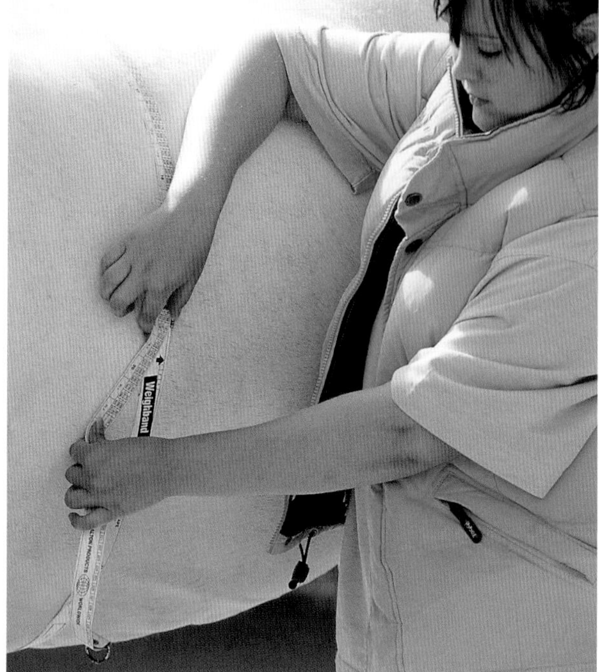

9. Weight

To the eye, your horse should be well covered but not fat, his ribs just visible. Use a weigh-tape regularly; although not guaranteed to be accurate, it will provide an indication of whether he has put on weight.

TIP

Use the back of your hand to double check heat – it is more sensitive.

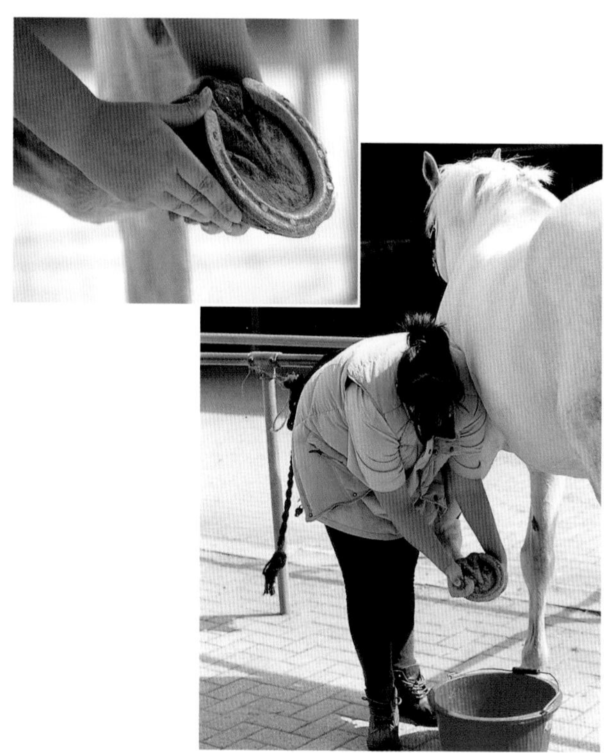

A HORSE'S TPR

You may read or hear people talking about a horse's TPR. This means temperature, pulse and respiration, and knowing all three will give a good indication of a horse's general health. To establish your horse's TPR, take all three readings at the same time of day for four days, when your horse is relaxed and settled in his stable or on the yard and before he expects a feed. Make a note of the readings.

10. Respiration

A fit horse's respiration at rest is quite difficult to detect. Stand behind the horse and to one side and watch the flanks moving in and out as the horse breathes; each breath, in and out, is counted as one. Once again, time the horse for 30 seconds and then double that figure to establish the breaths per minute, which should be between 8 to 15 for a resting horse. Pay attention to coughs or unusual respiratory noises as these can indicate many things from stress to respiratory airways obstruction (RAO, formerly known as COPD), and should not be ignored.

11. Temperature

The simplest way to take your horse's temperature is with a digital equine thermometer. A veterinary mercury thermometer is also available, but is more difficult to read and can therefore be inaccurate in inexperienced hands.

TIP

If you think or know that your horse may pull away suddenly, fasten a piece of string or baling twine to the thermometer at one end and a peg at the other. Clip the peg to the horse's tail.

Lubricate the bulb of the thermometer you are using with petroleum jelly or saliva. If it is a mercury thermometer, shake it smartly to return the mercury towards the bulb. Stand behind and to one side of the horse and lift his tail towards you. Gently insert the thermometer in the horse's anus. Allow it to enter at an angle and follow the wall of the rectum; this ensures you are not reading the temperature of a ball of droppings. Leave it in place for 30 seconds – and don't let go! If the horse objects it is important to remove the thermometer immediately ensuring that it does not break. Clean and sterilize the thermometer before putting it away.

The normal temperature for a horse is about 38°C, or 100.4°F; if it goes above 39.5°C, contact your vet.

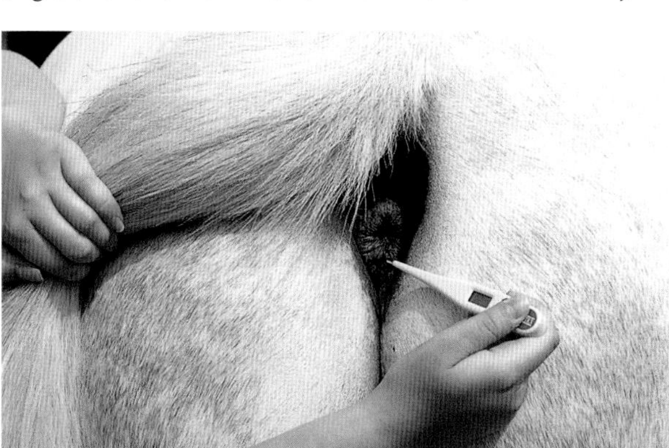

12. Saddle region

Run your hands over the area of the horse's back where your saddle would be. Ensure that there are no areas of discomfort – he will react to your touch – or sores or cuts. If you are in any doubt, have your saddler come and check as soon as possible. Now run your hands over the rest of his body to check that there are no bald patches, sores or injuries. Watch out for rain scald and sweet itch.

TROTTING UP

In the early days of getting to know your horse, persuade a friend to trot him up so that you can watch his action from in front and behind.

His action should be easy and rhythmic. Note how the hind legs follow in the path of the fore legs so as to familiarize yourself with what is normal for your horse. Many successful competition horses dish (swing one leg out irregularly), but this is of no consequence: it is irregularities in stride that you are looking for.

30 minutes to Give Your Horse a Massage

When it's pouring with rain, your tack is dirty and you really don't feel like getting on board, spend 30 minutes giving your horse a massage – you'll both feel the benefits.

Horses are by nature tactile animals. The majority enjoy a thorough grooming session (although there are always exceptions, usually created by over-zealous grooming or the use of harsh brushes on very fine skin), so think how much pleasure a massage might bring: not only will your horse benefit from this relaxing exercise, but it will also give you an opportunity to check him out for injuries, heat spots and sensitive areas. This focused attention is also a great bonding opportunity.

When to use massage

- Before or after work
- The day before a challenging competition, and as soon as possible afterwards
- Regularly for an elderly or retired horse
- To calm down an excitable horse
- With your vet's permission, on a horse on box rest
- On a youngster to familiarize him with human touch

Note: *Don't feed your horse for an hour and a half before a massage, and keep him warm afterwards.*

RELEVANT POINTS OF THE HORSE

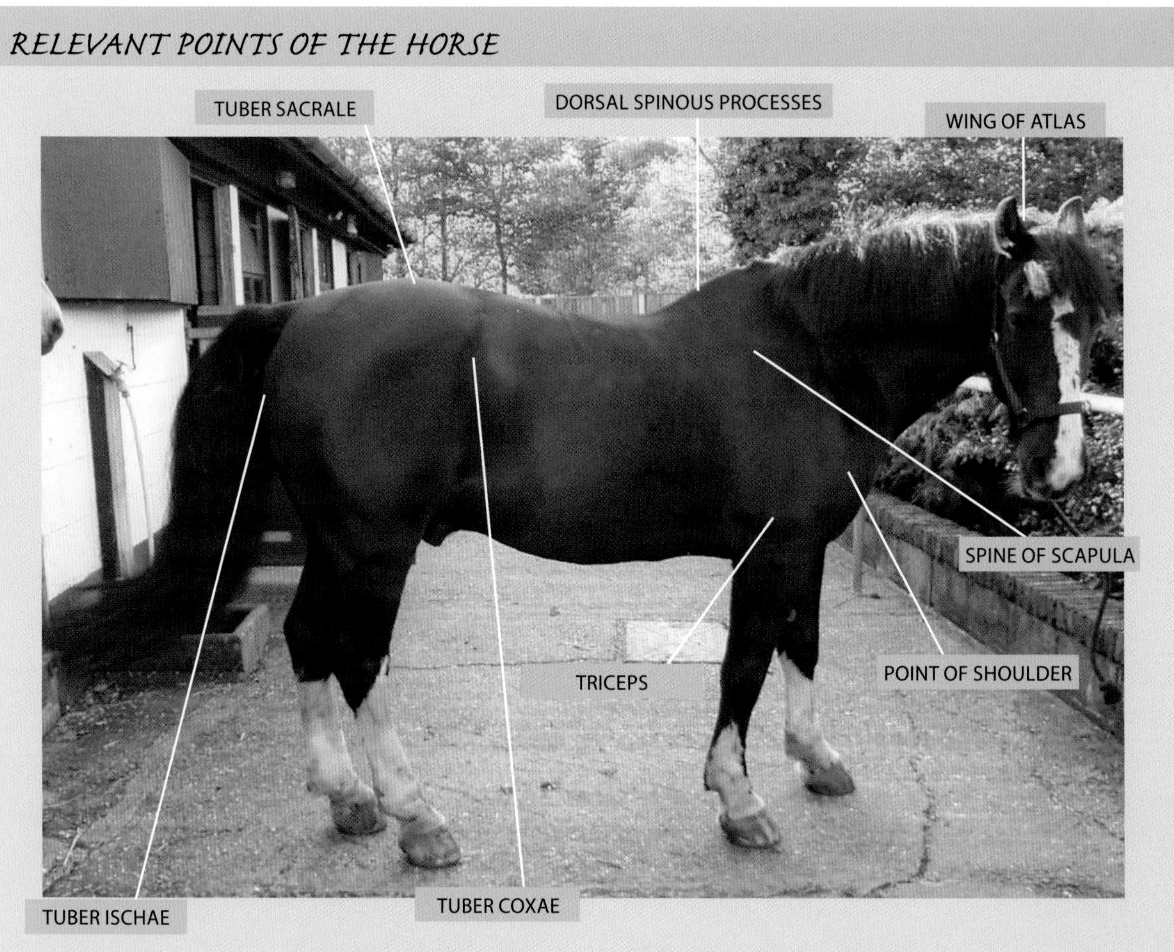

Begin your massage on the horse's left side, as this is the side he is most accustomed to being approached from (for photographic purposes, we have in fact begun on the right, the offside – *see* next page).

Position him somewhere quiet where you will not be disturbed and where he can relax and not be distracted. If necessary give him a haynet. If it is cold, throw a rug over his quarters to begin with, covering the shoulders when you are working on the quarters. As you work, allow the hand that it not working to rest on the horse's body in a reassuring manner. Feel your horse's body – his muscles and bones – as you work, and allow your hands to work where they best fit its contours.

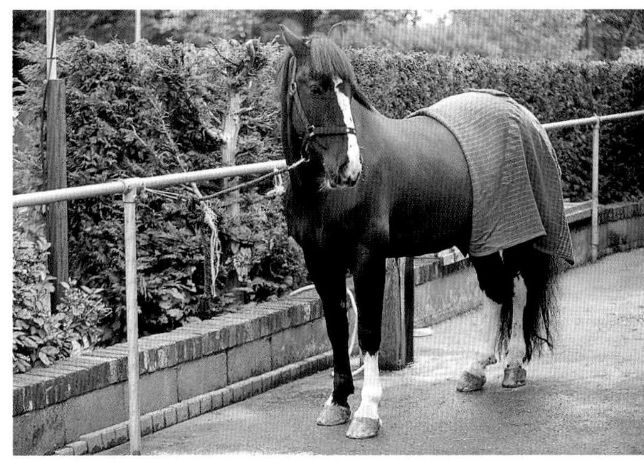

⇧ *If your horse is likely to feel the cold during treatment, use a summer sheet, or something heavier if necessary, over his quarters, whilst you massage him.*

THE TAPOTEMENT MOVEMENTS

These are used along the bigger muscles and are chosen according to what your horse finds most comfortable and how much resistance you find in the muscle.

HACKING

CUPPING

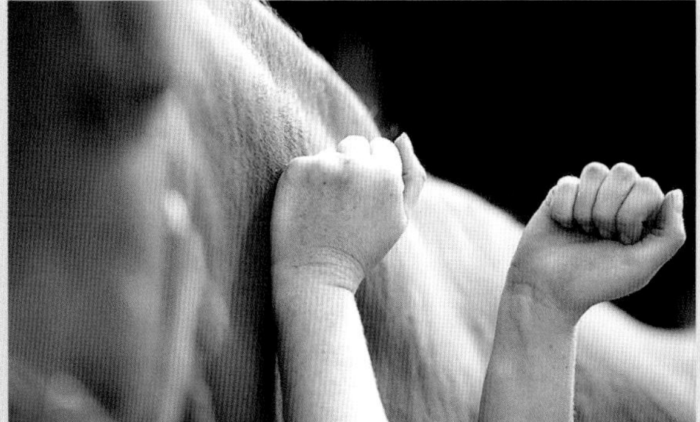

POUNDING

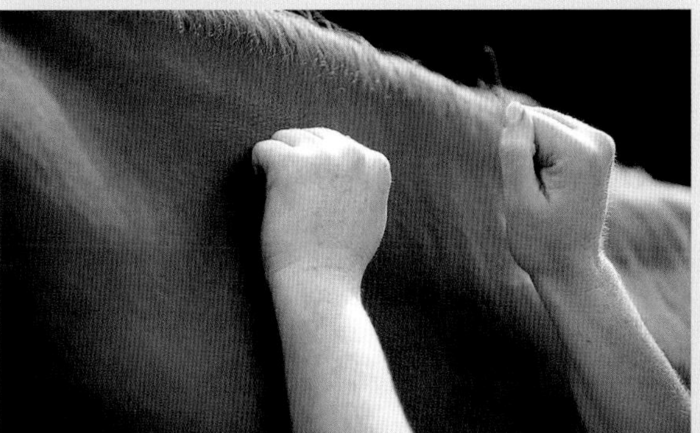

BEATING

These techniques must be performed with soft wrists, otherwise it is quite painful for the horse, resembling more of a karate chop than a therapeutic movement!

1/2 Begin at the wing of atlas, working from just behind your horse's ear, down his neck towards his shoulder in slow stroking movements. This is known as effleurage. Cover the entire neck, as this warms and prepares the muscles for the next movements.

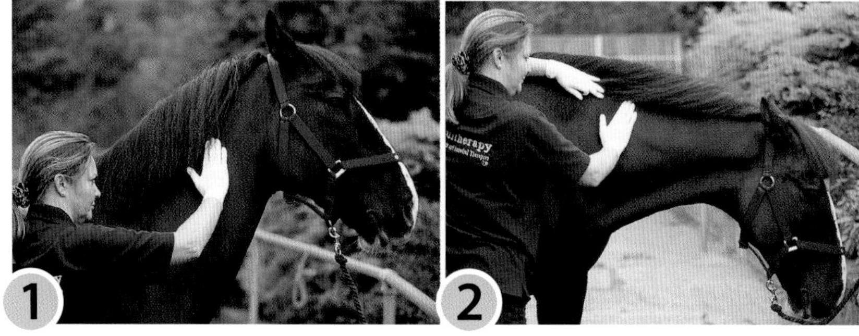

3/4 Now 'knuckle' (see photograph 3, which shows knuckling on the withers) down the neck as shown, taking care to avoid the cervical vertebrae that you will be able to feel at the bottom of the neck. Knuckling will cause a gentle contraction of the neck muscles, so you will now need to repeat your effleurage over the same area.

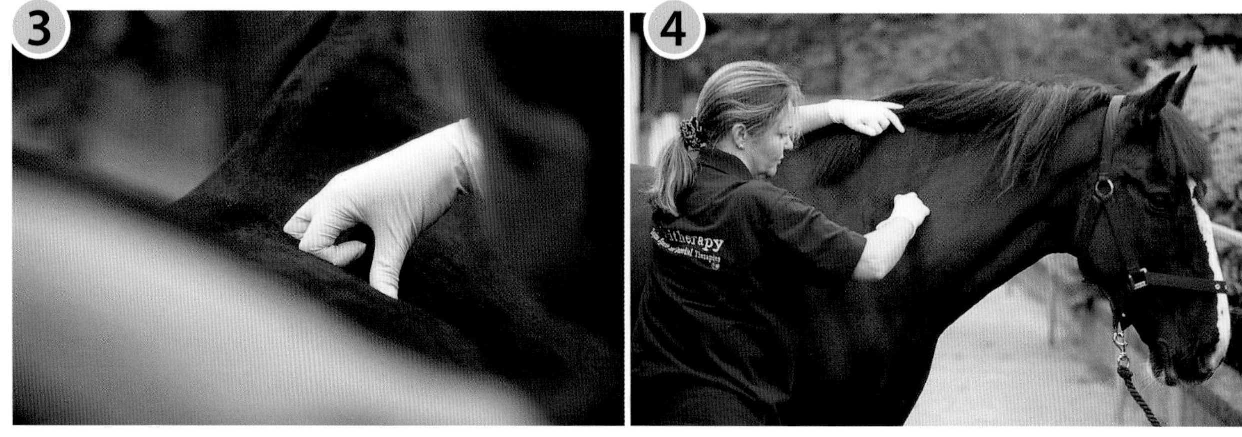

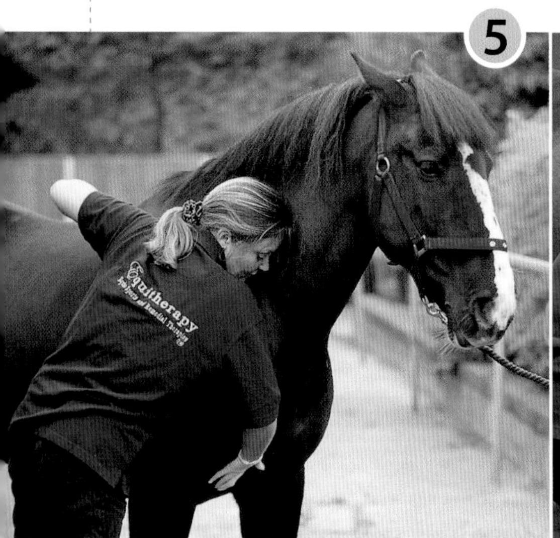

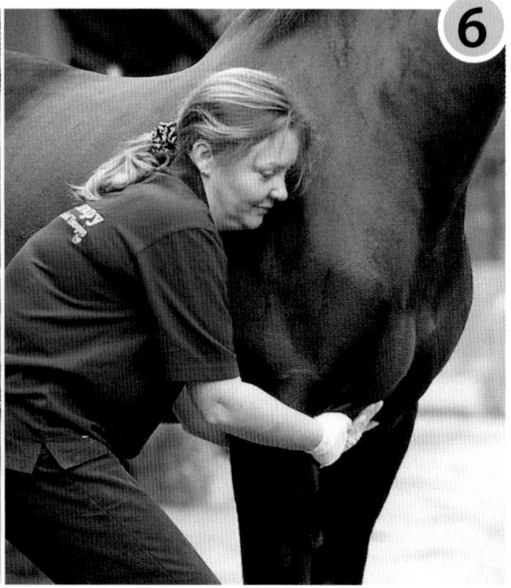

5/6 Having completed your effleurage on the neck, allow your hand to progress around the chest and under the forearm. Bring the other hand under the forearm from the opposite side, reaching up to meet and overlap the right hand.

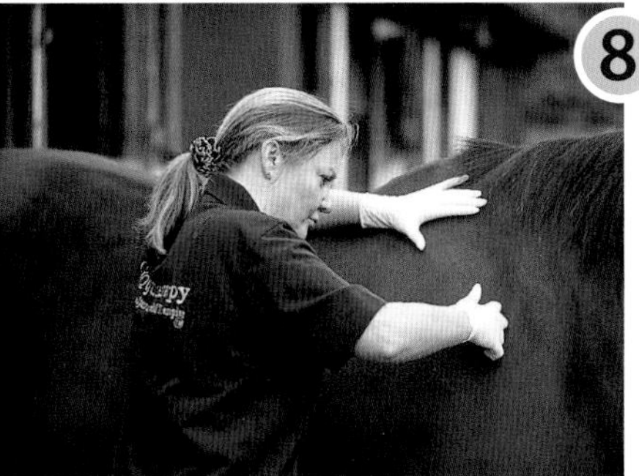

7/8 Move to the top of the shoulder, always keeping one hand on the horse's body. Using your fingers, effleurage from above the scapula to the point of the shoulder. Follow this with gentle knuckling, and then repeat the effleurage.

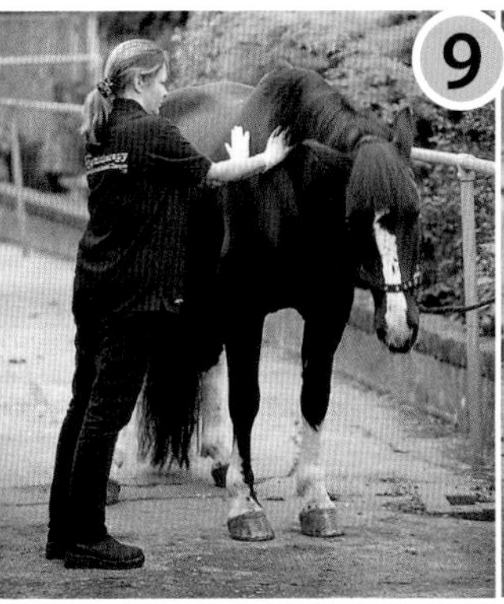

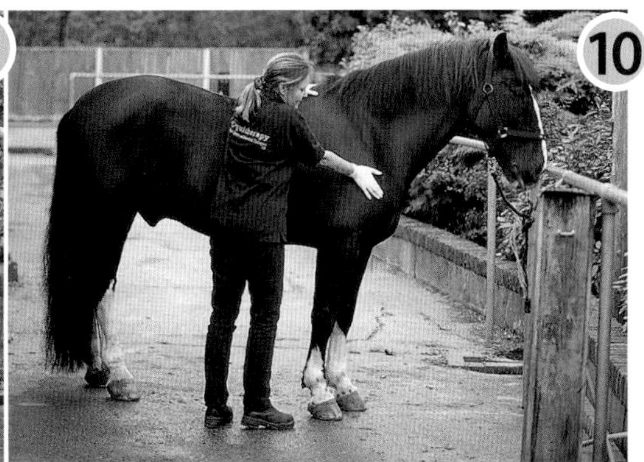

9 Now locate the spine of the scapula (a bony ridge across the horse's shoulder blade): effleurage firstly above and then below the spine of the scapula.

10 Working with two hands, gently ease your hands apart to stretch the muscles. Then knuckle each muscle and repeat regular effleurage.

11/12 Effleurage the triceps in the normal way, and then follow with deep effleurage (see photograph 11) using your fist. Finish off with normal effleurage.

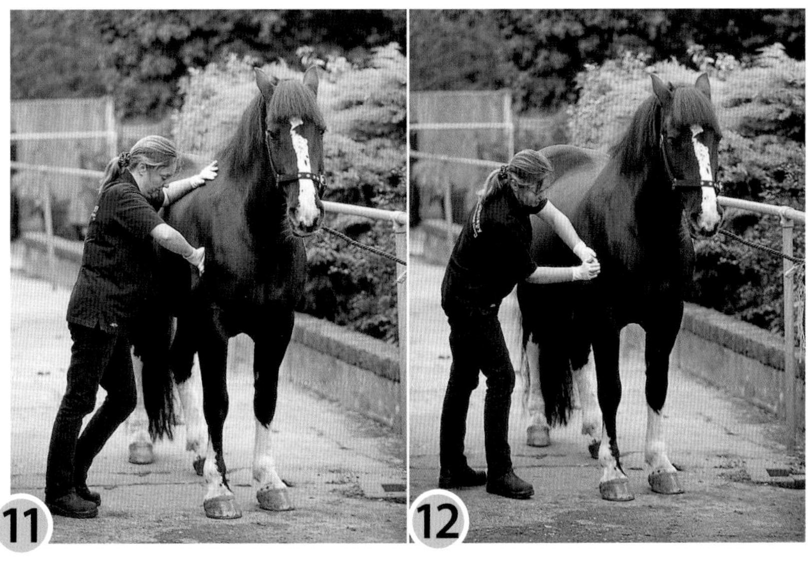

13/14 Working across the top of the wither and taking care to avoid the cartilage at the top of the scapula, effleurage with one hand using the heel of the hand or your fingers. Now knuckle into this area. This is a good example of technique fitting beautifully into an area.

15 Effleurage along the muscles of the horse's back, parallel to the spine (the paraspinal muscles).

16/17 Use two-finger rotations or petrissage (see photograph 17), circling along these muscles. Then knuckle the same area.

18/19/20 Now hack, cup or pound, according to what your horse finds most appropriate, and effleurage to finish.

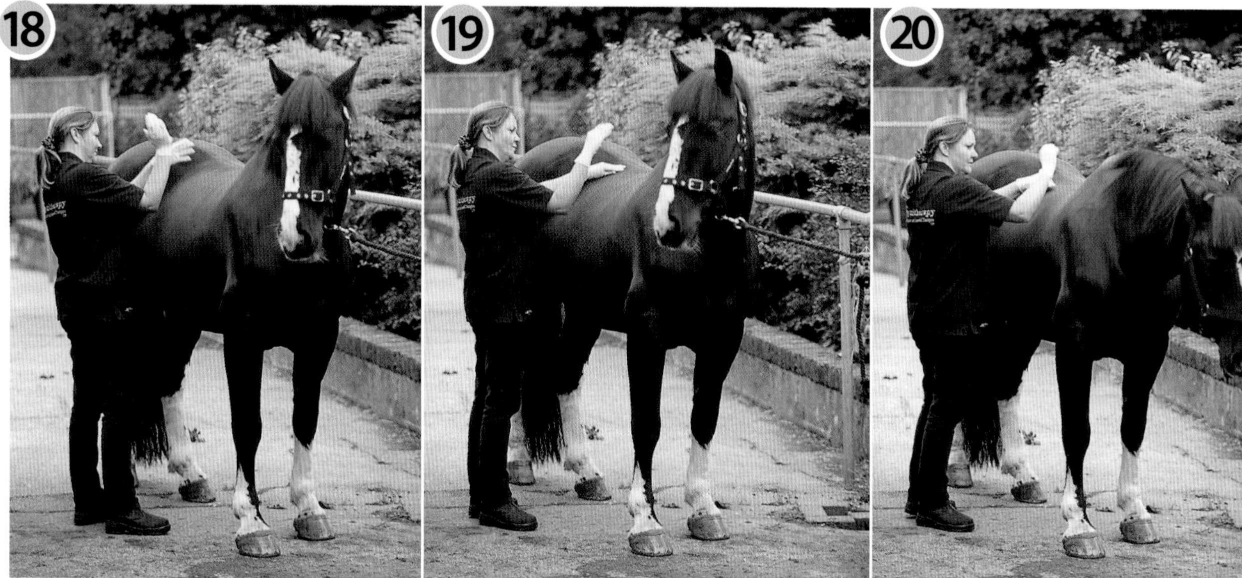

21 If you know your horse to be sensitive around the tummy, leave out this step. Gently effleurage over the ribs, allowing the fingers to sit between the ribs, which soothes the intercostal muscles (the muscles between the ribs).

21

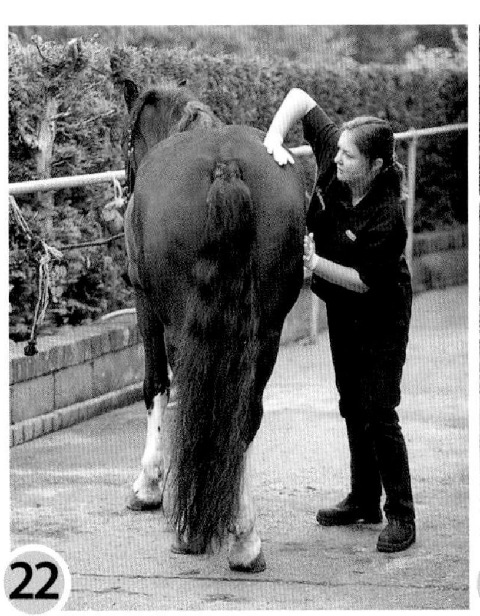
22

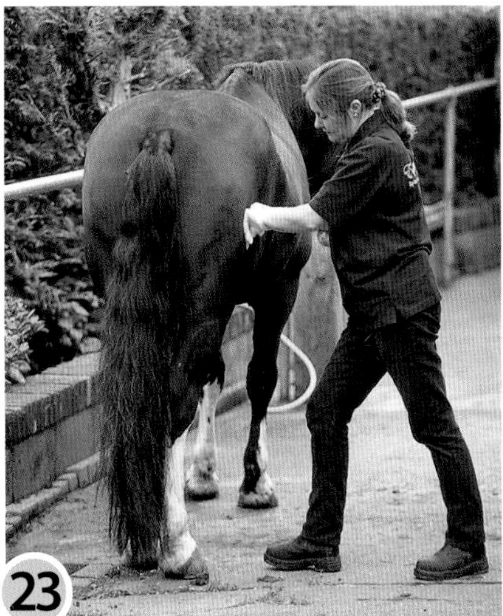
23

22/23 Next, effleurage the gluteal group of muscles. You may perform deep effleurage (see photograph 23) on these muscles if you feel it is appropriate. Be careful to avoid the tuber sacrale and the tuber coxae.

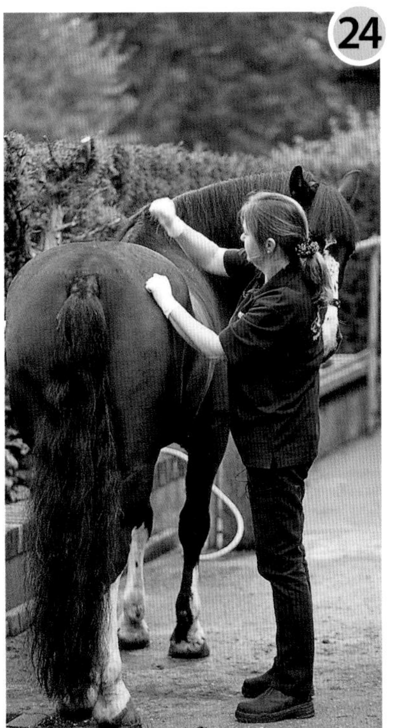
24

24 Knuckle this muscle group, and then perform all the tapotement movements. Finish off with effleurage.

25/26 Allow your hands to run down over the hamstrings, and effleurage from top to bottom. Work into the dock to address two muscles from the hamstring group. Use the petrissage movement once again from top to bottom, and then effleurage to finish this group.

Now, running your hands along your horse's body, repeat these movements on the opposite side.

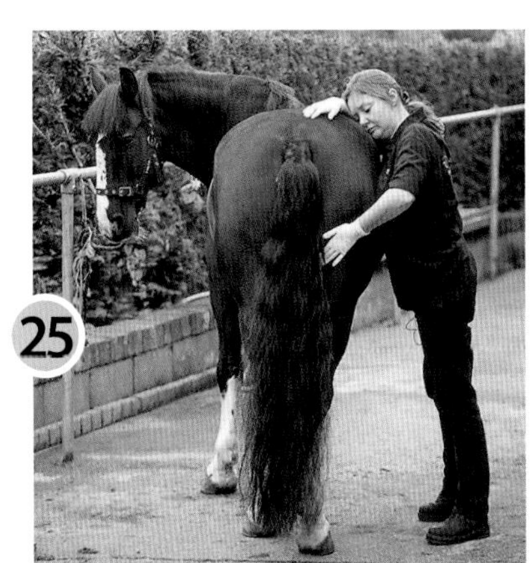
25

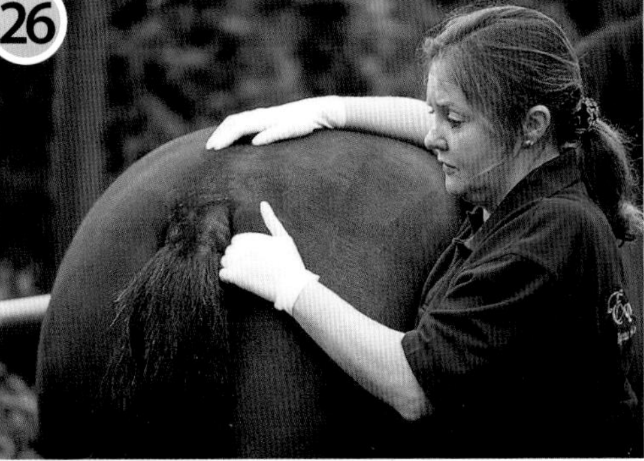
26

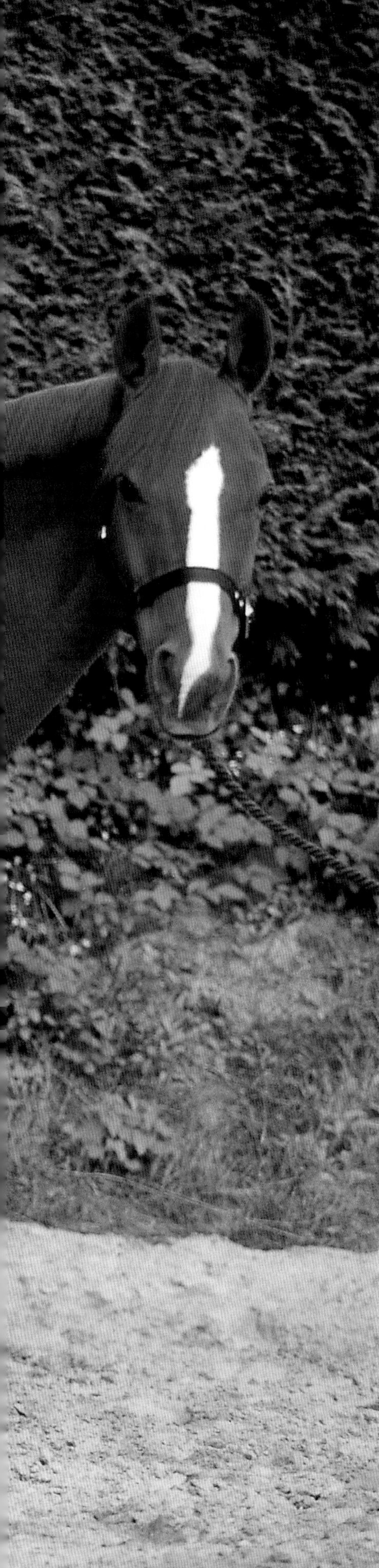

2 30 MINUTES TO A SMARTER HORSE

- 30 minutes to give a thorough groom
- 30 minutes for a top tack clean
- 30 minutes to a mane and tail make-over
- 30 minutes to competition ready
- 30 minutes to clip and tidy up

Nothing quite beats the satisfaction of standing back to look at your horse when you've turned him out for something special, with coat and tack gleaming. It isn't possible to completely avoid the hard work that this requires. However, regular grooming and – yes, it's true – keeping your tack clean after every ride, make this much easier.

The best time to groom your horse is after you've ridden him, when his pores are open and the scurf that accumulates on the skin is easier to remove. Spend 30 minutes when you return from a ride, giving him a groom that he'll enjoy too.

Whilst a daily wipe over will keep your tack reasonably clean, once a week a thorough session is needed. And for special occasions remember: it's the finishing touches that make all the difference.

If you find the prospect of pulling your horse's mane or sorting out his tail daunting, don't despair, because it really is possible to do the job in just 30 minutes.

Even getting ready for a competition can be achieved in 30 minutes in an emergency, and if all you have is half an hour, you could spend it tidying up your horse's winter clip.

30 minutes to Give a Thorough Groom

When it comes to grooming, riders tend to fall into two groups: those that love it, and those that find it a chore. However, as with most tasks around the stable yard, if you organize yourself beforehand and practise a regular routine, it soon becomes second nature.

For the stable-kept horse and his owner, a thorough grooming session has several benefits:

Benefits to the horse
- It keeps the skin clean, the pores open, and removes debris from the coat.
- Most horses find the attention of a grooming session a pleasure.

Benefits to the rider
- It gives you an opportunity to check your horse for injuries.
- It enables you to familiarize yourself with your horse's lumps and bumps.
- It helps to keep your tack clean.
- It provides a quiet opportunity to bond with your horse.

When you are grooming your horse, focus your attention on him and use the opportunity to note how he feels that day. Is he sore or stiff, tetchy or relaxed, warm enough? If you put this time to good use, getting to know your horse better, you will gain added value from a day-to-day routine.

GROOMING A HORSE THAT LIVES OUT

If you keep your horse at grass, the natural excretions of his coat are part of his protective system, keeping him warm and waterproof! Therefore his grooming requirements are quite different from that of a stabled horse. Before riding it will be necessary to brush him off beneath the saddle and bridle areas to prevent sores and help keep your tack clean. His feet will need to be picked out, and it is also important to run your hands over his body regularly (daily if possible) to check for injuries. But this will be sufficient, unless you are entering a competition, in which case a more thorough grooming will be appropriate.

Don't forget: Sick horses may find intensive grooming a little too much to cope with, as might tired ones.

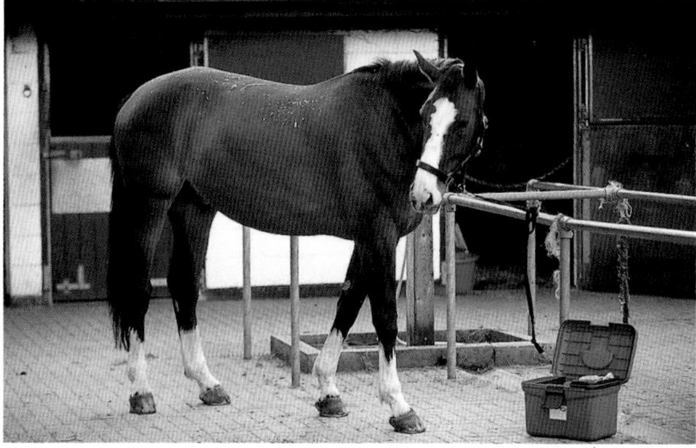

Before and after!

When and where to groom

The best time to groom a horse thoroughly is usually after exercise when he is warm and his pores are open. For this reason most riders will give a horse a quick brush off before riding and then a thorough grooming afterwards. However, a hot and sweaty horse should be allowed to cool down and dry off before he is groomed.

If the weather is particularly cold, groom your horse with his stable rugs on: first fold back the front half, brush him, and wrap him up again when you have finished; and repeat the process with the horse's back and haunches, folding the rear half of the rug forwards.

It is often easier to groom your horse outside on the yard than in his stable, because then you have a clear view of, and access to, his feet. Also, if you drop a brush or sponge it will not become covered in bedding, nor will the bed end up soaking wet if you knock a bucket over. Always use a headcollar and leadrope, and tie him up to fillet string using a quick-release knot, as you should normally do.

Your cleaning kit

Before you begin to groom your horse, ensure that you have everything you need to hand. Time will be saved if you don't have to stop and search for that missing sponge or brush.

Most riders develop their own preferences regarding brushes and types of curry comb, but here's a checklist of potential basics:

Cleaning kit checklist

Dandy brush (**1**)
Body brush (**2**)
Flicky brush (**3**)
Metal curry comb (**4**)
Plastic curry comb (**5**)
Rubber curry comb
Hoof pick (**6**)
Water brush
Sponges
Stable rubber (**7**)
Mane and tail brush and/or comb (**8**)
Scissors (**9**)
Finish products such as mane and tail conditioner and coat sheen (**10**)
Hoof oil/conditioner and brush
Hoof cleaning brush (**11**)

WHAT'S THE DIFFERENCE BETWEEN ALL THOSE BRUSHES AND CURRY COMBS?

Dandy brush Firmer than a flicky brush or a water brush, this is used to remove mud, dirt and sweat from a thick coat. Fine-skinned or clipped horses will not like this brush. It is also a little firm for legs and bellies, but can be used for cleaning hooves.

Body brush A shorter-bristled, 'flat' brush that usually has a strap to fit it against the palm of the hand. This brush can be used all over the horse's body.

Flicky brush Similar in shape to the dandy brush but larger and with longer, softer bristles, this brush is great for flicking off dirt and sweat. Be judicious about its use on sensitive areas.

Water brush A softer version of the dandy brush, used mostly for laying manes and tails.

Mane and tail brush Many riders use a hair brush for this purpose, but there are brushes intended for this use available on the market.

Hoof-cleaning brush This could be anything from a dandy brush to a washing-up brush!

Hoof-oil brush There are various shapes and sizes available. To prevent the rest of your grooming kit becoming oily, put the bristles inside a small plastic bag.

Metal curry comb Used to clean brushes.

Plastic curry comb Used to clean brushes, or to brush the dirt and mud off the less sensitive areas of the horse.

Rubber curry comb Used to remove dirt and mud from the less sensitive areas of the horse's body.

Step by step to a well-groomed horse

1 Pick your horse's feet out from frog to toe.

2 Scrub out the inside of the foot – a dish-washing brush is particularly good for this. Check that the foot appears and smells healthy.

3 Scrub the outside of the hoof, checking clenches and the condition of the hoof.

4 To prevent dirt and dust from the mane falling on to the coat after you have brushed it, begin by sectioning and brushing through your horse's mane. Use either a special hair brush or a body brush, according to how effective the result is on your horse's

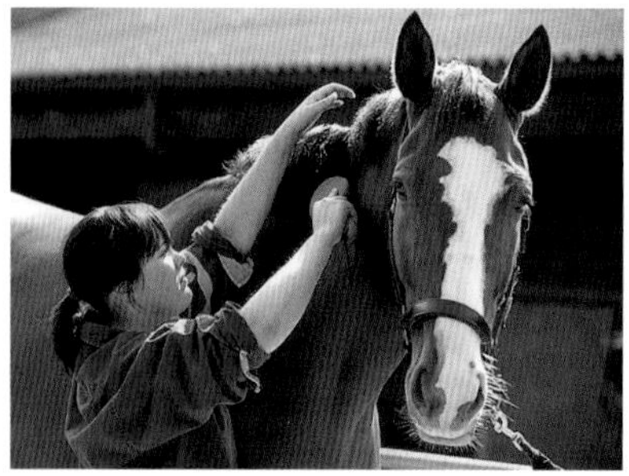

mane. Brush all the hair over to the opposite side to which it lies, to enable you to reach right into the roots, and then bring it back again, section by section.

5 With a damp water brush – by this I mean shake off any excess water – lay the mane by brushing through from the roots to the ends. This helps to control flyaway sections of hair.

6 Using a plastic or rubber curry comb, if your horse is particularly muddy and dirty, or a flicky brush, begin at the horse's neck and work your way along his body to his tail on one side, removing as much dirt as possible. Then repeat on the opposite side. Do not use either the curry combs or the flicky brush on the sensitive areas such as the face and belly, or the thin-skinned areas such as his legs. At every third or fourth stroke, clean the flicky brush against your metal curry comb to remove residue dust. The rhythm of this action can be comforting to the horse – many have been known

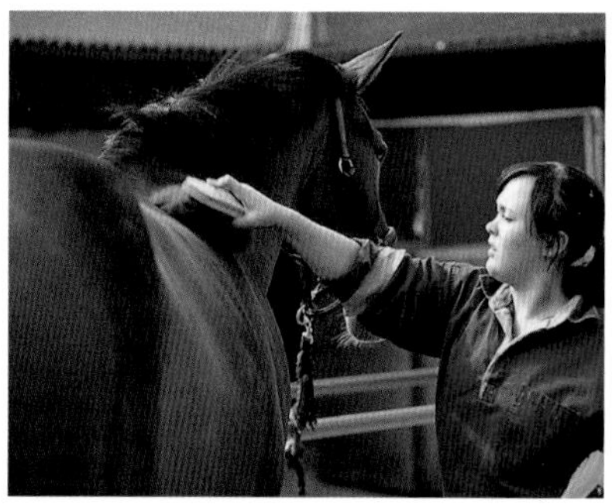

to fall asleep at this stage. Also the gentle pressure that you apply to your brush strokes (which should be strokes, and not blows!) has a therapeutic effect on the muscle and skin beneath.

7 Repeat step 6, using a body brush but including the legs, tummy and face on this occasion.

When brushing the face, slip the lower part of the headcollar off your horse's nose for a few minutes. Be very careful around the face; some horses cannot tolerate a large brush in this region, and it may be advisable to try to find something smaller. Don't forget to brush the ears and under the jaw, and pay particular attention to where the bridle lies.

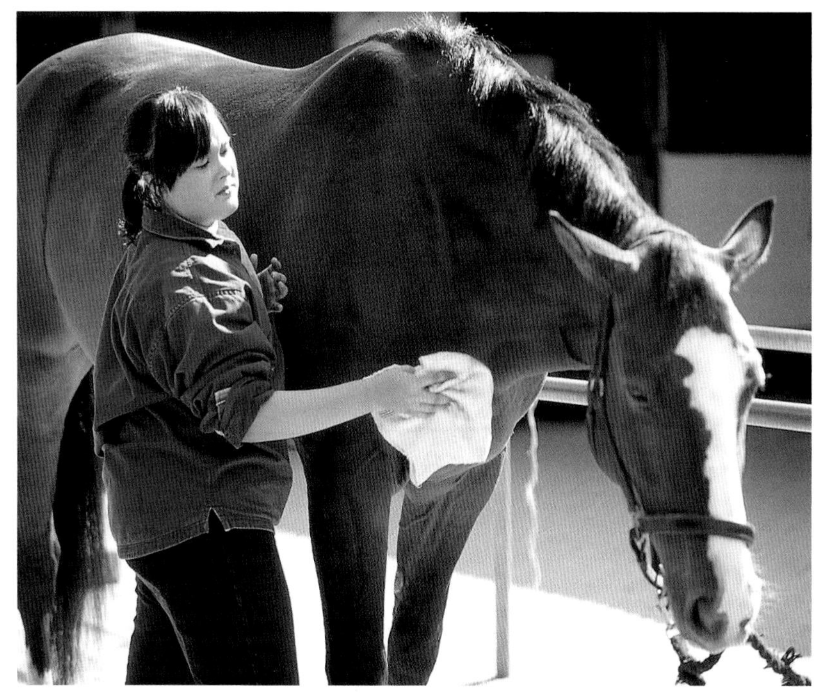

8 With a small damp sponge, wipe your horse's eyes, nostrils and the corners of his mouth.

9 Now, standing to one side of your horse, brush through his tail, if necessary dividing it into sections before you begin. Use a clean sponge to wash under his dock and around his anus.

10 Lay the top of your horse's tail, using the water brush once again.

11 Using a damp stable rubber, wipe all over your horse's coat, even around his face if he will allow it. An old tea towel makes a great stable rubber.

12 Finish off by applying either hoof oil or conditioner to your horse's feet.

FINISHING TOUCHES

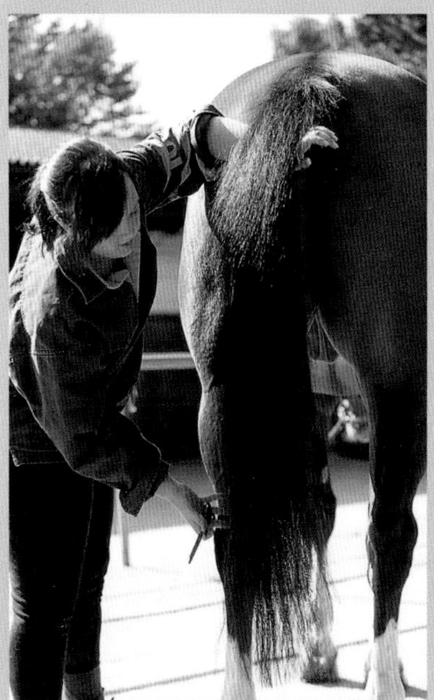

A thorough grooming session is always a good opportunity to trim the odd whisker, level off your horse's tail, or pull a stray hair from his mane without it becoming a traumatic experience for him.

30 minutes for a Top Tack Clean

Choosing the correct saddle, the best bridle and most appropriate bit takes time and effort, and is costly. It therefore makes sense to look after these items once the choice is made.

Tack should be cleaned after every ride. Saddlers confirm that a wipe over with a cloth that has saddle soap on it to remove mud and sweat is enough, provided that the relevant items are given a thorough clean every week. An occasional feeding with specialized products may also be necessary, should the saddle and bridle become stiff, or following a thorough soaking if you are caught in the rain.

As you clean your tack, check the stitching, especially on the stirrup leathers, reins and girth. Pay particular attention to areas where the metal fittings rub against the leather.

Keep your cloth or sponge as dry as possible. Not only will excess water make more work for you, but it may also damage or mark your tack, and should only be used if the tack is absolutely caked in mud. In this event, 'polish' the leather dry with an appropriate, clean cloth.

Taking the time out from your valuable riding hours may seem a waste, but if you consider the contribution that good tack makes both to your riding performance and safety, and to the comfort of your horse – suddenly 30 minutes once a week doesn't seem so bad.

Before you begin

Collect together everything you may need before you start.

Tack-cleaning checklist

- 2 buckets of water (one for the stirrup irons and bit)
- Saddle soap
- Sponges
- Toothpicks
- Metal polish
- Leather conditioners

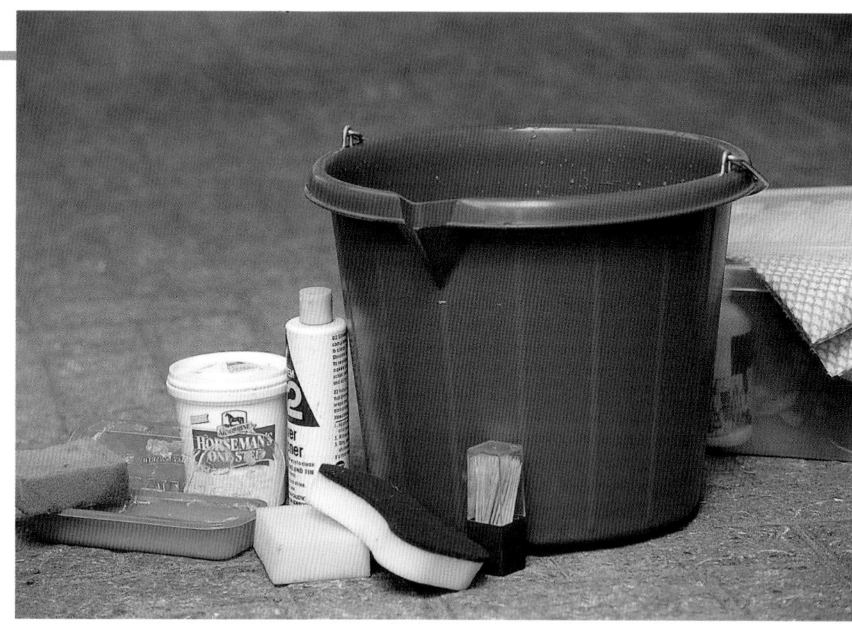

The saddle

A saddle seat doesn't need to be cleaned every day provided it is being used on a clean horse with a clean numnah. However, the girth, leathers and saddle flaps should be wiped over or brushed as frequently as possible. Synthetic saddles should be cleaned according to the manufacturer's instructions.

CLEANING A FABRIC GIRTH

If your girth is not made of leather or something similar, it can be brushed clean or washed in warm soapy water. Be sure to rinse it out thoroughly, as soap can irritate the horse's skin, and hang it up to dry. If you prefer to use a fabric girth it is advisable to purchase a spare.

1 Take the saddle 'apart', removing the stirrup leathers and the girth. Remove the stirrup irons from the leathers and place the irons in a bucket of warm water.

2 Using warm water, with a splash of washing-up liquid or a teaspoon of vinegar to break down the grease, wipe the leathers and girth, if made of leather. Clean the stirrup-leather buckle holes with a toothpick.

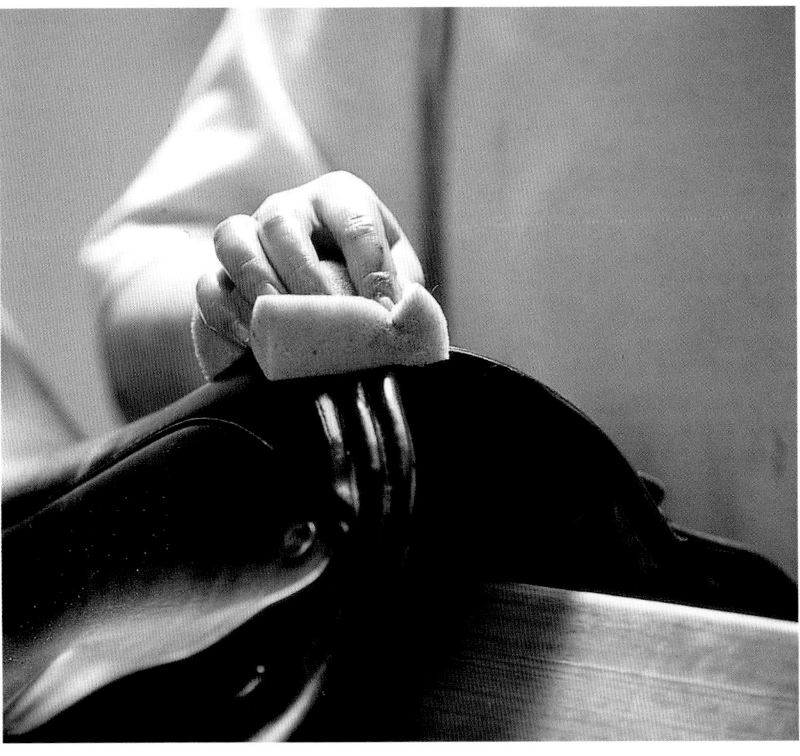

3 Wash all parts of the saddle with a damp sponge. Don't forget to wash beneath the saddle flaps, and particularly around the stirrup bar. If the saddle has any suede patches, these should be brushed once the surrounding leather has been cleaned and dried. Don't forget to check all stitching, and for signs of wear as you are cleaning the saddle. Ensure that all the parts that are meant to move – the stirrup bar and D-rings, for example – actually do so!

4 Now wipe the saddle, leathers and girth with an appropriate treatment. If you don't normally use a leather conditioner or oil regularly, it is a good idea to do so about every four weeks.

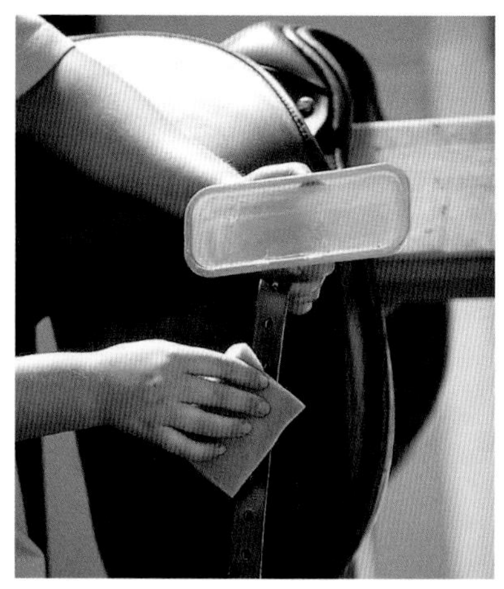

5 Wash and dry the irons, paying particular attention to the treads. A toothbrush is useful to clean mud and dirt from the tread. Use an appropriate metal polish to finish.

6 Put all the components of the saddle back together. Ensure that the leathers are at a suitable length, and that they are level.

The bridle

1 Take the bridle to pieces. As you are doing so, check to see what holes the cheekpieces and noseband are on. Put the bit into hot water. Wash each leather strap with a damp sponge, using a very soft or old scouring cloth (see photographs) to remove stubborn grease.

2 Check each buckle and keeper and the stitching. Clean any built-up grease from the buckles using the scouring side of your sponge. Polish the buckles with an appropriate product.

3 Clean the straps with saddle soap or your choice of cleaning product.

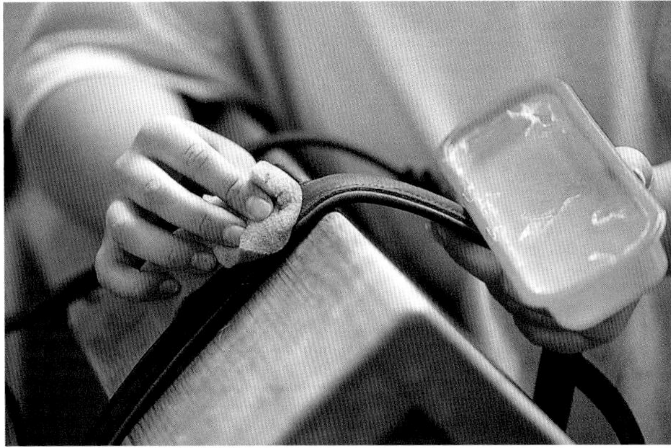

4 Clean out the buckle holes with a toothpick or matchstick.

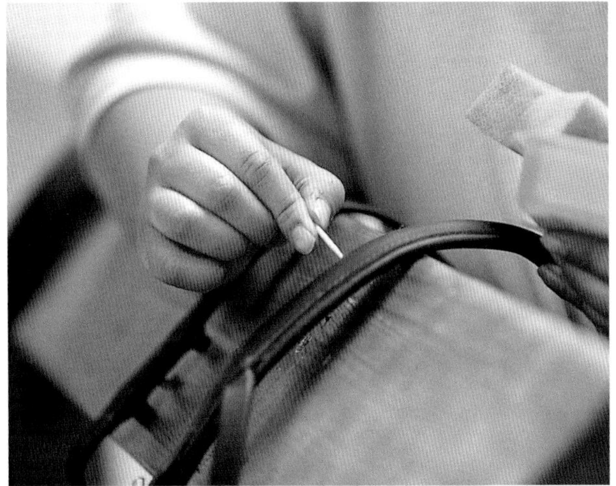

5 Scrub the bit using the scouring side of your sponge to remove any build-up of dirt.

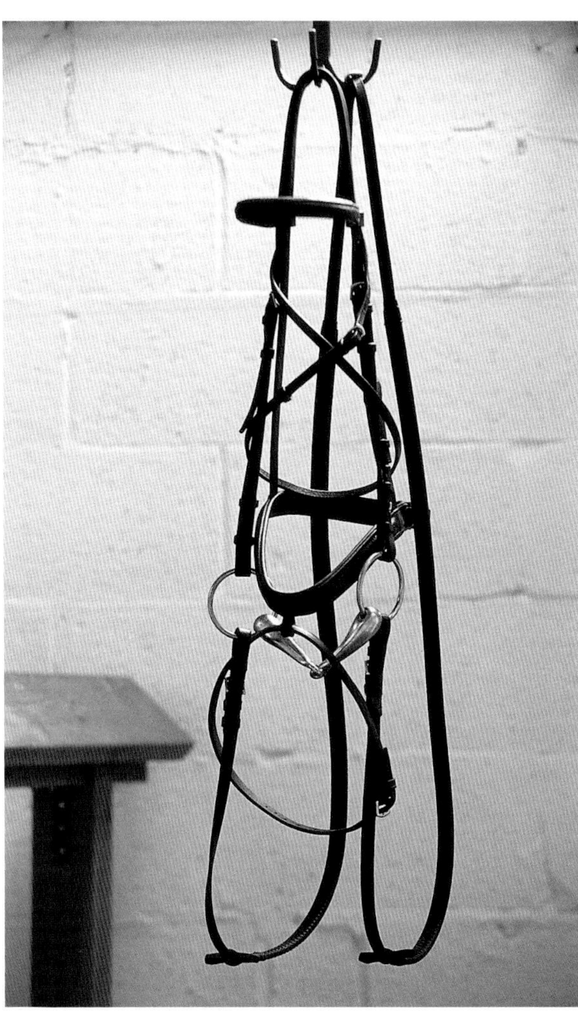

OILING YOUR TACK

When to oil tack:
- if it is new;
- if it has become dry and stiff;
- if it gets very wet;
- if you are storing it away.

Ensure that the leather is properly cleaned (see above). Apply the oil to the item with a brush or piece of clean cloth, and massage it in. Give the oil time to be absorbed into the leather, then re-treat it with saddle soap to bring back the shine.

30 minutes to a Mane and Tail Make-over

In normal circumstances, pulling a mane or tail is not a task to be performed in a hurry. However, the demands on time to be spent in horsey pursuits can be precious, and jobs such as pulling manes and tails sometimes get left until the last minute.

Sam Gardner runs a showing yard in Kent, where she has 10 liveries: 'I have to make the best use of my time for every task I undertake, and I've become an expert at preparing horses.'

Once the initial task of pulling is complete, maintaining the smart results can become a weekly, or even a daily chore taking just a few seconds.

Tidying up the tail

1 Whilst it would be normal to begin with the mane, the tail will probably have to be bandaged to help it lie flat, so with only 30 minutes to spare, begin with the tail to give the tail bandage more time to do its job.

If your horse has a thin tail, it might be possible to pull it, but horses are more sensitive about having their tails pulled than their manes, and this job should not be done in a hurry. Also, this horse has quite a thick tail so, faced with the pressure of getting him ready quickly, Sam decides that trimming the tail is the only way.

⇧ *Sam prefers to pull a tail by hand as it makes the horse less sore; however, a tail such as this should be pulled over several days, not in 30 minutes.*

PULLING A TAIL

Before pulling your horse's tail, ensure that, if you compete in any particular discipline, a pulled tail is appropriate. Horses may object to tail pulling, so be sensitive and stand clear of possible kicks.

The hair is pulled from underneath and down the sides of the dock, beginning at the top of the tail. Most people find pulling by hand (winding the hair around your finger rather than a metal pulling comb) more sympathetic to the horse. Unless the tail is very thick, avoid taking hair from the middle.

2 Now it is time to cut the ends of the tail. Bearing in mind how high your horse carries his tail, place one arm beneath the dock and raise the tail. Run your hand down the tail and grasp it firmly just below the hock. The tail should end at about the middle of your horse's chestnut.

Cut off the hair at the point you have noted. Allow the tail to drop, then trim off any stray hairs and ensure that it is straight.

⇦ *If your horse carries his tail really high, it's worth enlisting some help to hold up the tail whilst you measure the ends.*

⇩ *'I'd always recommend really sharp scissors for this job,' says Sam. 'And in the case of a really thick tail, I'll use clippers.'*

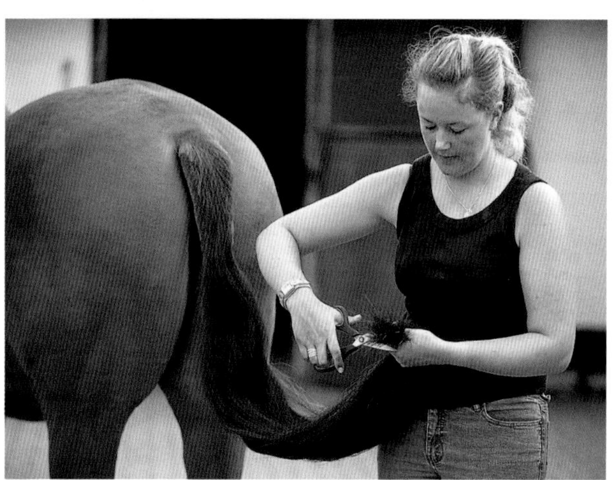

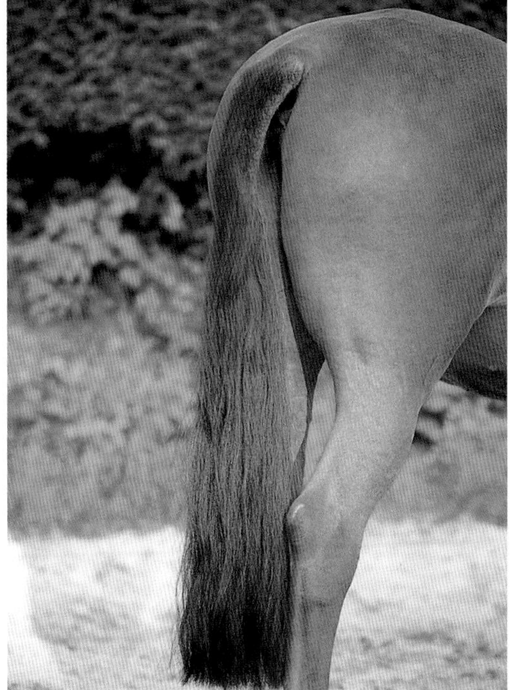

3 A tail bandage will help to flatten tail hairs to give this neat end-result.

TAIL BANDAGE TIPS

- Wrap a tail bandage round your horse's tail firmly, but not too tightly. Leave it on as long as possible, but not overnight. 'If necessary, spray the tail with hairspray before applying the tail bandage. It will brush out,' suggests Sam.
- Before a competition, leave the tail bandage on as long as possible, provided your horse is comfortable. Sam recommends putting a bandage on the morning before a show, and leaving it for about an hour if possible.
- If you're using a 'tail shine' product, don't put too much on the top part of the tail as the bandage will slip off.
- If you have problems keeping tail bandages up, start tying them at the middle of the dock and then go up to the top of the tail and back down again.
- Always use a tail bandage that stands out against your horse's tail: 'I can't tell you how many people I've seen riding into the show ring with their horse's tail bandage still on,' says Sam.

⇦ *Sam likes to use a damp bandage on her horses' tails, but it's a fine art to tie a tail bandage just right, and a damp bandage will shrink. This is probably one tip best left to the professionals.*

HOW TO TRIM A COMPETITION TAIL

If time is not an object, always pull a tail. However, if you find yourself up against the clock, here's how to trim a tail without losing your place in the line-up.

1. Sam's first tip is: don't be afraid! Give the tail a good brush and, standing to one side of the horse, start to trim it in a line up the tail. She advises: 'If you're going to be doing this regularly, it's worth buying a pair of left-handed scissors to do one side.'

2. Once you've removed the longer hairs, carefully trim as close to the dock as possible. Take care here, as you don't want to trim too much hair away from the top of the tail. Where a pulled or trimmed tail ends will play a part in the appearance of the horse's quarters, so trim gradually, until you have decided just about where trimming should finish for your horse.

3. Having decided approximately where you wish to trim the tail to, pull out any stray hairs to the sides to judge whether these should be removed, and to even up both sides of the trim.

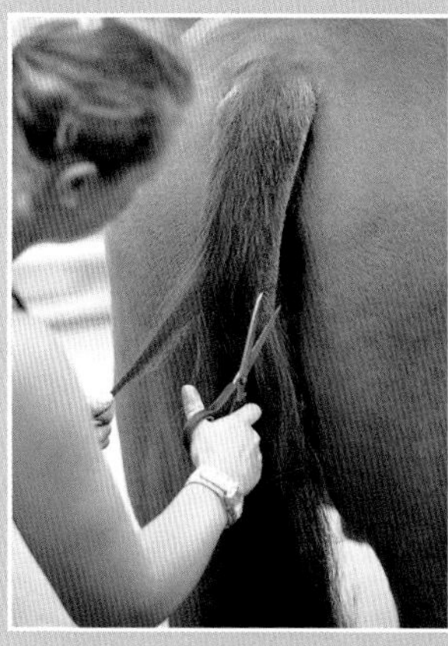

4. Your aim is to remove all the hair on the underside of the tail, leaving it in its natural state on the top.

Tidying up the mane

1 Firstly, give the mane a good brush through. Sam begins by cutting off and levelling the mane to a sensible length. 'As with the tail, with a mane this long it would be cruel and unnecessary to try to pull all that hair, even if we had all day.'

⇧ *Only blunt trim a mane with scissors if it is very long. It is a waste of time to pull a long mane to a good finished length.*

2 Sam sections off the forelock, combing it forwards to create a straight bridle path. Next she takes a 2.5cm (1in) section of hair and backcombs it to 1.5cm (½in) above the desired finished length of the mane.

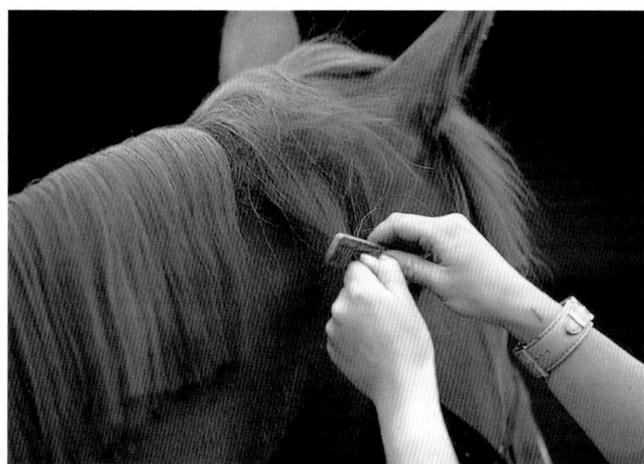

⇧ *Regularly comb out the backcombing as you progress down a mane to ensure that you are not creating steps.*

3 She wraps the remaining straggly hair around the metal mane comb.

⇧ *Tip: If you wish to protect your hands and nails whilst pulling, wear thin surgical gloves, available from most supermarkets and chemists.*

4 Then takes a strong grasp, and with a fast, firm tug, pulls the hair away.

⇧ *This is a bit like having a plaster pulled off – the quicker it is done, the better!*

SAFETY REMINDER

The pulling of manes and tails can be quite traumatic for a horse. (A distracting haynet is often advisable.) Do not balance on boxes or steps to pull a mane until you know how a horse is going to behave. Likewise do not stand directly behind a horse when working on his tail. A bale of straw is a safer thing to stand on, and you can put it behind the horse when pulling his tail. Even if you know him well, an awkward 'pull' could surprise both him and, as a result, you. If necessary enlist help.

5 Finally, the professional touch that makes all the difference: Sam uses very sharp scissors held at an angle, to make random, small snips into the line of the mane to prevent it looking too rigid.

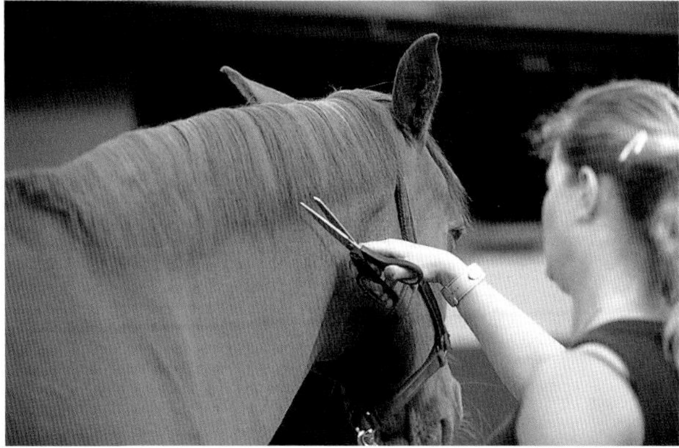

⇧ *Don't get carried away when you have the scissors in your hands! Make a few snips and then stand back to see what is needed.*

TIPS FOR MANE PULLING

- If you have the opportunity, work the horse until his veins are up before pulling the mane. This helps open the pores and makes pulling less uncomfortable.
- Don't wash the mane or tail before pulling. However, washing it afterwards will be soothing.
- First of all, make the mane thinner, and then work on the length.
- Work from poll to wither, and don't worry too much about straggly ends during the first sweep. Then go back to the top and pull out any stray strands.
- Don't pull the mane the day before you are going to plait. Your horse won't be pleased to see you approaching his mane for a second day running!
- If a horse is a youngster or having his mane pulled for the first time, do just a little bit at a time.
- Keep brushing as you pull, in order to avoid a stepped look.
- If your horse has a particularly fine mane, trim it with scissors (see step 5).
- If a horse has found this a particularly painful experience, arnica may help.

⇩ *A well pulled mane that looks natural and flatters the horse's neck.*

30 minutes to Competition Ready

The pre-planning before a big day is part of the fun and organization – which is what competing is all about. However, sometimes things go wrong – you oversleep for example, or a friend has a problem loading – and you find that your well made plans have gone awry. But that's no excuse to stay at home: here's a 30-minute plan to get you off the yard as fast as possible. It's not easy, but it can be done. Showing expert Sam Gardner says:

In reality, your horse should have been prepared as much as possible the day before – bathed and plaited up, with a summer sheet, hood and tail bandage to protect the results. Before beginning this countdown, make sure you have everything you are going to need to hand. I sew a plait more quickly than I can plait using rubber bands, but you should just do whatever comes most naturally to you. If you are going to sew, arm yourself with needles, double-threaded with knotted thread, before you begin.

WHAT YOU WILL NEED

- 2 buckets of water
- water brush
- comb
- scissors
- needles and thread or bands
- butterfly clip or similar
- coat shine
- stain remover or instant shampoo
- good quality hairspray
- fly spray
- talc

The clock starts now...

30 minutes to go...

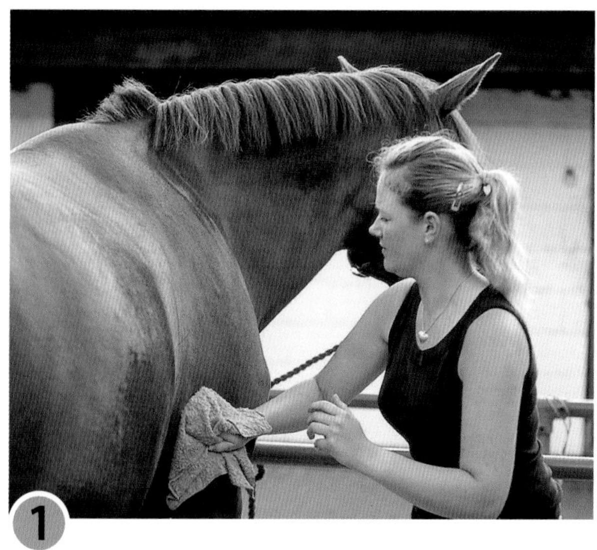

1 If your horse is not too grubby, use a stable rubber, dampened with warm water and a little disinfectant, to remove dust and bedding quickly. The more the stable rubber is wrung out, the better. If you have any stable stains, wipe them off with a spray stain remover or a small amount of shampoo: wipe it on and wipe it off – this takes 30 seconds (if you have everything to hand). Finish off with a coat shine, except for under the saddle.

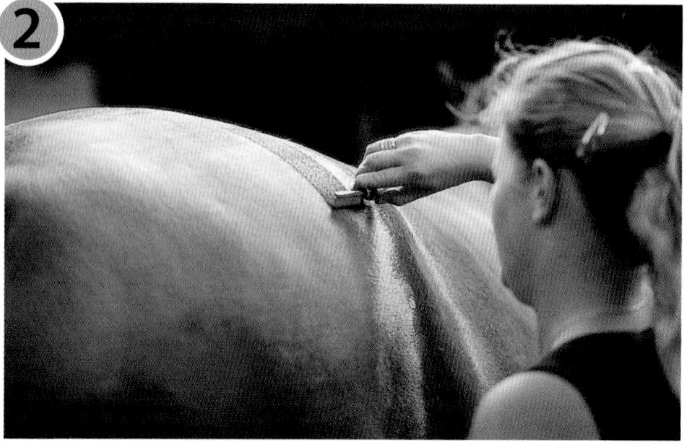

2 The next step is quarter marking. Thoroughly soak the quarters with a sponge until the coat is standing up properly, then remove the excess water. Use a flea comb to create the markings of your choice. The important thing is not to waste time being indecisive about your choice of markings. Sam chooses three strong bars across Abbie's quarters. These are simple and effective.

3 & 4 She then uses a body brush, as shown, to create shark's teeth.

5 Finally set your markings in place with a good coat of hairspray.

25 minutes to go…

6 The next step is to plait the mane. If you are racing against the clock, make a wider plait. It takes Sam 15 minutes to sew 10 plaits into Abbie's mane.

HOW MANY PLAITS?

There used to be various rules about the number of plaits necessary, but fashions have changed. Many people still prefer an odd number of plaits. What is important, however, is that the plaits are even in width, so once you have decided the width of one plait, do all the others the same. It is now acknowledged that plaits can be used to enhance the appearance of your horse's neck and crest. Here are some guidelines:

- The smaller the horse, the narrower the plaits should be.
- The longer the horse's neck, the fewer plaits are needed.
- If your horse has very little crest, make the plaits more 'hooded' to create the illusion of a crest.

10 minutes to go…

__7__ Before moving on to the horse's tail, put baby oil on his nose to the point where the hair-line begins.

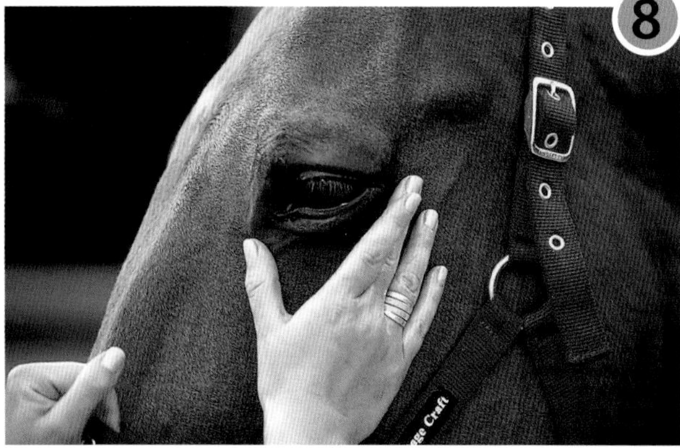

__8__ Then put baby oil around the eyes – in a V-shape on the eyelid to the brow-bone and under the eye from the corner to the end of the projecting cheekbone.

7 minutes to go…

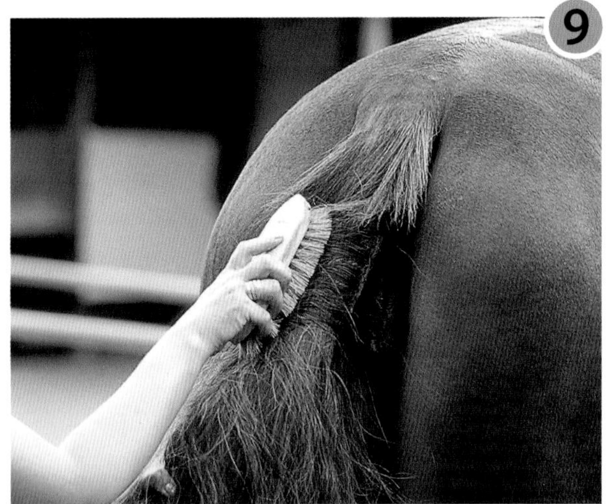

__9__ Now move to the tail. Abbie's tail needs pulling, but there isn't enough time for this. In the circumstances Sam decides to do the best she can with plaiting. Cover your hands with hairspray to help you grip the tail, and begin to plait hairs from the sides of the tail in a funnel around the dock and tail hair, picking up additional strands as necessary. Take minute pieces of hair – the finer the horse or pony, the finer should be the strands that are used for plaiting.

5 minutes to go…

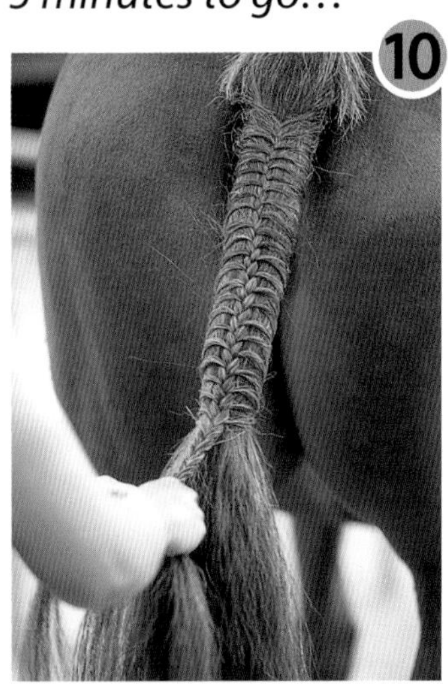

__10__ If you are in a 'condition and turn-out' show you must plait to the end of the dock; otherwise, finish plaiting around the tail at the point that looks most natural. Now plait the remaining hairs right to their ends.

__11 & 12__ Stitch and bind the ends of the plait in the same way as you would for the mane. Thread the needle through the top of the individual plait and pull top and bottom together, doubling it up (see 12). Secure the plait.

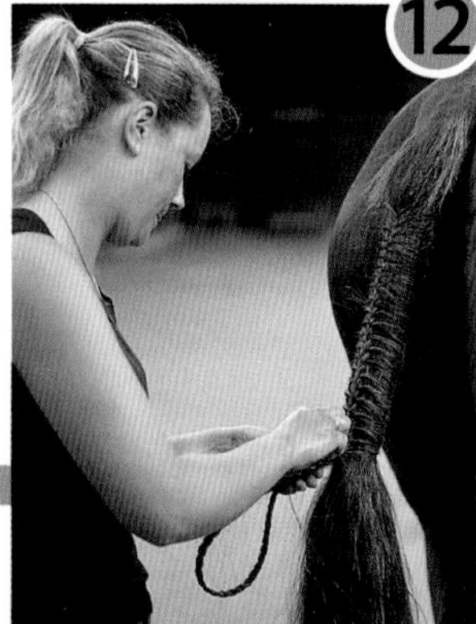

Time's up...

Taking advantage of a few final seconds, Sam brushes talcum powder into Abbie's white socks, and slicks baby oil over her hooves as a final touch. 'I would usually finish with a quick spray of fly spray to keep the horse's mind on the fact that there's a job to be done.'

TAKE 30 MINUTES TO SEW PLAITS INTO A MANE

If this is your first attempt at plaiting, don't even *try* to follow our 30-minute plan. Rather, put 30 minutes aside when you are not in a hurry, and practise plaiting your horse. Most professionals prefer a sewn plait as it is neater, less obvious, and more secure than a plait held by an elastic band.

1 Comb or brush through the mane. Do not wash a mane the day before you are going to plait as it will be too slippery; wash it a couple of days before.

2 Decide what width you would like your plaits to be. Section the forelock and comb it forwards. Wet the mane thoroughly, and then section off the hair for your plaits using a butterfly clip or similar to control the surrounding hairs.

3 Make the plaits as even as possible to the bottom of the mane.

4 Using a plaiting needle, double-threaded and knotted at the end, push the needle through from the back to the front.

5 Loop the thread around the plait a couple of times, then push the needle through, from back to front, once again. Fold in the loose ends and repeat this step to make the plait secure.

6 Now push the needle through the plait at the crest, and draw up the end. Stitch this through one more time to secure it.

7 Repeat the process, folding the plait in half and securing it once again.

8 Roll the plait into a neat shape and finally secure it, stitching from back to front and wrapping the thread first around to the left, and then around to the right. Do this about three times. Then thread the needle through the plait from front to back to secure, and cut off.

Work down your horse's mane from his poll to his withers. Don't expect beautiful results the first time: practice makes perfect.

30 minutes to Clip and Tidy up

The challenge was to find a clip that could be completed by someone who had clipped before and could do it in 30 minutes. It can be done, but is not recommended if you are in a hurry.

Although it is just possible to do this clip in 30 minutes, this is more about ease than speed, as clipping should never be done when you are in a hurry. Nor should a 30-minute clip be attempted if you have never clipped your horse before. However, if your horse is only in light work, hacking and competing occasionally, it is possible to give him a variation on the blanket clip that will smarten him up, is easy to do, and takes just 30 minutes to complete at a comfortable pace.

So before we begin this clip we are assuming that this is not the first time that you have clipped your horse, and that you know how he will react to the noise and feel of the clippers.

1 Once you have checked everything for safety, begin by placing your finger at the top of the withers, and then remove the hair in a straight line from the point of the shoulder to your finger.

2 Comb the mane over to the opposite side and, starting at the withers, clip up the mane line to the headcollar.

3 Clip the neck following the natural line of the jaw and removing all the hair.

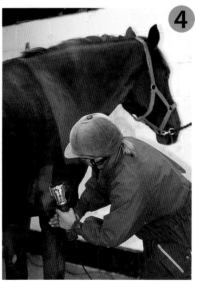

4 Remove the hair between the shoulder and the elbow, beginning to shape the elbow as shown, see picture 11 page 52.

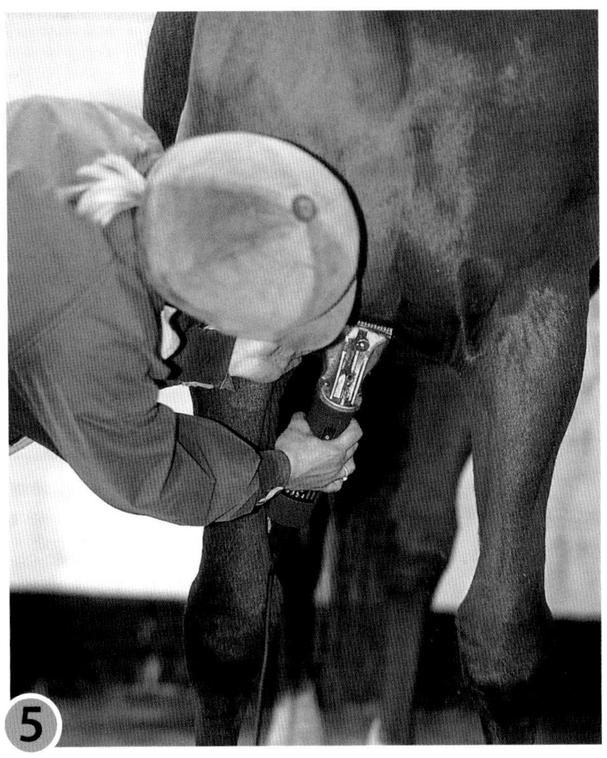

5 Holding the skin back to pull out any wrinkles, remove the hair from the chest.

6 Starting at the middle of the tummy, remove a line of hair up to the point of the shoulder.

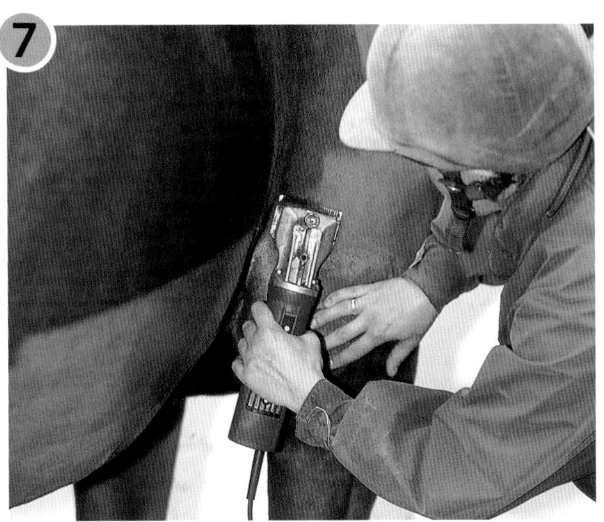

7 Then remove the rest of the hair underneath the tummy and below your line.

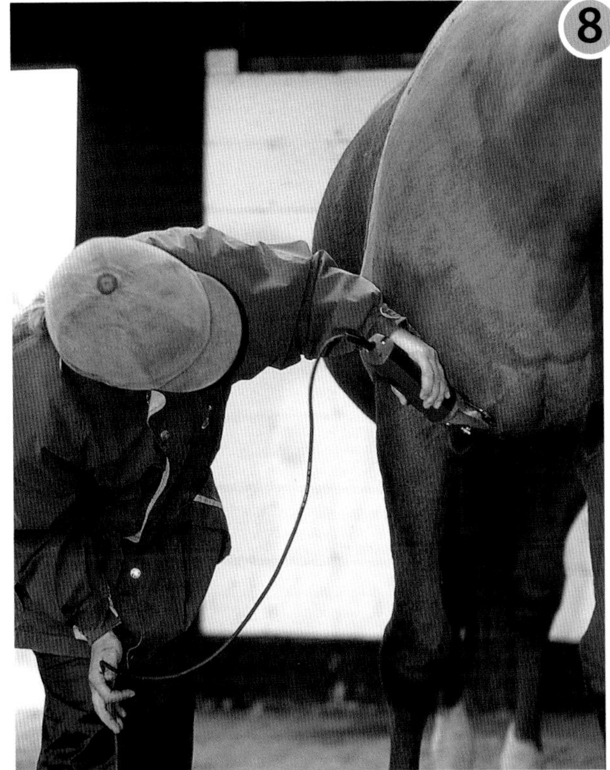

8 Tidy up the area around the point of the shoulder.

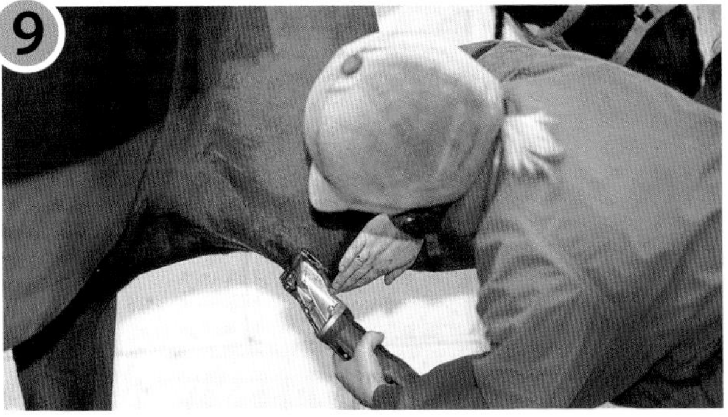

9 Ask someone to hold the horse's leg for you whilst you trim this awkward area.

10 As you clip the remainder of the horse's tummy, working back towards the stifle, keep one hand on the horse for your safety and his reassurance.

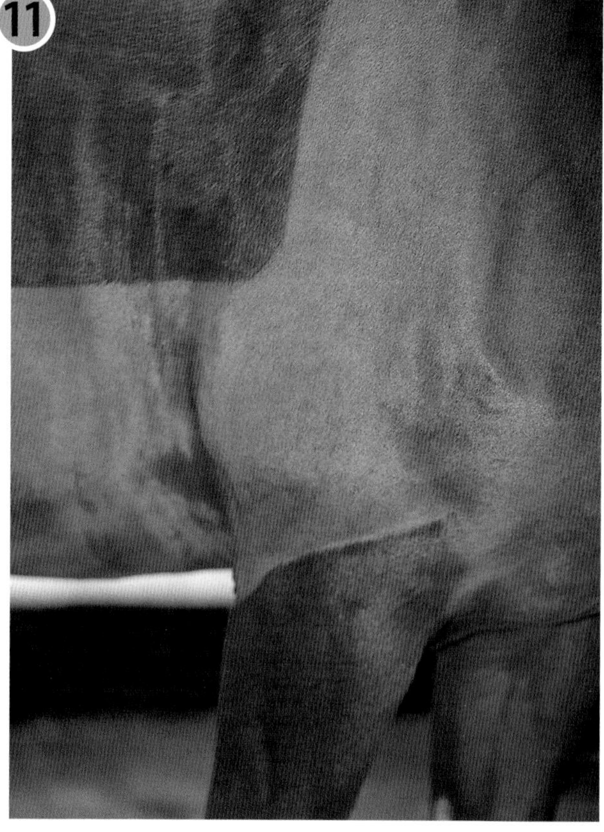

11 Now tidy up your line and round off the corner above the point of the shoulder.

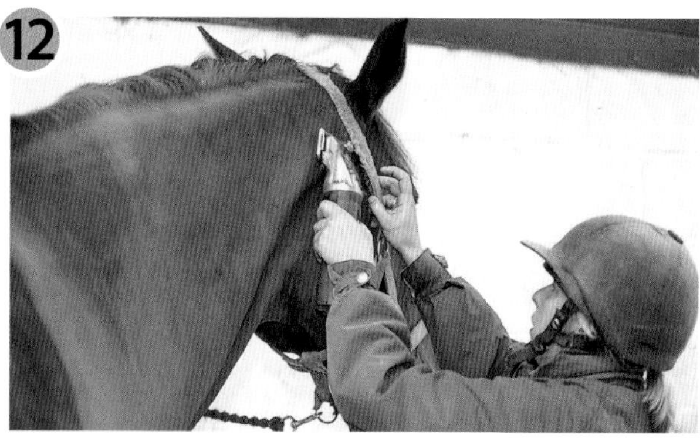

12 Clean up around the jaw line.

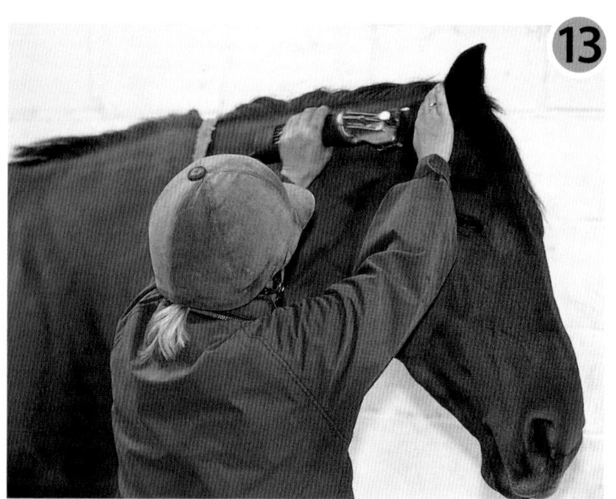

13 Take a line down the face from the back of the jawbone, following the imaginary line of the cheekpiece to the chin.

14 Clean up underneath the jaw and behind the ears and on top of the head, stretching the skin to avoid wrinkles.

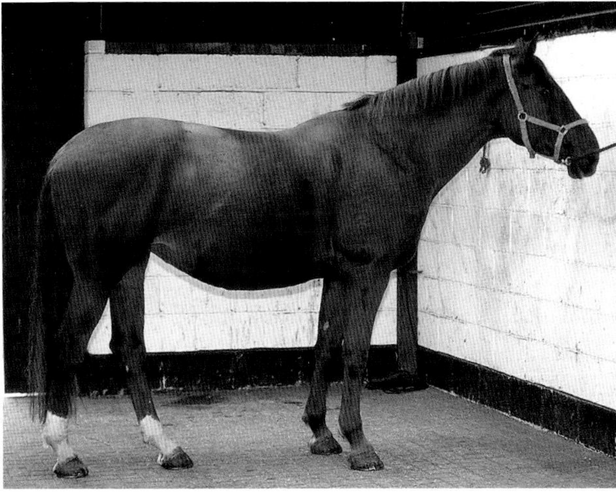

Before

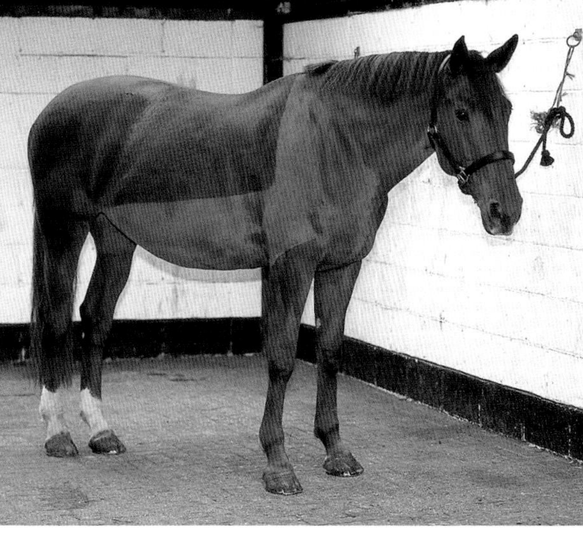

After!

GETTING STARTED

- Check your blades thoroughly before you begin.
- Approach the horse holding the clippers but with them switched off.
- Place the blades on the horse without having them switched on.
- Run the clippers away from the horse, so he can hear and see them.
- When he is happy about the noise and the blades touching him, start the clippers and run them on the shoulder in the direction of the hair growth (this way it pulls less on his skin, but you won't get such a close clip).
- Finally clip a section of hair away from the shoulder area, this time going against the lie of the hair (this way you get a closer clip).

Fifteen top tips from the expert

1 Always wear an old riding hat.
2 If you are not confident about running a line freehand at any point, use chalk.
3 To ensure your shoulder and tummy lines match on both sides, make sure your horse is standing square.
4 Begin on the horse's left-hand side, as this is the side that the horse is most accustomed to being handled from (push the mane over to one side).
5 If you encounter a whorl, change the direction of the clippers so you are still clipping against the lie of the hair.
6 Most horses are ticklish around the stifle area so begin clipping the tummy at the middle, work forwards, and then go back to the stifle area.
7 If you are trimming a line from the stifle to the shoulder make it slightly uphill as this will make the horse look lighter on the forehand.
8 If you are slipping a headcollar around the horse's neck to clip the head, thread the leadrope through the ring on baling twine, just in case the horse pulls back suddenly.
9 Always use a power breaker.
10 Whenever possible choose a dry, quiet day, with good light, and make sure the area where you are working is clean.
11 Settle into a comfortable pace, and don't hurry the speed of the clippers.
12 Never clip alone, but always have somebody else about who is prepared to help.
13 Be careful of tickly spots.
14 Don't use a haynet unless the horse won't stand quietly without one.
15 Be careful of the cable; safety is paramount.

3 30 MINUTES TO A BETTER BEHAVED HORSE

- *30 minutes of helpful handling*
- *30 minutes working on equine ethology*
- *30 minutes of inspiring lungeing*
- *30 minutes to learn to long-line*
- *30 minutes to control spookiness and napping*

We all dream of owning a horse that is problem free. Sadly, most difficulties arise either from a breakdown in communication or from rough treatment by a previous owner, and it takes time and consistently kind handling to overcome them. The lessons begin with the way you handle your horse from the ground. Picking out his feet, asking him to move over, tying him up – all these day-to-day activities are the first steps to let him know that certain types of behaviour are acceptable.

Communication is the key to a successful relationship with a horse. Most will behave well when they know what is expected of them. This they discover by watching your body language and listening to your signals. Spend 30 minutes on groundwork, and communication between you and your horse will be improved.

If you've always looked on lungeing as a last resort, you're missing the opportunity to watch how your horse is going, reinforce your vocal aids, and bring some variety into your training programme. And have you ever tried long-lining? It's a good alternative to lungeing, working your horse in a way that is nearer to the contact you have in the saddle.

Napping and spooking can both be the result of genuine fear, and the only way to deal with this is to work on the confidence that your horse has in your leadership. However, quite often this behaviour is due to boredom, laziness and naughtiness. Tackling it in 30-minute sessions may be the best way to deal with it.

30 minutes of Helpful Handling

You begin training your horse the moment you walk into the yard. The way in which you handle your horse from the ground sets up the foundation upon which the rest of your training will be built; it's therefore important to get it right. The majority of handling problems result from either bad or inconsistent handling and confusion on the part of the horse. If you have trouble with

- putting on a headcollar or bridle
- leading
- picking up feet
- barging
- tying your horse up

it is quite likely that one of these is the reason. Even if you've owned your horse from birth and can't recollect an incident that may have been the cause, sometimes the slightest thing will register in the horse's mind and be reinforced by seemingly innocuous behaviour on your part. And sadly, misunderstandings that start on the ground often persist when the horse is under saddle. Equine behaviourist Richard Maxwell encounters many horses with these sorts of problem during his working week. Addressing them begins with establishing that the horse understands pressure and release, and then halter training.

PRESSURE AND RELEASE

Halter training is based on the principle of pressure and release, a principle that is used throughout riding (think 'leg aids' for example). 'I really want to emphasize to people that pressure does not mean force,' Max explains. 'Horses are very quick to assess what's right and what's not. Punishment does not come into this equation, and if you abuse the technique, your horse will soon work out what's right and what's not and consequently ignore you.' In the initial stages of halter training, pressure is applied to your horse's poll and nose via the halter, and released the moment he stops resisting you and does as you are asking. Release should be backed up by verbal praise or a pat.

Pressure can come in various forms, either physical – from the halter, from the halter via the line, from your hand or fingertips, from the bit via the reins, from your leg; or visual – from a hand gesture or from your posture. Once the principles of halter training are understood by the horse, you can advance from physical pressure to visual pressure.

At every stage of training your aim is to apply the lightest pressure possible. Always begin with the lightest pressure and very gradually increase it until your horse responds. You then want to work your way back to using the lightest pressure once again.

TRAINING HALTERS

There are various types of training halter available. The important thing is that the fibre of the halter allows the pressure on the horse's poll and nose to be released. In too many cases friction prevents this happening. For this reason Max has developed his own halter and line, which we have used here. These halters are available from his website: www.richard-maxwell.com

To have control of your horse on the ground (and to have his respect) you need to have control of forward and backward movement, and the quarters. All of this comes through halter training – and the good news is that this can be learnt and used by any rider. What's more, you can use this technique with any horse, whether it is new to you and you're building up a relationship, or you want to address problems that have developed over a period of time.

Like any training concept, used inconsiderately or with force it can do harm – even a basic headcollar can inflict pain in the wrong hands.

The key points to remember are:

- release pressure as soon as your horse offers the slightest response;
- praise him for doing the right thing.

Take 30 minutes to introduce your horse to halter training

Your aim is to gain your horse's attention, focus and respect.

Step 1: Establishing that your horse understands pressure and release
If this is the first time that you have worked your horse on a training halter, stand quite close in front of him. You want to be able to reach out and pat him if he takes the smallest step towards you. Apply gentle pressure on the line. This will apply pressure to the horse's nose and poll. If he responds by moving towards you, release the pressure immediately. 'Remember that it isn't how quickly you put the pressure on that impresses the horse, but how quickly you take it off,' Max advises. If he pulls back, go with him, retaining the original tension through the line. Remain passive – don't drag against him, or give. Your horse needs to work out for himself what it is he needs to do to relieve the pressure.

Step 2: Getting control of forward movement
Once your horse understands the basic principle of pressure and release, gradually increase the length of line between you (see photograph, below). Each time,

SENDING YOUR HORSE ON TO A CIRCLE ON THE HALTER

To ask your horse to go off on to a circle on the left rein, once you have him at the end of the line, grasp the line about halfway down its length in your left hand. Now take the hand out in the direction you wish him to go (to the left), whilst spinning the other end of the line in your right hand.

Note that there is no tension in the line. Repeat on the other rein.

To bring him in, take a gentle pull on the line and draw him in, as shown, left.

apply gentle pressure on the line until your horse walks towards you, then make a fuss of him. In this way he is doubly rewarded for working out what it is you want, and for doing the right thing.

Step 3: Getting control of backward movement
There are three ways in which you can ask your horse to move backwards, using pressure and release:
(**a**) via direct pressure from the halter
(**b**) via pressure from the halter down the line
(**c**) via hand pressure

(**a**) Stand in front of your horse and, holding the halter by the clip and using pressure and release, ask him to move backwards. Reward him as soon as he takes a first step.

(**b**) Now stand a few feet in front of him and ask him to go backwards by making waves along the line (see photograph, above). Once again, as soon as he understands, reward him by releasing the pressure (stop waving the line) and praising him.

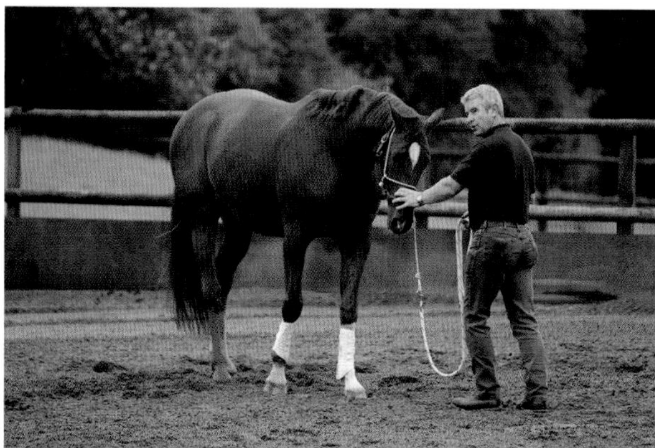

(**c**) Use a hand to create gentle pressure on his nose to teach your horse to move backwards (see photograph, above). Release as soon as he moves.

Step 4: Getting control of the quarters

For this, the source of pressure is the spinning rope. Stand by your horse's shoulder, holding the line as shown in the photograph. Now spin the end of the line near his quarters – not touching them. The halter contact should remain slack. As soon as he moves his quarters, stop spinning the line. If he doesn't understand immediately, be quietly persistent until he does.

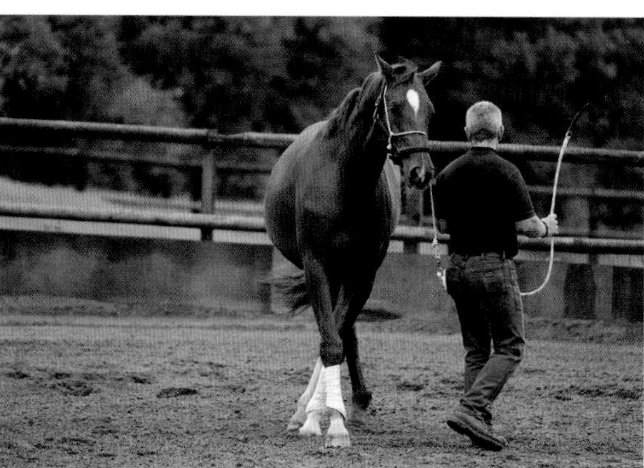

In the more advanced stages of training, this technique can be developed to teach your horse to perform a turn on the forehand (see photograph, above). And the same principle can also be applied to gain control of your horse's shoulders.

Take 30 minutes to tackle your handling problems

So often riders can be heard bemoaning the fact that they can't put a headcollar on their horse without a battle, that their horse barges them in the stable, or that leading the horse to the field is a logistical challenge. In almost every case these problems originate from bad handling. And although to the rider who doesn't experience them they may seem trivial, they can make your equestrian life a nightmare.

Your horse likes to know where he stands with you. If you allow him to push you around in the stable, but expect him to stand still on the yard whilst you groom or tack him up, you have no right to be angry with him when he doesn't understand what is required. Every time you handle your horse you should do so with consistency, remembering that this is the first step in his training.

Once you've taught your horse the basic principles of halter training he should have respect for your intentions whenever you are handling him. Sometimes this is enough to make handling problems a thing of the past; sometimes you need to directly apply the techniques you have both learnt.

'My horse won't stand still whilst I pick out his feet'

Once you've taught your horse the principles of halter training, asking him to stand still to have his feet picked out should not be a problem. 'You may find that you need to spend 20 minutes halter training every day, before you attempt to pick his feet out. It may seem a chore to do this for three or four days but you'll be saving yourself a lifetime of hassle.' Max advises. 'The problem with most handling issues is that we tackle our horses "cold". If you were to split up two horses for 16 to 18 hours and then reintroduce them, the leader would reassert themselves. And that's just what we need to do.'

By going over the halter training you are re-establishing that you are in charge, and that if you want to touch or pick out the feet, that's okay. Gradually you should be able to reduce the amount of time spent halter training.

Some people will pick out a horse's feet 'going around the four corners', others like to pick all four feet out from one side of the horse. Neither is wrong, the important thing, once again, is consistency. If you have a horse that will not stand still to have his feet picked out or cared for, begin by establishing a location in which this will take place.

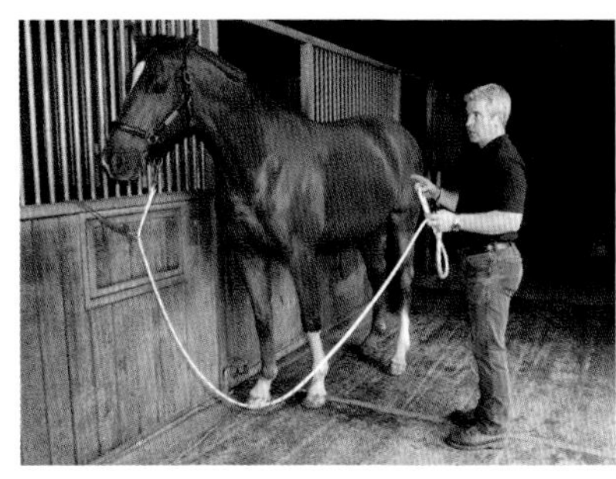

Max recommends running a lead rope through a ring or baling twine, but not tying it. 'This way you have handling control but the horse does not feel trapped. You can keep his attention and at the same time he will learn to trust you.'

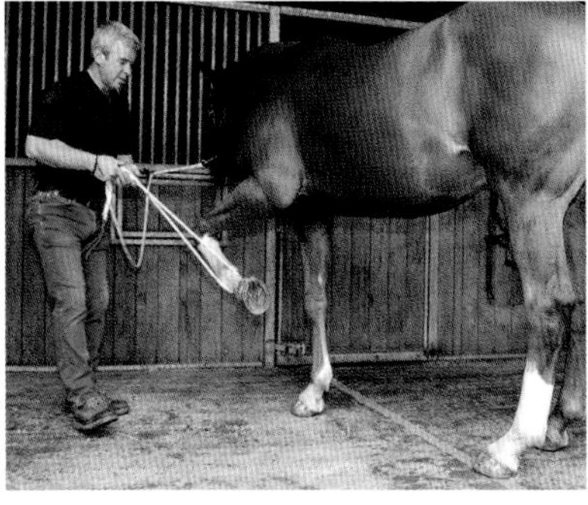

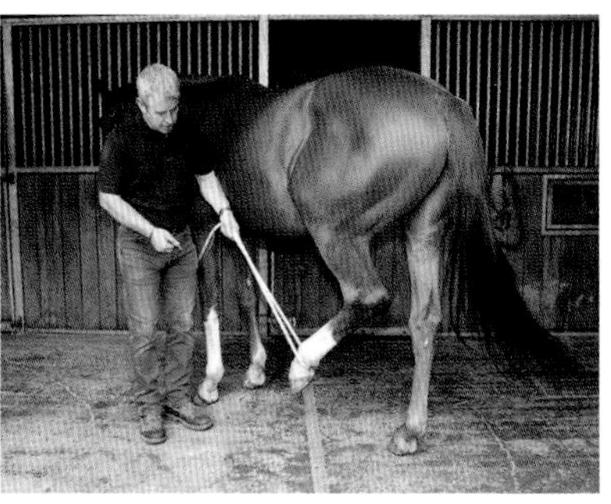

If the horse is a youngster or you need both hands, the end of the rope can be tucked in a belt loop, pocket or waistband, loosely enough to break free if necessary.

Now you're in a better position to control the horse whilst you pick out his feet. If your horse is really difficult, loop the line around the leg and gently lift the foot, using the rope (see photographs, above); not only will this put you in a much safer position, but if the horse has physical problems such as arthritis, or if he's a shiverer, you will actually be helping him to rest the leg.

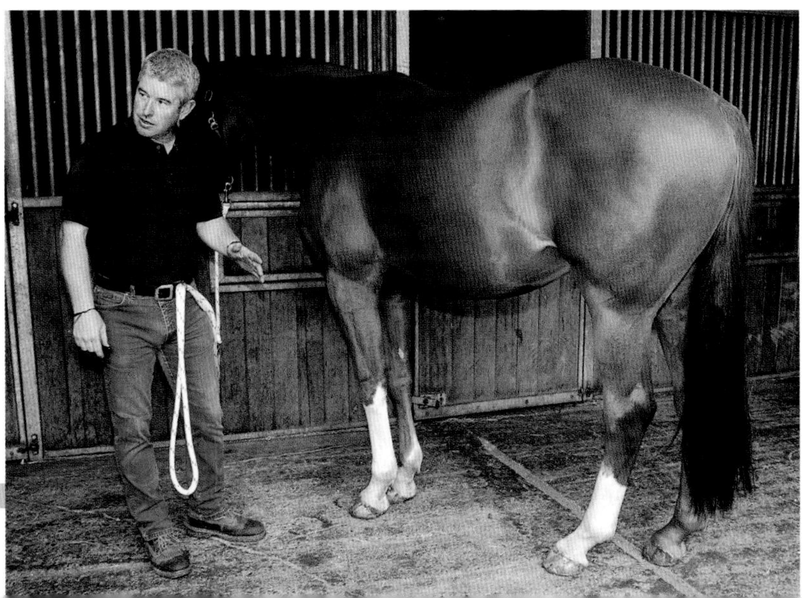

'I can't get a headcollar on my horse without a battle'

If you have problems putting a headcollar or bridle on your horse, you're off to a difficult start. A horse can make a fuss about being handled around the head for a variety of reasons:

- as the result of an incident;
- due to problems caused by physical discomfort;
- because he's just decided he's bigger and taller.

Whatever the cause, Max recommends using a halter to begin with: 'We're all too quick to get around the horse's face,' Max observes. 'Say "hello" first.'

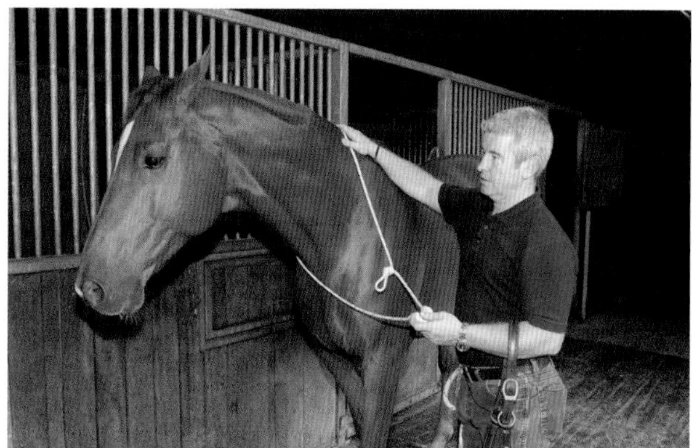

1 In the stable, begin with the halter over the base of the horse's neck, as shown. For the purpose of our photo, Max is working in the barn, outside his stable.

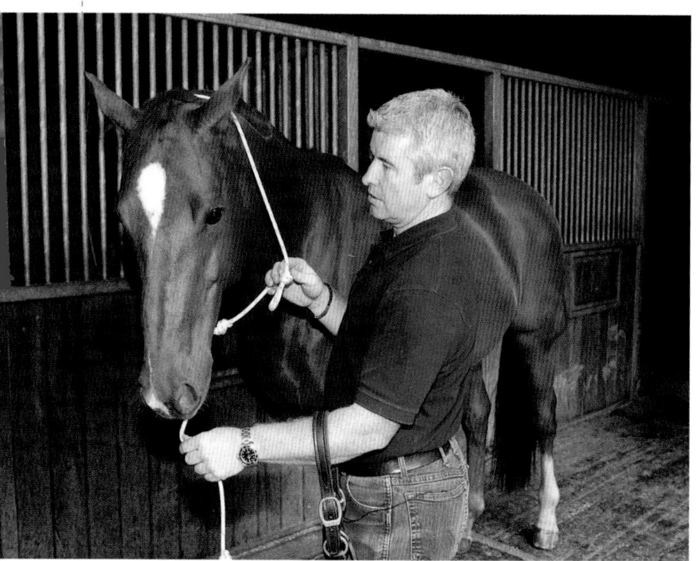

2 Gradually bring it up the neck, allowing the horse to become familiar with the sensation.

3 Drape it over the nose. Take your time, and when your horse is settled, slip the end through the loop and attach a lead rope.

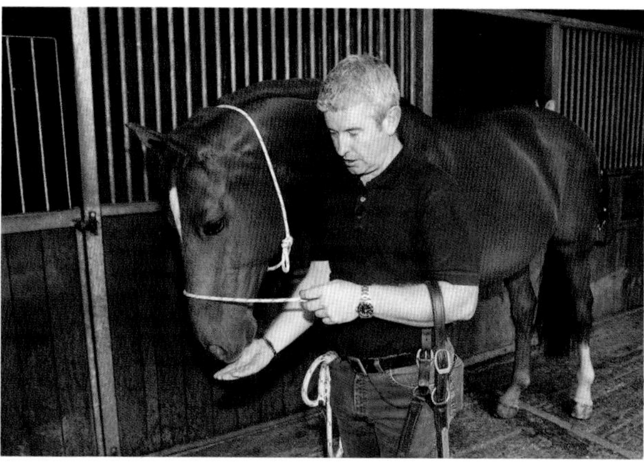

The halter gives you control, and if your horse throws his head up or around, you can use pressure and release to show him where you want his head to be.

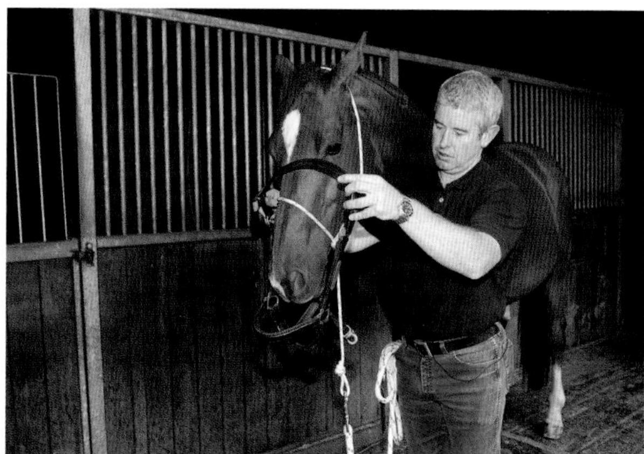

4 Max prefers a headcollar that clips together under the jaw. Gradually raise your headcollar over your horse's nose and ears, returning to the halter for control if necessary. Once your horse is settled, fasten the headcollar.

5 Your aim is for your horse to be seeking the headcollar or bridle and almost putting it on himself. Don't forget to make a fuss of him whenever he does the right thing.

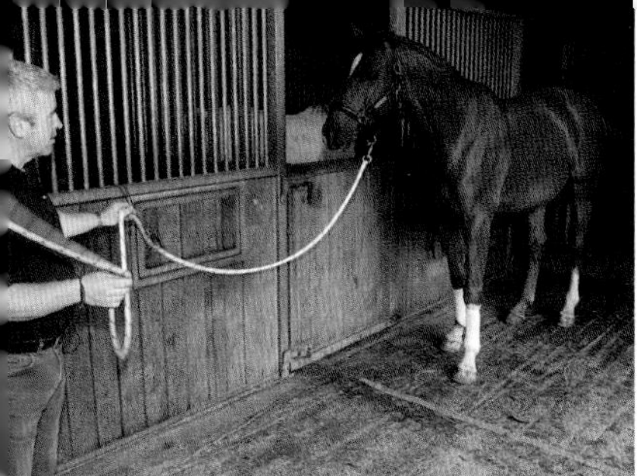

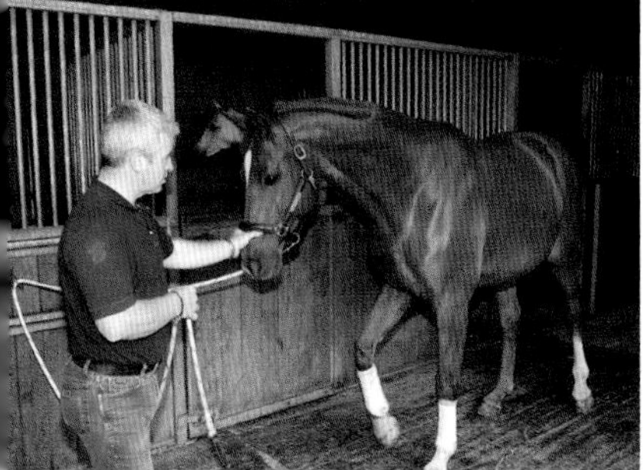

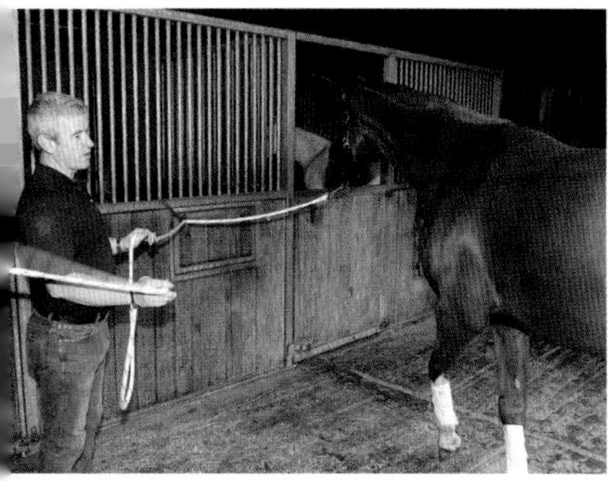

'My horse barges me out of the way in the stable'

With halter training firmly in place, barging, whether in the stable or when tied up on the yard, should become a thing of the past. If your horse walks into you whilst being handled, with the line through the ring like this, you can ask him to move backwards or sideways as he has learnt through halter training.

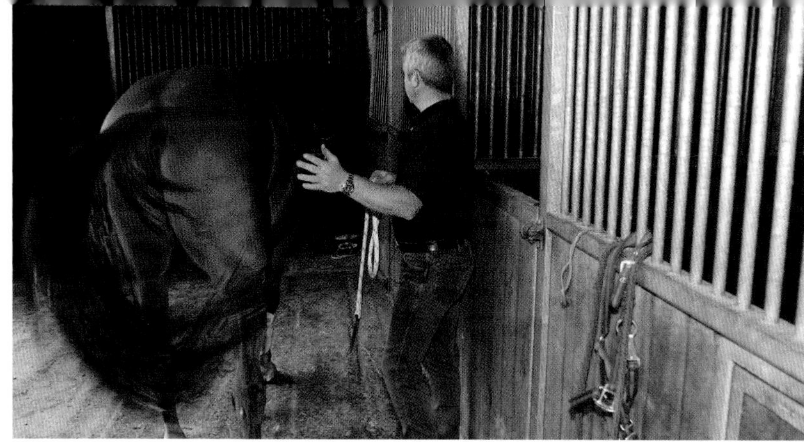

In the photograph above, Mattie moves sideways as a result of a simple hand movement from Max.

'Be aware of subtle barging – nudging and bumping – that begins as a game and becomes an established pattern of behaviour,' Max warns. 'As a handler you need to focus on the subtleties. The more you let the little things happen, the more of an argument you are going to have one day to sort it out.'

'My horse won't be tied up'

Some horses have a fear of being tied up. This is usually due to a bad experience, and most horses will subsequently react badly as soon as they feel the 'snag' on their headcollar. By threading the line through the ring or baling twine and holding on to the other end (see photograph, below), you give your horse sufficient range to make a decision about pulling back for himself.

'My horse drags me all over the place when I try to lead him'

If you are having problems leading your horse, the first thing that Max recommends is that you lead with energy and purpose. 'Don't dawdle along. You can be efficient in your movement even when leading.' If your horse is determined to take control, work on the halter in the yard, making changes of direction, turning him on his forehand and on the quarters, and getting him to thoroughly engage his mind before he has the opportunity to decide to do otherwise (see photographs, below).

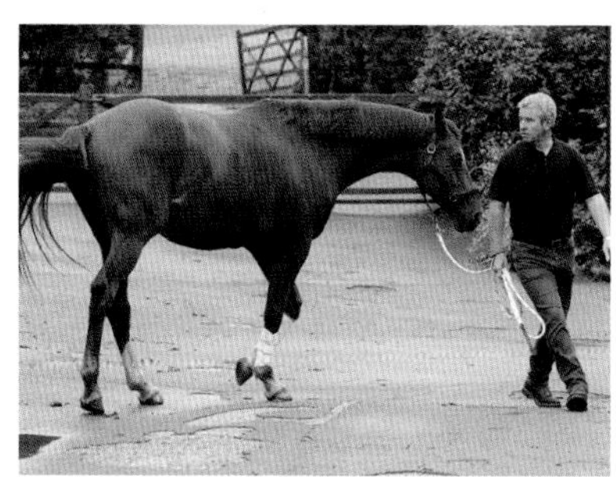

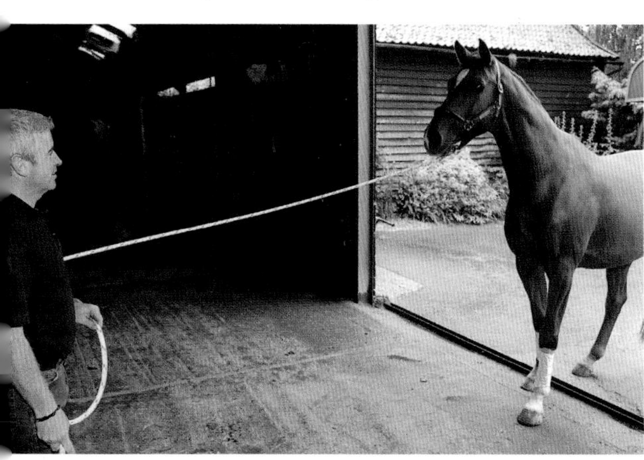

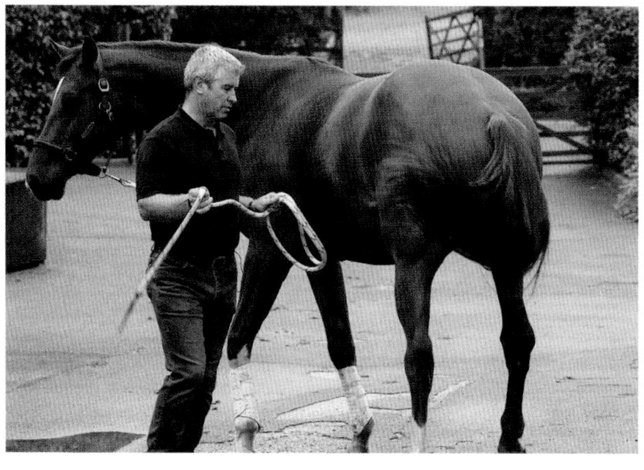

30 minutes Working on Equine Ethology

Whether you're in the early stages of setting up a relationship with a horse, or you've known him for some time, working with him on the ground brings a fresh dimension into your relationship. Lungeing and long-lining, used well, are great methods of physical and, to a limited extent, mental training. However, the seven tasks, the first phase in equine ethology training, engage the horse's mind in a different way and exercise all his muscles, whilst also helping in the development of human–horse communication.

WHY SET TASKS?

'What we're establishing with the seven tasks is a language,' says Dave Stuart, Director of Programme Development National Equine Ethology Centre. 'Through building a language comes leadership. And once a language is established we can communicate, and start to put the horse to task on a lunge line to help build his confidence. The more confident we can get him on the ground, without the rider interfering on his back, well, that's got to be confidence-giving to the rider as well. Once back on the horse, we have a pattern established that's going to make it so much easier under saddle.'

Equine Ethology was developed and accredited by the French Equestrian Federation. It is based on learning to have a better understanding of horse behaviour to enable you to earn your horse's trust and respect. The ability to read the signs of acceptance and respond immediately, and to use body language as a tool, are key to its success.

How you break down your equine ethology tasks into a 30-minute-a-week training programme is very much in your hands. As every horse and rider/handler combination is different, it is impossible to dictate exactly how far you should progress at each session.

Spend your first 30-minute session on Task 1: Desensitization, helping your horse to overcome his natural fears. If he resents the moves it's going to take you two or three sessions to settle him, but this is really important. If things aren't going well, use the approach and retreat method (see box, right). End on a positive note and then begin again at your next session. Don't try to rush things. Once your horse is comfortable with task 1, move on to task 2, but remember always to begin with task 1 and work through the tasks in sequence.

The first three tasks, known as the 'principle tasks', are the most important, as all the others depend on your horse's acceptance of these. As your horse progresses, you will need to spend less time on each task, and it is likely that you'll soon be running two or three sessions together to develop your skills..

How to begin

As already mentioned, body language is very important in the tasks, and advice on your stance is given in the instructions. However, there are three things to remember:

- Smile
- Stay relaxed
- Be patient

For these moves you will need to work with the lunge line over one arm. Keep it slack in the first instance, to reinforce the sensation that your horse is free to move where he likes, unless you need to catch his attention. As you work through the exercises, ask yourself how your horse would rate your feel: is it smooth, comforting, pleasant, too light, too harsh, too rough, too ticklish? Try to convey your affection for your horse in your touch.

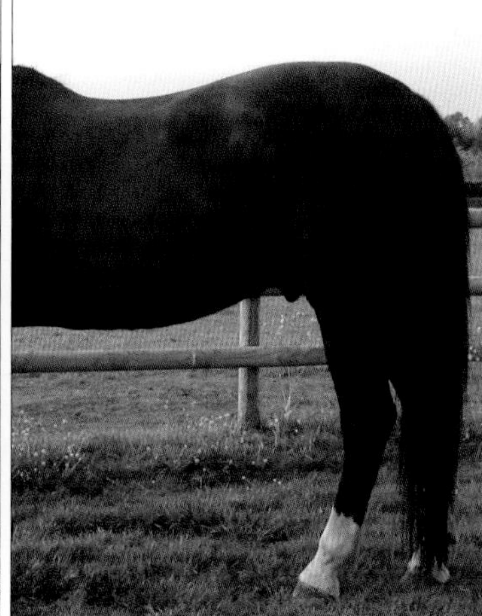

➪ ***THE DRIVE LINE:** If you stand in front of the drive line your horse will turn or move backward. If behind it the horse will move forward or rotate his hindquarters depending on where he feels pressure. Only by standing at the drive line will the horse remain comfortably still.*

What equipment do you need?

Unless stated otherwise, you will need a:

- halter;
- 3.6m (12ft) lunge line;
- communication stick;
- 1.8m (6ft) universal string.

These can all be obtained from www.equineethology.com, but if you're keen to get started in the interim, you can improvise; thus for task 1 you can use many things to desensitize your horse, from your hands to a plastic bag. After this you will need to have equipment that can help you to become more effective:

***'Touch your horse with your heart, put your heart in your hand,'* Pat Parelli**

Task 1: Desensitization

This is the most important task. If your horse accepts this task in the first session, call it a day and let him absorb the lessons he has learnt.

Aim:
Your horse should be able to accept your touch all over without tail swishing, tensing or flattening the ears.

Objectives:

- To gain his confidence, acceptance and understanding.
- To prove you are not there to hurt him.
- To teach the horse to relax to your touch whether from hand or communication stick.
- To teach you rhythm, relaxation and retreat.

Uses:

- To reassure your horse whenever he gets confused, scared or offended.
- To reassure your horse that he is doing the right thing.

All this is an indication of trust and acceptance. Put on a halter and attach a 3.6m (12ft) lunge line. Hold the lunge line about halfway along its length, with your horse's head towards you and the communication stick in your opposite hand. Beginning at the nose and progressing slowly through to the tail, rub your horse all over with the stick (see photographs, page 64). Be rhythmic in your movements, relaxed in your posture, and retreat (see box below) if your actions are causing your horse offence.

Don't restrict your horse's ability to move his front feet around. As a flight animal it is natural for him to want

WHAT IS APPROACH AND RETREAT?

If your horse has a difficult spot, carefully get as close to it with the communication stick as you can, but retreat before the contact becomes intolerable to your horse. Keep your movements rhythmic, and don't express any feelings of anger or reproof. With repetition your horse should begin to accept your touch.

TIP

Ask permission to enter your horse's space. Put the back of your hand out and allow him to sniff it before moving into his space. Likewise allow him to familiarize himself with the communication stick before beginning task 1.

TROUBLESHOOTING

- Don't give up. If your horse is troubled, keep trying until he realizes what it is you want, and that he is doing the right thing. If he is scared of the stick, begin by rubbing him all over with your hands.
- If your horse refuses to let you touch him with the communication stick, begin by stroking the lunge line with the stick in the same rhythmic manner, and gradually work along it, as he calms, until you can stroke his neck. It's okay for him to move his feet around, but keep him facing you. If he tries to run away, gently 'bump' his nose back towards you (to 'bump' means to make gentle pulls on the lunge line, take and give, stopping the moment he stops). Allow him to lick his lips (a sign of acceptance), and then continue.
- If your horse tries to kick or bite, you should use your communication stick as an extension of your arm. If he is kicking, keep his head turned towards you, and if he is biting keep him out of your personal space. Using the principle of approach and retreat, allow your horse to kick and bite at the communication stick.

to do this, and being over-restrictive can pressurize him into a violent reaction, such as striking out or rearing. If your horse is defensive about an area, don't make an issue of it now: make a mental note of it, and come back to it later, using approach and retreat. Once your horse accepts the contact of the communication stick, repeat the procedure with the universal string and then your hands, remembering to approach and retreat whenever you come to any of his more sensitive areas.

NEED HELP?

In some circumstances it takes an experienced handler to communicate with a horse. If you feel out of your depth with your horse (and you'll easily see the signs), seek professional help; likewise if you wish to develop your training within equine ethology. Be sure, however, that you use a registered equine ethology instructor, because in the wrong hands, like many training aids, more harm than good can be achieved. For more information and knowledge on equine ethology and natural horsemanship, visit www.equineethology.com, or email info@equineethology.com.

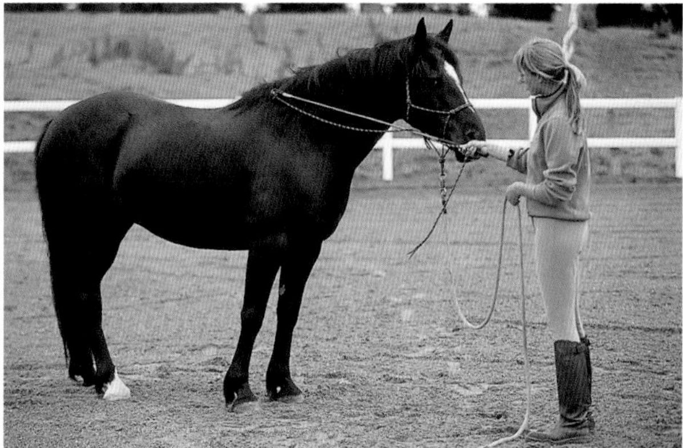

➪ *Finish every session by 'rubbing your horse to a halt'.*

Don't forget: Your horse should accept you touching his most vulnerable spots, and should appreciate that your intentions are non-predatory. If you feel that this is not working, it may be better for you to ask for help from a qualified equine ethology instructor.

SIGNS OF ACCEPTANCE

These signs can vary from a step in the right direction, to licking and chewing and lowering the head. If your horse's head is above his withers, he is not relaxed, and you will not have made a change or achieved acceptance.

Task 2: Sensitization using direct (or steady) pressure

This is a little more difficult to teach the horse, as his natural tendency is to move into pressure. However, all your riding aids are based on asking your horse to move away from pressure.

Aim:
To ask your horse to yield from steady pressure applied, initially with the communication stick and eventually with your fingertips, to his chest, front end and hindquarters.

Objective:
- To teach your horse to respond with movement to feel or pressure, reinforcing your riding aids.

Uses:
- To move your horse out of your personal space.
- To move him into a required position.
- To lower his head.

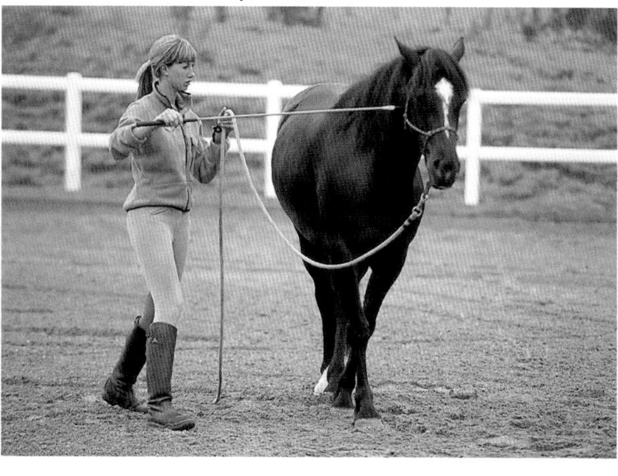

To ask him to move his front end sideways, stand at his neck, and apply pressure in the groove where the jaw connects with the neck. Work towards him walking in a circle around his hindquarters.

To ask your horse to move backwards, stand at his nose holding the lunge line about halfway along its length, and apply pressure with the communication stick to the centre of his chest. Use steady pressure, don't poke him. In the first instance just ask for one or two steps, but work up to walking him backwards for several steps.

To ask him to move his quarters sideways, stand by his ribs or hindquarters, and apply pressure just below the point of his hip bone. Now work towards him walking in a circle around his forehand.

HOW TO BE EFFECTIVE

Use increasing degrees of pressure with your tools in order to be effective. Being assertive is important but getting emotional – angry or frustrated – is counter-productive, as is getting aggressive.

Try this test with a friend: ask them to stand still, and tell them not to move until the pressure you apply gets uncomfortable enough for them to want to move. Once they move, stop, rub and start again. Note what happens. It's important that you start with a very light touch and get progressively more assertive until a response is given. Then immediately stop.

Remember, if you watch horses in a paddock they can get very assertive with each other. They will use a turn of the ear, then the head, then the neck might snake down, then the teeth will be bared. Finally, if all this posturing doesn't get the desired result, they will turn their hindquarters and, if there is still no response, a kick will ensue. These are all phases of firmness communicated by a dominant horse to a less dominant horse. We are attempting to imitate this behaviour to gain a higher place in the hierarchy.

Don't be tempted to poke or prod to get a response. Maintain the pressure and do something else to get a response (use a combination of tasks 2 and 3).

Above all, don't give up. Horses are the best people trainers in the world.

As soon as he has moved away from the pressure point, release the pressure and use task 1 to let him know he has done the right thing. Once he is happy with this manoeuvre, try the same thing using your fingertips.

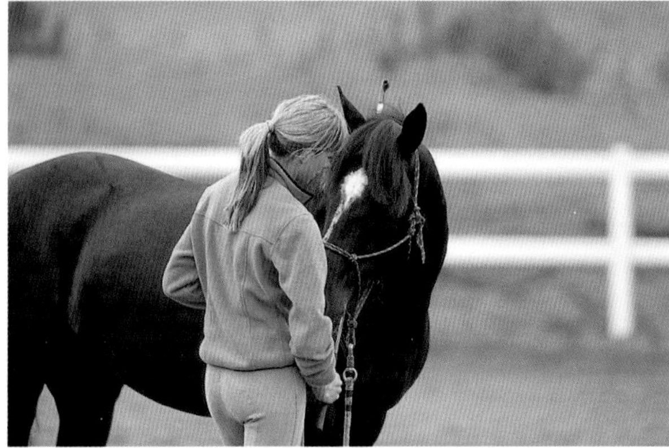

The next step is to ask him to move backwards from the bridge of his nose with your fingertips, and from the clip of the lead rope to step backwards and forwards.

POSTURE AND PERSISTENCE

Focus on your intention in your facial expression and posture. Don't give way to pressure from your horse, but remain firm, so that he learns that he will find release of pressure if he moves away from the source. He is then responsible for his own actions and will see this as a reward.

'He knows that you know and you know he knows.' Ray Hunt

TROUBLESHOOTING

- *Don't forget:*
  Don't jab or poke.
  Don't apply too much pressure, too quickly.
  Don't forget to rub your horse before and after.
- Plan what you are asking of your horse before you ask for it. For example, which direction are you going to ask him to move in, and how far do you want him to go? Where should you be standing?
- If your horse tries to escape from the communication stick or your hand, this is a fearful response, and you should react with sympathy and patience. Firstly, slow things down, asking for one stage at a time and being quick to reward the slightest positive response. Intersperse task 1 with task 2 to reassure your horse.
- If his reaction is to throw his head in the air or plunge to the ground, try to stay with him, picturing the communication stick or your hand gently glued to his head. If you do not feel athletic enough to do this, or your horse is too tall, use the halter and lunge line as an extension of your hand, and gradually work towards him using just your hand.
- If he tries to kick or bite, use the communication stick, as with task 1, and allow him to do so but remain passively persistent.
- If your horse just won't move, increase the pressure until you note some response, such as twitching or swishing of the tail. Do not increase pressure further, but wait – it may seem like ages – until you are given the slightest sign of positive response (see Recognizing a Response, page 70).

Task 3: Sensitization using indirect (or rhythmic) pressure

This is the next step on from sensitization using direct pressure, asking your horse to move on a signal, rather than as a result of pressure. In this task he will learn to move backwards, forwards, sideways from the forehand, and sideways from the quarters.

Aim:
To teach your horse to respond to a gesture rather than an action. Your intention is to teach your horse to read your body language, and not to be afraid of the communication stick; you must therefore ensure that he does not feel fear.

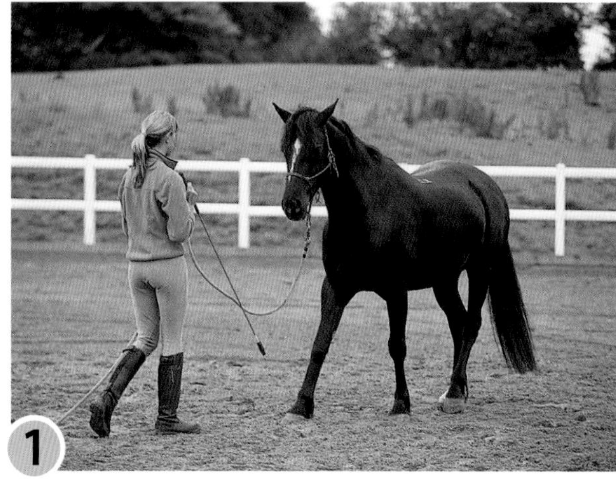

Objectives:
- To teach your horse to recognize your body language.
- To teach you to communicate via body language.

Uses:
- It helps you to control your body posture in the saddle.
- It teaches your horse to move backwards and sideways.

CONTROL YOUR LIFE

Having the ability to 'have your life up' (be purposeful and focused) or 'have your life down' will help you control your body posture in the saddle. For example, next time you have trouble stopping your horse, check whether your 'life' is up or down.

To ask your horse to go backwards, stand by his nose and hold the lunge line halfway along its length. Look purposeful, and be focused on what you are asking of your horse.

2

Now, rhythmically tap the line in front of your hand with the communication stick (see photograph 1, left). Your aim is for your horse to move backwards. If he doesn't understand and fails to respond immediately, increase the taps and advance up the rope until he does back away. Respond immediately, allowing the rope to slip through your fingers, hopefully to the very end. Now ask him to come forwards by stepping backwards, softening your facial expression (smile!) and posture, and stroking the line with the communication stick. Reel your horse in towards you as you step backwards.

Repeat both movements until your horse is performing them with ease. Now try to move him backwards by pretending to tap the rope.

Once your horse understands what is being asked of him and accepts the action, try asking him to move backwards by 'tapping' the air towards the front of him. (In photograph 2 Hannah raises her forearm and uses her fist to tap the air.)

To drive your horse's forehand away, position yourself by his neck with the communication stick held in front of you and level with his cheekbone. Walk towards your horse tapping the air with the communication stick (see photograph 3).

3

4

As soon as he responds by moving sideways, relax your body position, smile, and rub your horse with the communication stick (photograph 4). Once your horse is confident with a step or two, aim to be able to turn him in a circle from the front end, but go easy, step by step, and be sure that he is happy with each one.

To drive your horse's quarters away, with your communication stick in one hand, and a purposeful expression, approach his hindquarters in a wide arc (see photograph 5) – you don't need to be too close for this exercise. Your horse's head should turn towards you as he moves his hindquarters away. As soon as he does this, stop, smile, and rub his head with your hand.

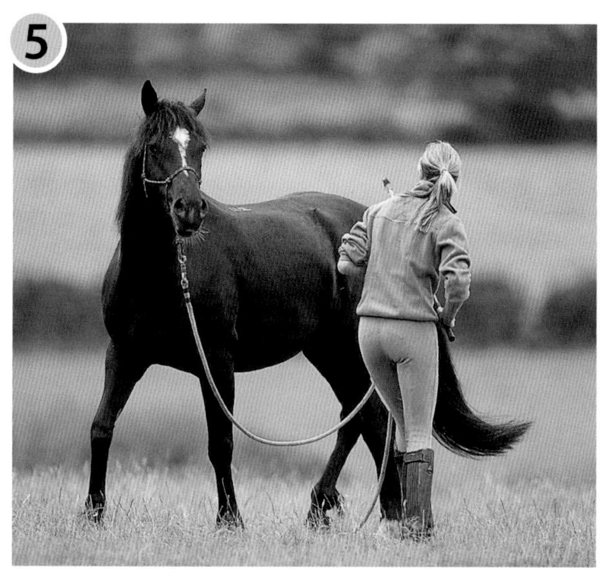

Once you have achieved your aim, soften your posture and expression, and walk down your horse's side with the communication stick outstretched, and rub him on the hip as in task 1 (see photograph 6). You need to ensure that your horse is not afraid of the communication stick. If he does try to move away, repeat task 1, beginning at the neck and working through to the hip, allowing him to move his feet until he feels confident enough to stand still once again. At this point, run through the first three tasks to ensure your horse is responding in a relaxed and confident manner. If you uncover any trouble spots, work on them before moving on.

DEGREES OF PRESSURE WHEN DRIVING THE QUARTERS

Step 1: Start from near the horse's head and move in an arc towards the hindquarters.
Step 2: Put rhythm into the stick as you move towards the hindquarters (see photograph 5).
Step 3: Move the stick with more energy.
Step 4: If your horse still hasn't moved, start tapping him on the hindquarters and increase the intensity until he takes a step.

Remember, these are just suggestions. You need to be effective to be understood, and don't give up. Rome wasn't built in a day, and persistence and tenacity will win through – but also reward the slightest try. By doing so you will enable your horse to learn what you want.

TROUBLESHOOTING

- If your horse turns his head away, use three gentle bumps on the line to bring him back to you, bumping to the right if he is turning to the left, and vice versa. Make sure that you bump horizontally and don't pull down on the line.
- If your horse tries to walk away from you, shorten the line to bring his head around and keep approaching his quarters. As soon as he looks to you and moves his hindquarters away, stop, smile, and rub his head.

Task 4: Balancing forwards and backwards

This is a combination of 'steady pressure' and 'rhythmic pressure'.

Aim:
To make your horse step backwards, and then bring him back towards you with a simple hand gesture.

Objectives:
- To improve balance forwards and backwards.
- To teach your horse to be straight.
- To teach your horse to carry his weight on his quarters.

DEGREES OF PRESSURE WHEN BACKING UP

Step 1: Start by vibrating the rope.
Step 2: Put more energy into vibrating the rope.
Step 3: Move towards the horse.
Step 4: Use rhythmic pressure with the stick as necessary.

Stand by your horse's nose and keep your feet still. It is important with this task that you remain in one spot.

To ask your horse to move backwards, use task 3 whereby you drive your horse backwards until he is about 1.8m (6ft) away from you (see photograph 1). Allow your rope to droop to the ground, but keep hold of the end. Now, with a firm and purposeful look and keeping a focus on what you are wanting your horse to do, ask him to back up once again using as little pressure as necessary (see box). As soon as your horse responds at any stage, reward him by stopping the action and smiling (see photographs 2 and 3).

To ask your horse to move forwards, standing on your spot, smile, bend towards your horse and comb the rope towards you with flat open hands (see photograph 4). Keep your movement inviting, smooth and rhythmic. It is unlikely at the first attempt that your horse will respond, so move on to the next step – put a little pull into the rope by closing your fingers slightly, all the while maintaining the same rhythm and posture. If your horse doesn't respond to this, move on to the next step and put more drag in the line, so that your signal is a little more insistent. If he doesn't respond to this, lock on to the line with hands tightly closed. Maintain the contact but don't pull – allow your horse to give.

1

3

2
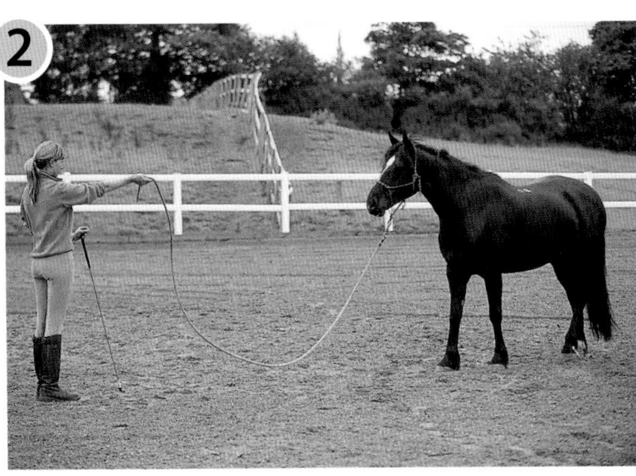

4

RECOGNIZING A RESPONSE

Be watchful for the slightest signs of acceptance. These may begin with just a shift of weight. Correctly acknowledged and rewarded, the next response may be half a step backwards, and then a full step. The sharper you are at acknowledging and rewarding the horse's tries, the better a relationship you will establish through your training.

The instant he gives, and stops pulling back, open your hands and smile. Rub your horse for a moment or two to give him a sense of having achieved what was asked of him and to reward him.

TIPS

- *Be focused, rhythmical, and full of positive energy.*
- *Ensure you are in the correct and consistent position.*

Once your horse has mastered backward and forward movements at the lightest of gestures, begin to work on his straightness, keeping his two eyes towards you and looking initially for just a couple of steps before moving on.

CORRECTING STRAIGHTNESS

Once your horse has learnt to step backwards, then you can work on his straightness. If your horse goes crooked there are usually two reasons:

- He has turned his head away from you and is only looking at you with one eye. In this case, you need him to look at you squarely. If he moves his nose to your right, lift the lead rope and give him three little bumps to the left.
- He has moved his quarters out to one side. In this case, you'll need to hold his head still while you correct his quarters, using the communication stick.

There are occasions when your horse will go crooked as he comes towards you, but this is simpler to rectify. Try to reel your horse into you faster, and position your hands on the opposite side to that on which he is evading you as you reel him in.

TIPS

- *Keep your feet still.*
- *Don't shake the end of the rope at your horse: think of the rope as an extension of your finger.*
- *Begin with the gentlest movements.*

TROUBLESHOOTING

- If your horse will not go backwards, go back to task 3, working at your horse's nose, and work on him going backwards easily when you tap the rope with your communication stick. Are you rewarding even the slightest response (see Recognizing a Response box, above)? When finally you have your horse at the end of the rope, leave him there for a couple of minutes to reinforce the notion in his mind that this is what you are asking for.

- If your horse drags backwards when you apply pressure, maintain the pressure and drag with him. As soon as he comes forwards, even if it is just a weight shift, stop, relax the pull, smile, wait a moment, and then start again at the beginning.

If you continue to have problems, it is recommended that you seek the help of a recognized equine ethology trainer (see Need Help? box, page 64).

- If your horse rears up don't punish him, but don't relax the pressure, because if you do you will be teaching him exactly the opposite of what you want. So don't release the pressure until his feet touch the ground once again. Then calmly begin again.

Once again, seek help if you feel that you are moving outside your ability zone.

Task 5: Developing responsibility through circling

Does your horse go out on a circle to left or right when you ask him to? Does he pick up the pace you ask for and hold it until you ask him to change? This task will help to establish these actions.

Aim:

Your aim is to be able to send your horse out on a circle in the direction of your choice just by his feeling your reaction on the lunge line, with perhaps the slightest of support from the communication stick or line end.

Objectives:

- To teach your horse to move confidently in arcs and circles.
- To train your horse not to change direction or pace until told to do so.
- To establish instant and smooth transitions.
- To teach your horse to stop from walk or trot.

Before beginning this exercise, run through task 3 and ensure that your horse is totally happy with it. Use your communication stick to yield his forehand and his quarters, and don't forget to reward him with task 1.

This exercise is begun by doing a **short-range version** that helps your horse understand what you are asking of him, and that is easier for you, the handler, as you don't have to negotiate a long lunge rope.

There are three parts to this task:

- the send;
- the allow;
- the bring-back.

The send: Hold your lunge line in your left hand about 90cm (3ft) away from the horse's head. Using task 3, send your horse backwards until he is just out of reach. Now, lead his nose forwards in the direction you want him to go (see photograph 1).

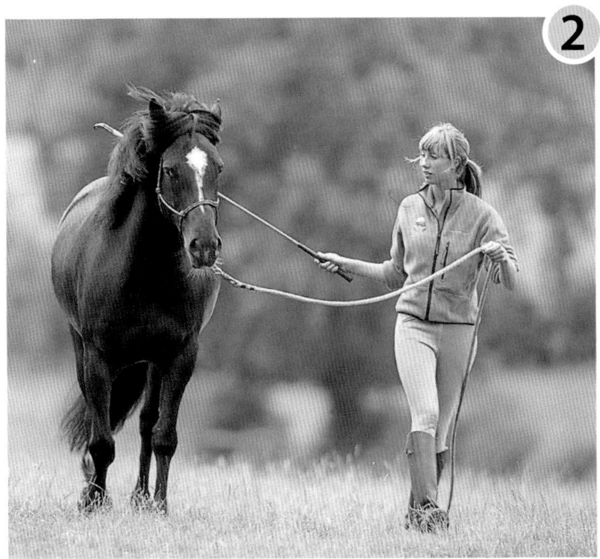

Touch your horse on his neck to support the direction you've given him (see photograph 2).

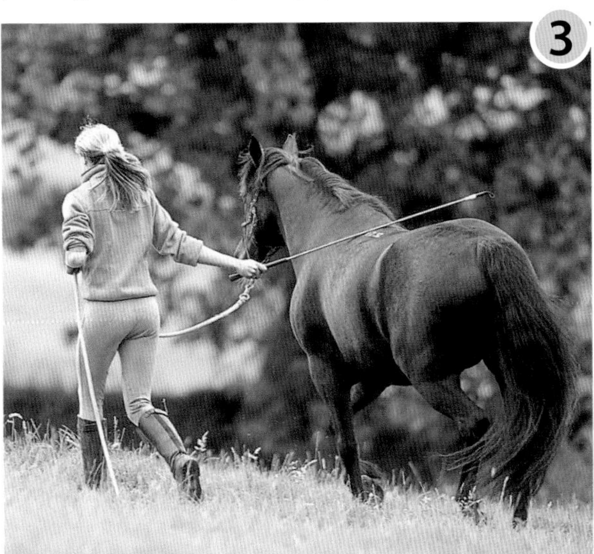

The allow: With your hand open and the end of the communication stick in your palm, rest it softly against his ribs (see photograph 3). This is meant as a friendly and reassuring gesture, and the stick should not be allowed to bounce. However, if your horse stops, tap him with the stick on the top of the rump, and then return it to its original position.

The bring-back: Tap the side of your horse's rump to bring him to a halt and to bring him back to you (see photograph 4). His hindquarters should disengage and he should be facing you. Finally, work through task 1, with special emphasis on the areas in which you have been using the communication stick.

4

Extending the range Once you have mastered this task on a shorter line, begin to allow the line to run out to its full length. Keep your feet completely still throughout this exercise. Send your horse backwards until he is at the end of the line. Then lead his nose forwards in the direction you want him to go, at the same time swinging your communication stick in one complete revolution. Allow the lunge line to pass from hand to hand around your back as your horse circles. Allow the communication stick to relax. This is your neutral position, and your horse will learn to feel secure when you are in this position (photographs 5 and 6).

To bring your horse back in from the lunge line, run your hand halfway down the line, drawing it in to your belly button; then 'swooping' down (see photographs 7 and 8), tap his rump with the communication stick (in fact Hannah only needs to swing the end of the lunge line). Your posture and expression should be friendly and welcoming as you bring your horse all the way in. Once your horse understands his responsibilities – to maintain gait and direction – you can develop the circling pattern through lungeing for his athletic development. Note: at this point you are bringing the horse in to you at the end of the circling pattern to reward his progress. It is important that you do not confuse this task with lungeing. In the future, you will develop the task so that you can ask the horse to stay out on the circle, to back-up on a circle, or to change direction. Repeat this process until your horse can do it equally well on both reins, and right at the end of the lunge line.

5

6

TIPS

- *Be clear about which direction you wish your horse to go in. To enable him to feel free to go forwards on to the circle without your body being a barrier in his way, try the following: to send him out to the right, assuming that you are facing 12 o'clock, your right hand (holding the lunge line) should point to 4 o'clock, and your right foot, hip and shoulder should turn in that direction, too. To send him out to the left, point to 8 o'clock.*
- *Be careful not to bore your horse. Task 5 is not lungeing, and is aimed at teaching him specific skills. Aim for a minimum of two laps, and a maximum of four laps performed voluntarily by your horse.*

Don't:

- *step outside your circle and chase your horse;*
- *prevent the rope from sliding freely through your hands;*
- *continue to swing the communication stick or rope end after your horse has done as requested.*

DEGREES OF PRESSURE WHEN CIRCLING

- Lift the rope to lead your horse in the direction of travel (remember to put more direction into the rope to guide the horse).
- Lift the stick to enable you horse to notice a change leading to your next phase.
- Start swinging the communication stick and string towards your horse's neck.
- Touch your horse's neck with the swinging rope.

TROUBLESHOOTING

- **Your horse stops behind your back.** The first time this happens turn, smile, and bring your horse in to you. Then send him out again. If he continues to do this, bring him back towards you with a stern look and send him out again immediately. Then smile when he's back on the circle.
- **Your horse changes gait without you asking him to.** Initially this task is done in walk until you and your horse are more proficient (the circle is too small for most horses to canter safely). If your horse does go into trot or canter, this is probably because he is nervous or confused. Don't worry about it for the present, as your aim is to get him on to the circle: just remain in a neutral position until he stops. If he really takes off on the circle after two laps, bring him back (see page 72). Rub him for a bit, then send him gently out on to the circle again. Keep repeating this until he relaxes.If your horse changes from trot to walk without your instruction, repeat the course of action for horses that stop (see above).
- **Your horse takes backward steps when you try to send him out on the full line.** This is usually due to confusion. Go back to working on the short-range circle to ensure it is clear and easy to your horse. Check that you are leading your horse clearly in the correct direction. You could also try task 3, task 4, and task 1.
- **Your horse leans against the rope during the allow.** This is an indication of your horse's wish to run away! Don't shout at him, be neutral and friendly, and repeat all three parts of the task until he understands what is intended of him. Do task 1 for a little longer than usual each time you bring him back.

Task 6: The ability to move sideways from pressure

Moving laterally is not natural for the horse because he has to cross his legs. As well as improving his flexibility, these exercises cause him to use the left brain to think about what he is doing, and add suspension to his movement, which is useful for more advanced exercises.

Aim:
To teach your horse to move sideways.

Objectives:
- To increase his athletic abilities.
- To encourage him to think with his left brain.

Uses:
This exercise is useful with an excitable horse because he has to use his left brain, and this focuses him on the here and now, and suspends his flight instinct.

Your horse must be comfortable with task 3. Hold your line loosely about 90cm (3ft) from the clasp.

The short-range task Hold the halter on the clip, keeping your arm out straight. Using your communication stick, drive your horse's head away to get a 360 degree turn (photograph 1). Turn with your horse. Repeat, driving his rump in a complete circle (photograph 2). Now drive his head sideways for a couple of steps (his rump should remain still), then drive his rump sideways for a couple of steps (his head should

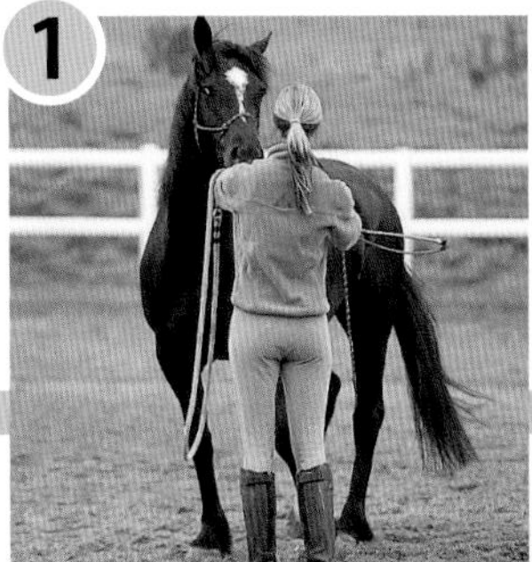

remain still). Repeat these two actions several times, driving your horse sideways first from the forehand and then from the quarters. Allow your line to slide out to its full length as you keep moving forwards at the same pace. Do not speed up. To stop, relax, slow down and halt and allow your horse to do the same. Do this from both sides.

When you have finished, use task 1, focusing on the areas you have been driving away.

The long-range sideways task Once your horse is familiar with the short-range task, stand approximately 45cm (18in) away from the fence. With the hand that is closest to the fence, hold the lunge line at approximately halfway along its length. Hold your communication stick in the other hand. Start walking, and don't stop, no matter what happens. Flap your communication stick up and down behind you with rhythm (see photograph below).

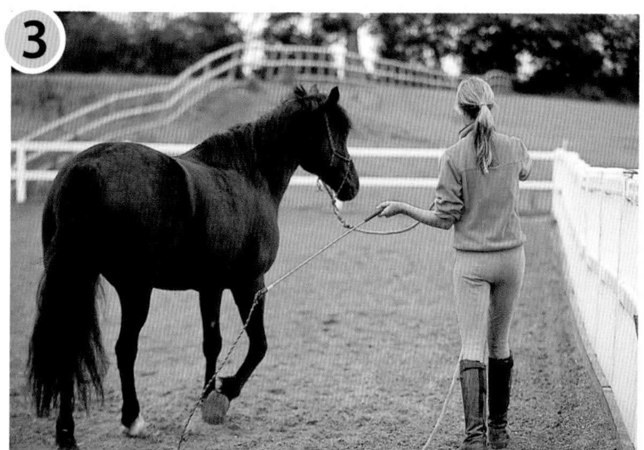
3

4

This should drive your horse out and around you until he comes to the fence in front of you. When he does this, allow the line to slide through your hand to its full length and stretch your arm out. Bring the communication stick around in front of you, keeping the rhythmic movement and walk going: this should drive your horse sideways (see photograph above). After a few successful steps, stop and smile and rub your horse with the communication stick.

TIPS

Keep walking forwards whatever your horse does. Straighten up and exude energy as you move towards him. If you are positive and committed, he will feel the force of your forward motion and realize that it is his job to find his place. Once he is moving, switch off, relax, smile: your horse should feel the difference and relax himself.

- *Don't hold the rope too short and too close to the horse.*
- *Don't drift away from the fence.*
- *Don't pull back on the line.*
- *Set an even pace as you walk.*
- *Work on both your horse's good side and his weaker side.*

TROUBLESHOOTING

- **Your horse runs backwards during the short-range task.** Once again this is due to fear and confusion. Use tasks 1 and 3. If he still goes backwards, hold your position by his neck (this may be quite difficult) and be passively persistent until he makes the slightest move in the right direction. Then stop and work on task 1. Then begin again, and continue in this manner until he is relaxed and confident.
- **Your horse runs backwards during the long-range task.** Stay by the fence and keep trying to move forwards. Keep the rhythm with your communication stick until your horse works out where he needs to be. If he won't come forwards and around you, revisit tasks 4 and 5 to see where he has lost his way. It might also help to go back to the short-range task.
- **Your horse moves sideways, but drags his hindquarters.** This may be because he really is having trouble moving sideways. Accept this initially, but start asking for a little more from his rump by rolling your communication stick out in that direction in a rhythmic fashion, as he becomes more confident. Focus all your attention on this area. Fairly soon a look is all it should take.
- **Your horse tries to kick you when you drive his rump.** Stay calm and don't become tense. Keep at the end of the line so you are well clear of his back end. Keep your rhythm going if possible, even if he is bucking or kicking. The moment he moves, smile and stop. Then begin again, and it won't take him long to realize that it's more comfortable to try to do what you want.
- **Your horse turns his forehand towards you.** Walk down your line towards him and gather it up as you go, then swing the tail of the line towards his nose and send him off sideways again.
- **Your horse turns away and the line goes over his back.** Hold the line low to prevent him from doing this.

Task 7: Desensitization to claustrophobic situations

Task 7 builds your horse's confidence and trust in you not to put him in harm's way. To a horse this includes potentially claustrophobic situations, such as squeezing through tight spaces (maybe 3m/10ft), going into trailers or horseboxes and, in some cases, even the action of moving him to a fence before jumping.

Aim:
To help your horse become more confident in enclosed or tight spaces such as trailer loading.

Objective:
- To help him overcome claustrophobic tendencies.

Uses:
- Task 7 can help with loading difficulties.
- It can be used to put your horse over a small jump in a way that you can see his performance.
- If your horse rushes into his fences, this task should help to slow him down.
- Bringing your horse back in to you at the end of this task teaches him to come back to you after a situation that has put him under pressure. In effect he sees you as the place of comfort.

Position yourself close to the fence with your shoulder towards the fence and your horse facing you and parallel to the fence. Holding your lunge line halfway down its length in the hand nearest to the fence and your communication stick in the opposite hand, start walking backwards, moving away from the fence with each step.

Direct your horse's forehand into the growing gap, clearly showing him that the way to go is between you and the fence. Slap the ground to your outside with the communication stick to encourage him forwards.

The moment he goes forwards, stop and relax and allow him to continue by himself, being sure to let the line slip through your hand as he goes.

Once he has passed you, ask him to yield his quarters so that he is facing you once again. Repeat the exercise until he becomes confident.

Once your horse understands and is comfortable with task 7, try sending him between two barrels, two jumps or any other obstacles that may help with his training. You can also send him over a small jump.

TROUBLESHOOTING

- **Your horse turns and runs back out and around you.** This is quite normal on the first attempts. Keep walking backwards, making the gap wider and tapping the ground with your communication stick to discourage him from running out that way. Don't allow the line to slide through your hands until he goes through the gap. Be prepared to widen the gap as much as he needs. It may take your horse a long time to gain his confidence. Remember that every horse is an individual, and his attitude towards narrow spaces will be based on his confidence, spirit and experience. Be patient with him and remain relaxed. Go into neutral when he finally rushes through the gap, and be sure not to restrict him with the line. Likewise stop tapping the ground with your communication stick the moment he decides to go forwards.

TIPS

- *Be sure to lead your horse into the gap between you and the fence.*
- *Don't overstretch your horse too soon, asking for too narrow a gap or too high a jump.*

30 minutes of Inspiring Lungeing

⇧ *This horse is beginning to work through his back and to track up, and is obviously listening to the person lungeing him.*

As part of your schooling programme, lungework can be inspiring, educational and fun for both you and your horse if you use a little imagination.

Lungeing is a safer way of working with a new or difficult horse as you can watch what he is doing from the ground and from a relatively safe position. It is also an excellent forum in which to begin to establish a language between you and your horse. Finally, if done properly, it is a great way of getting maximum benefit in minimum time.

Twenty minutes is more than enough time on the lunge, as working on a circle is strenuous for a horse. Always divide your time between both reins (although if your horse does have a problem side you may decide to work on that rein for either a little longer or a little less time, according to the cause of the problem). Alternate between each rein on a regular basis, rather than doing all your work on the left rein and then progressing to the right, for example. At the beginning allow several minutes for your horse to warm up in walk without side reins; similarly he should be allowed to cool down and stretch at the end of each session.

WHEN TO LUNGE

- If your horse is a little over-exuberant when he first comes out of the stable, a few minutes of lungeing before you ride will give him the opportunity to settle into his work.
- A youngster can learn the first steps of communication and training in the hands of a person with good experience of lungeing.
- Give yourself the opportunity to get to know a new horse by watching how he performs on the lunge line.
- Horses that have learned bad habits can begin retraining on the lunge.
- In certain circumstances lungeing can be used to bring a horse back into work after some forms of illness, or when he cannot be ridden.

Try one of each of the following ideas during a 30-minute session to establish which work best for you and your horse. Once you are comfortable with each of the concepts, you can work them into your lungeing routines to keep these varied.

Changes in pace

Using changes in pace, whether on the lunge or whilst riding, will increase your horse's impulsion because he has to engage his hind legs. This is quite hard work for your horse so don't rush progress, and do work through the permutations over several lungeing sessions.

Once you have warmed up your horse on both reins, working in trot, and thinking of your circle as a clock face, ask him to come back to walk at 12 o'clock, walk a circle, and then go back up to trot when he returns to that point. You are looking for immediate responses to your requests. Once he has the idea, introduce a second point at which to ask for a change of pace, at 6 o'clock. For example, your horse will go from trot to walk at 12 o'clock, and then back to trot at 6 o'clock. When you have established this in trot to walk to trot, introduce halt.

Once this is mastered, it should then be possible to introduce indirect changes in pace. And depending on your horse's temperament and abilities, it may be possible to introduce canter into the permutations, and also transitions at 3 o'clock and 9 o'clock in the slower paces.

Don't forget: If your horse starts to anticipate changes at the quarter-circle markers, count the number of strides instead. For example, trot for four strides, and then go into canter or walk for four strides, and so on.

Changing the size and position of the circle

Lungeing tends to be done on a 20m (65ft) circle, but it is possible to gradually decrease or increase the size of this circle. This is great for your horse's balance. Bringing him in on the circle will also, in most cases, slow him down. If your horse does tend to become faster, he is probably trying to escape discomfort, indicating that he is not physically ready for such a tight circle. Remember this is much harder work for the horse than it looks.

Once your horse is working on a 20m circle in trot, gradually reduce the size of the circle, 90cm (3ft) at a time, though never below 10m (33ft) – maintaining the quality of pace. Do a couple of circuits on the shorter line, and then return to the 20m circle.

Don't forget that you can move around the school whilst lungeing: you don't have to be rooted to the spot. This is a great way of working with nappy horses or in an area where certain points in the school tend to cause problems.

For example, begin your lungeing in one corner of the school. Once you are happy with the way your horse is going, as he comes round the corner give with the lunge rein slightly and, using your voice or lunge whip, encourage him along the track to the next corner, running alongside. Now do another circle or two in this corner, and then continue to move around the school in this way, using each corner.

LEARNING TO LUNGE

There is no doubt that lungeing is a skill that develops with practice, and initially, if you have never lunged a horse before, it would be as well to organize a lesson or two with an instructor or a rider experienced in sympathetic lungeing.

When lungeing, the lunge line, your body and the whip should form a triangle, the base of which is the horse's body. Here, the lunge whip is shown in the driving position. It can be pointed towards the shoulder to send the horse further out on the circle, or in front of the horse to encourage him to slow down or stop. When not in use it should be turned behind the person lungeing.

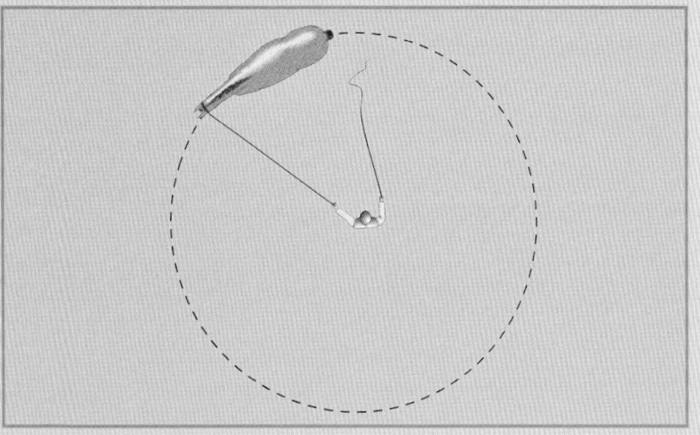

TACKING UP

The joy of lungeing is that as long as you have a lunge line of approximately 9m (30ft) and a lunge whip, you don't need to have any additional equipment other than your regular tack. The traditional way is to use a lungeing cavesson over a bridle, with a saddle or a roller and side reins. However, it is possible to use a bridle without the reins, and a roller.

In this case there are several ways in which the lunge line can be attached to the bridle:

1. Pass the lunge line through the inside bit ring, under your horse's chin, through the outside bit ring, over the poll and back to the inside bit ring, where it is clipped.

2. Pass the line through the inside bit ring over the poll and down to the outside bit ring, where it is clipped.

3. Pass the line through the inside bit ring and clip it to the outside bit ring.

Whichever method you and your instructor prefer, you will need to reverse the procedure when changing reins.

If you are going to use side reins, attach the buckled end to the roller in the appropriate place. (This should be approximately level with your horse's bit when he is working on the bit.) In the initial stages, clip the bridle end to one of the higher D-rings on the roller, until you are ready to use it.

Be cautious with side reins on the lunge, and never over-tighten them. They must allow your horse to stretch down into the bit, and should not strap him into a set position.

Opinions vary as to whether the side reins should be of exactly the same length, or slightly longer on the outside. Take advice from your trainer if you are inexperienced.

Always put boots on all the horse's legs when lungeing.

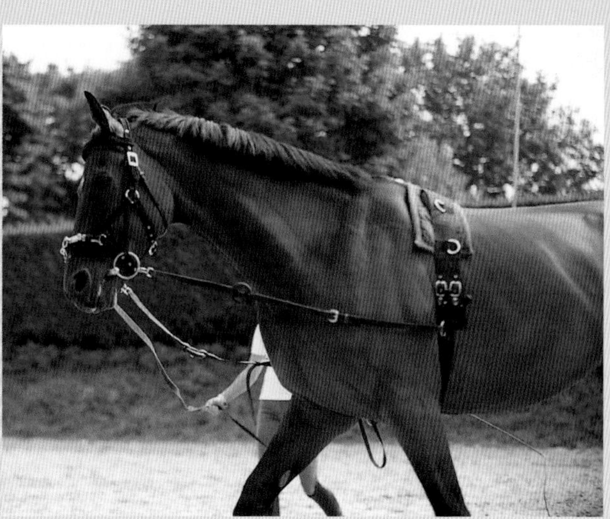

Working over poles

Introducing polework to the horse's work on the lunge, whether as ground poles or raised, has two key benefits:

- they are a great way of introducing a horse to jumping;
- they improve your horse's athleticism, encouraging him to pick up his feet and to use his front end.

Begin by introducing a singe pole on one of the quarter points of your circle. Allow your horse to look at the pole and to take it in his stride. It will not take him long to get used to it. Now introduce a second pole directly opposite on the circle.

Alternatively, arrange poles in a fan shape on one section of the circle: as a starting point, space them 1.4m (4½ft) apart at the middle of each pole.

Now try raising the outside ends of alternate poles on the curve; for best effect you may need to use five poles.

The next step is to introduce firstly a raised pole, and then a small jump to your circle. You will need to use blocks rather than wings to do this. Take this gradually and do not overstretch your horse until you are sure of his reaction.

Don't forget: Your horse may become excited at any point during polework and try to jump the poles. Use your voice commands and keep a consistent contact on the rein until he settles.

30 minutes to Learn to Long-line

Working a horse on two lines is like riding from the ground – and like riding, it takes a while to get the hang of it; but once this method of training becomes another tool in your box of skills, you'll find it invaluable.

Initially it will take more than 30 minutes to learn how to long-line. Behavioural specialist Richard Maxwell considers this method of training very useful, but estimates it would probably take twelve 30-minute sessions to become dextrous enough to feel confident and to progress your horse's training. In fact 30 minutes is long enough for any one session, as long-lining is, like lungeing, quite strenuous for any horse.

In your first 30-minute session you should aim for your horse to accept the lines, and have him working on them in walk and able to complete a slow turn. Subsequent 30-minute sessions should improve your skills, so that you move up through the paces, and making turns becomes second nature. Once your horse is working comfortably on the lines, in a good outline and at a regular pace, move on to polework and jumping exercises.

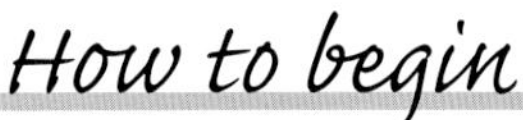

How to begin

Before you begin to work on two lines, try this test to discover how receptive your horse will be to a line passing around his back end. If you suspect that he might be worried by it, make use of the full length of a 9m (30ft) line to stay clear of his back end.

1. Tack up your horse in the normal way. Loop the reins through the throatlash, pull down the stirrups, and join them under the horse's belly with an old stirrup leather.

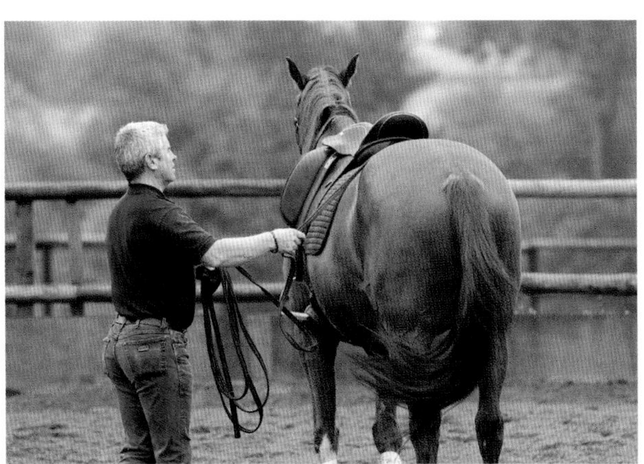

2. Now, attach your line to the ring of the bit on the horse's offside. Bring the line over his head, along his neck, over the saddle, and, with care, allow it to drape around behind his legs. Take a gentle feel on the line. As it is attached to the bit, your horse's nose will have to follow. You'll now have an idea of how he is going to react to the line behind his legs. If he is worried, gently persist, until he becomes accustomed to the line behind him.

3. Repeat this, attaching the line to the opposite side of the bit.

WHY LONG-LINE RATHER THAN LUNGE?

Long-lining is harder work for your horse than lungeing. With the length of his body contained by the two lines, it is very difficult for him to evade in any way and you have more control of his head – which is useful if he tends to turn in on you when lungeing – and his quarters – which is useful if he swings his quarters out on the lunge.

Work on two lines

Once your horse is settled with a line behind him, it's time to attach two lines. On each side, attach a line to the bit ring and thread the other end through the stirrup. Stand between the hip and the stirrup, and bring the outside line over the horse's quarters (photograph, below). Now, bring the outside line around the horse's quarters and you have your lines in position ready to begin (photograph, bottom).

BIT OR CAVESSON?

'Lines to the bit are controversial, but we ride off the bit, not off a cavesson or other things. If you can communicate with, and control a horse when your hands are thirty feet away from its mouth, when they're only three feet away the communication will be slicker and more efficient, and your timing and feel will be better.' Richard Maxwell.

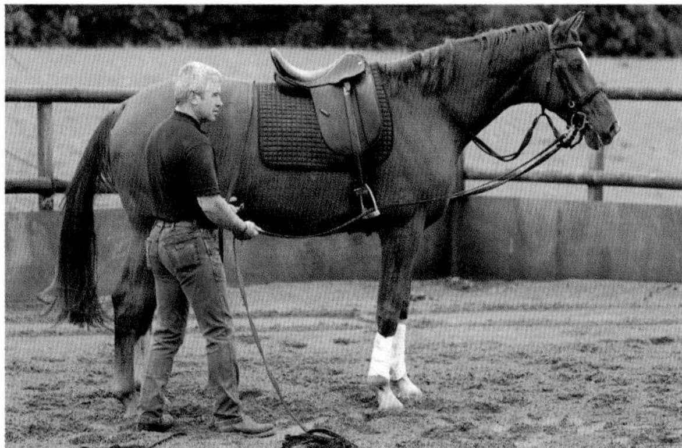

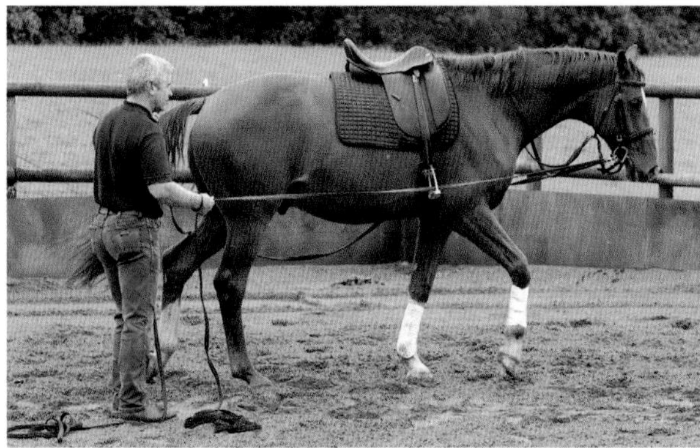

Send the horse away on a circle with a flick of the outside line and a vocal command. Max suggests using just two voice commands, one to send the horse on, and the other to slow him down. If your horse doesn't go forwards immediately, exaggerate the flick by drawing your outside hand across your chest and back again.

Don't worry if your horse goes off into canter or trot; allow him to settle down and become accustomed to the lines. If the outside line becomes caught in his legs, just let it go; it will untangle itself. Once your horse has settled a little, use your voice and a firm contact on the inside rein to slow him down.

Your aim is to work on a circle, maintaining a contact with your horse's mouth using the inside line and driving him forwards using the outside line. On the right rein, the inside line should be in your right hand, and vice versa (see photograph, below).

THE BENEFITS OF LONG-LINING

- **Control**
- **Engagement of the hindquarters**
- **Flexibility through the head, neck and shoulder**
- **Respect for the handler and the bit**
- **The lesson of moving away from pressure**
- **The lesson of responding with minimum resistance**

What are you looking for?

You want to see your horse going forwards, tracking up, stepping under his quarters, stretching his topline and reaching down for the bit. He will have to balance himself and make full use of his muscles. This should be achievable in all three paces, but start in walk as this gives you time to become familiar with the lines. Be sure to drive your horse forwards from behind, and not pull him in from the front. You need to change rein regularly, and for this you will need to make a turn (see opposite).

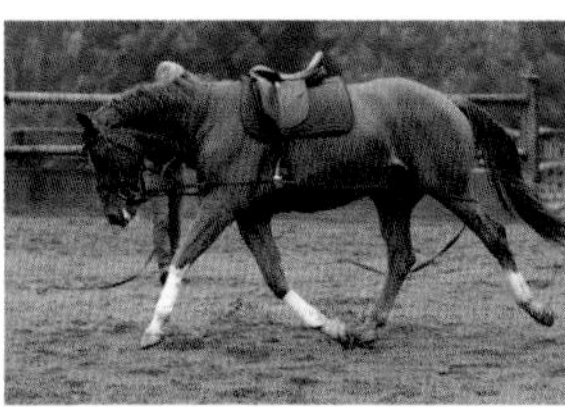

THREE STEPS TO A TURN

Learn to make a turn in walk.

1. Run your hand boldly down the outside rein.

2. Close your fingers on the outside rein and let your horse follow the feel.

3. Allow your opposite hand to open and the inside rein to slide through.

Long-lining over poles

Once you feel you have mastered the lines and your horse is working well, you can introduce poles and jumps to your circle. This has three significant applications:

- It can help build your horse's confidence over jumps.
- It can be used to add variety to your horse's training.
- It helps your horse to engage his inside hind leg.

Once your horse can cope with one pole, introduce a second on the opposite side of your circle.

30 minutes on Spookiness and Napping

Most horses will spook on occasion, but if you regard this as an opportunity to work on your training, rather than as an insurmountable hurdle, you'll soon get the better of this tendency.

Spooking is part of the horse's self-preservation instinct of flight, and can be inspired by a sight, smell or sound. It can also be caused by nervousness or anticipation on the part of the rider. Some horses seem to spook at everything, others are more selective and always pick the same subject, while a third group spooks totally unexpectedly. In most cases the horse will be scared, spook, be reassured by the rider, and then forget about it. However, some horses build upon the feeling, and as their fears mount up they behave purely instinctively and are therefore hard to control.

⇧ *Experienced horsemen recommend focusing on an object 100m/ yd beyond the problem, looking the other way, singing, or even counting to help get you past a potential problem!*

Opinions vary on how to ride past a spooky object. One school of thought recommends that you allow your horse to have a good look at it – but to do this, you have to be a confident rider yourself. The other recommends that you turn the horse away, even to the extent of riding shoulder-in past the obstacle. Whichever you do, make no mistake about it, spooking can be dangerous, but it presents the opportunity to flex all your training muscles. It demands an analytical approach to find the cause, a methodical approach to training, and a realistic approach to your abilities. It is not insurmountable.

⇧ *If your horse spooks on the road, desensitizing him to the source of the spook could make all the difference.*

Tackling the problem

Take some time to try to work out why your horse is spooking. The most common reason is fear, compounded by lack of confidence. A horse will have no confidence in a rider if:

- it hasn't had the opportunity to build up its own confidence;
- it doesn't understand the rider's signals;
- the rider isn't confident themselves.

Therefore the first step in dealing with a horse that spooks is to work on your own confidence and your horse's confidence in you, so that you work together as a team. This doesn't happen overnight but, like all aspects of training, if you take the time to build it up properly, it will be reflected in many other areas of your horse/rider relationship.

Spend 30 minutes building up your confidence

There are many strategies, both mental and practical, to help increase confidence, and these are dealt with in 30 Minutes to Build Up Your Confidence, page 140.

To deal with a spooky horse, a realistic approach to your abilities in the saddle is also necessary. Riding a spooky horse is unnerving, and it won't help if you are a nervous rider – in fact it takes a very confident rider not to be affected by a spooky horse. Therefore, until you have done more work on your confidence, both practically and psychologically, where possible avoid situations that might cause your horse to spook, and always ride out with another, more experienced horse-and-rider combination.

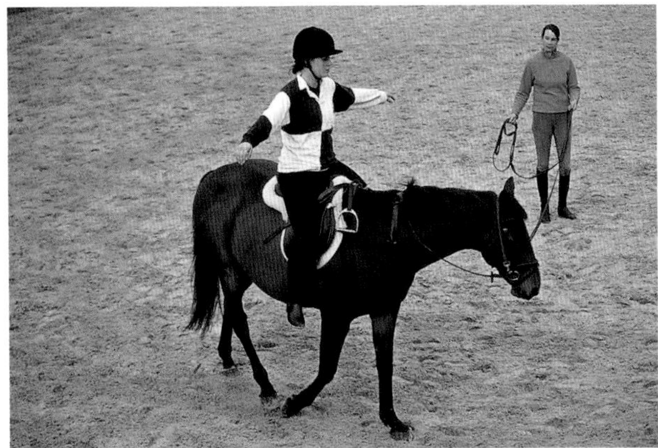

⇧ *If you need achieve a deeper seat, your instructor will probably give you ridden lunge lessons.*

The next step is to recognize where your particular shortcomings lie, and to work on them. If your seat is not sufficiently secure, for example, ridden work on the lunge will help to develop this skill. Or if you are at all unsure about your proficiency at giving the aids, work on this with your instructor, perhaps having lessons on a schoolmaster. And if you are still in awe of your horse, groundwork will help to familiarize you with his reactions and develop his respect for you. Spend as much time as it takes on groundwork until you are totally confident about your ability to control movement and direction. Pay attention to every detail, such as stopping with the horse facing where you want him to be and not where he wants to be; and take the discipline you have worked on back to the stable.

Your goal is to build up a relationship with your horse, and if you're not confident enough to do that on your own, enlist the help of a trainer. And as you see your horse's confidence in you developing, this will help your own confidence, too.

Spend a regular 30 minutes building up your horse's confidence

• *Plan to spend 30 minutes at least twice a week on groundwork.*

Read through the previous chapters to devise a groundwork training programme. Choose from halter training, long-lining, lungeing and groundwork tasks to establish a line of communication between you and your horse. Don't rush at this stage. Build up on each small success, and give your horse time to absorb what he is learning. Don't be surprised if you go back a step or two on occasion, but don't become frustrated either. Gently persist.

• *Go for a 30-minute hack with a confident rider and a more experienced horse.*

Hack out with a more experienced horse for as long as it takes (months, if necessary) to give your own horse confidence in his surroundings. Take the time to plan your ride carefully, perhaps walking it in advance, so that you have a good idea of any hazards you are likely to encounter.

• *Spend 30 minutes desensitizing your horse to any identifiable 'terrors'.*

Many of the obstacles that you encounter on a hack can be recreated either in the school, in the confines of a safe field, or on a private track or pathway. This method can be applied to most obstacles, from dustbins to tractors, but be sure that you are safe, and enlist some help if necessary. If you cannot progress all the way through the three stages of this process (see next page), work as far as you can, being sure to end on a positive note. Then start again from the beginning of your next session. With each attempt it should become easier.

⇧ *Practise desensitizing your horse to large objects such as tractors in a location where you feel safe and have help to hand.*

Working on desensitizing your horse

1. Walk your horse in hand past the obstacle until he becomes acclimatized to it. You must show no fear, and should lead him past confidently. If possible don't use a bit and reins, or any other form of compulsive headcollar, as you do not want the horse to feel that he is being punished. If you have to begin some distance away, do so, gradually working your way in closer and praising your horse for every step he takes in the right direction.

Allow him to proceed at his own pace. He may need a good deal of reassurance from you, or even a lead from another horse. If he appears curious and wishes to approach, smell or touch the obstacle, allow him to do so. Repeat this action until he shows no fear.

2. Now walk him past the obstacle on long reins. It's his turn to take the lead. Either walk beside him, in the position of a rider, or behind and to one side, taking care to avoid his back legs. Once again repeat this exercise until your horse is doing it confidently.

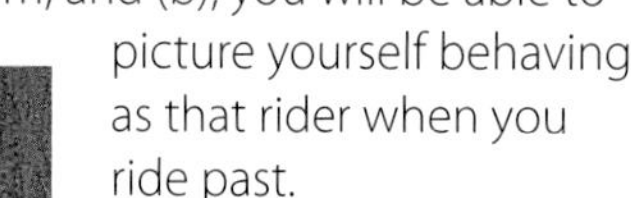

3. Once your horse will pass the obstacle confidently, it's time to mount up. Make sure you can remain relaxed; if you have any doubts, ask a more confident rider to ride your horse past for you. You will then (a) have seen your horse go past the problem, and (b), you will be able to picture yourself behaving as that rider when you ride past.

Ride past the obstacles as many times as it takes to feel confident. If possible, even try repositioning the obstacle in a safe field or footpath. Repeat the process until you can ride past successfully. Now you are better prepared to tackle a similar challenge should it arise.

Some strategies to cope with spooking

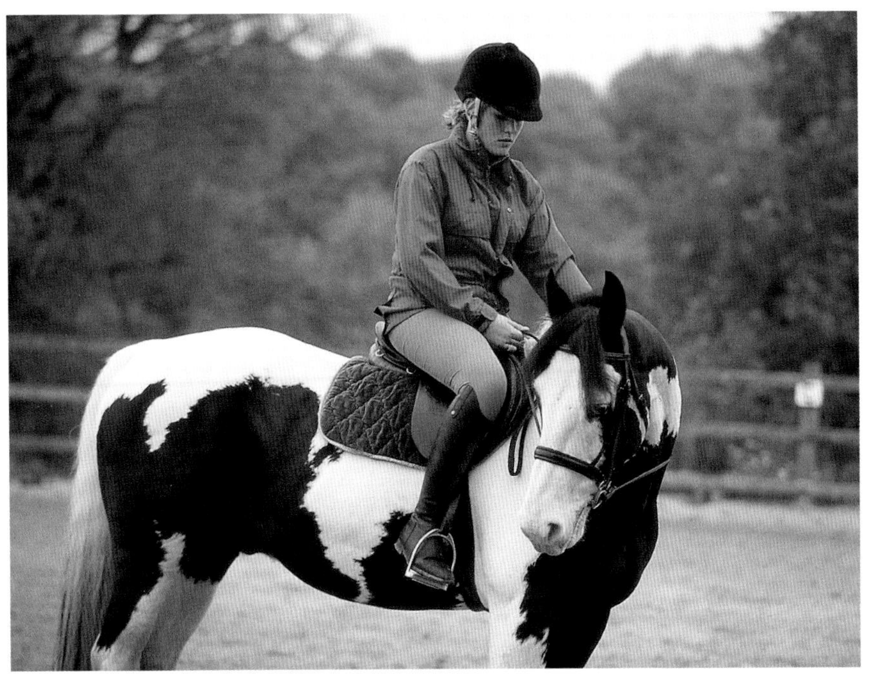

School your horse to work on simple exercises that will encourage him to use his left brain and so release endorphins that will slow him down.

Strategy 1: Get your horse focused on something else
When a horse panics and spooks he uses his right brain, the instinctive side of his mind. If you foresee being in a potentially spooky situation, have a routine prepared to divert his mind, which in turn engages the left brain. This then releases endorphins that calm and slow down the horse. For example:

Train your horse to bring his nose around towards your foot and the stirrup, when you raise one rein and give with the other. Practise until you have this perfect. When your horse spots a tiger in a bush on the left, regain his attention by asking him to turn his head to the right!

Lowering the head brings down the horse's heart rate and pulse, which in turn takes him out of 'flight' mode. Using the pressure-and release method (see 30 Minutes of Helpful Handling, page 56), teach your horse to lower his head, accompanying the movement by a verbal instruction such as 'down'. As his training progresses he will lower his head with minimal pressure, and eventually just on hearing the key word. Use this technique when riding, substituting subtle downward pressure on both reins.

Strategy 2: Get off and lead
This is quite controversial, as you will so often be told that if you get off, you are letting the horse win. However, if you dismount and lead your horse past the obstacle a couple of times until he realizes there is nothing to be afraid of, and then remount and ride past, not only have you made the best of the situation, but you won't have resorted to a battle with your horse either – so that's a win-win result!

Strategy 3: Learn to deal with a spook
What does your horse do when he spooks? Does he jump sideways, spin around, run forwards a few strides? Horses tend to be quite predictable in their reaction to spooky situations. Enlist the help of your instructor in dealing with your horse's reaction, and learn to be able to ride it. This will give you confidence, and in turn, more control of the situation.

Strategy 4: Develop your lateral control
Horse behavioural specialist, Richard Maxwell says: '80 per cent of evasions come through the shoulder.' Thus you might work on control of the shoulders by using lateral work (see 30 Minutes to Work on Focused Schooling, page 96).

Strategy 5: Have a health check
If your horse is spooking frequently and at varied causes, it may be worth having his eyesight and hearing checked. You should also check your feed programme if your horse suddenly and uncharacteristically starts spooking.

Strategy 6: Spooking at shows
If your horse only spooks at shows, it could be that you are overfacing either him or yourself. Go to a show first of all and lead him around until he's desensitized to the sights and sounds. If you feel confident enough, mount up and ride around. Work on left brain exercises (see Strategy 1) or other exercises you would normally work through at home. You could try finding a quiet corner and lungeing him, for example, or riding around the clear round arena but without jumping anything.

11

4 30 MINUTES TO A FITTER HORSE

- *30 minutes to set up a training programme*
- *30 minutes to workout your horse*
- *30 minutes to work on focused schooling*
- *30 minutes to spend on a rider workout*

Fitness is the ultimate goal of every horse and rider combination. However, fitness is appropriate to what you and your horse do and are capable of: what is important is that you understand what it means and how to achieve it.

Whether your equestrian ambitions are based on enjoying the countryside and your relationship with your horse, or you are aiming for national competition, you will both benefit from a training programme. Take 30 minutes out as soon as possible to devise a plan that suits you both.

It is possible to give your horse a total workout in 30 minutes if that's all the time you have to spare. Alternatively you can spend 30 minutes of a schooling session focusing on your horse's technical abilities, such as impulsion, rhythm and collection.

There's not much point in having a fit horse if you can't keep up with him. However, following a specially devised exercise routine for 30 minutes twice a week will probably be enough to tone you up sufficiently!

30 minutes to Set Up a Training Programme

Can you remember why you first started riding? What was it that drew you in? And what was it that you dreamt about achieving at that time? You've probably already achieved some of your dreams and thought of some new ones – or have you totally lost your way? Or are your goals second-hand, given to you by someone else? Whilst we work on our training and set our sights on competitive targets, very few of us actually incorporate into our dreams a programme for our horse's fitness. Fortunately, most horses seem able to keep up with us, becoming fitter as we do. However, this 'fingers-crossed' approach can lead to injury, over-facing and napping if we are not careful.

So how do you set up a programme that will ensure you and your horse develop together? Before going any further, there are three things to do:

- Recognize your goals and how to achieve them.
- Take stock of where you and your horse are today.
- Decide how much time you have available to put into your training programme.

Recognizing your goals and achieving them

Before embarking on any training programme, you need to know where you are going, and there are five well known rules to this end. Your goals must be as follows:

1. *Unambiguous.* It's not enough to say you want to be a better rider. What does that mean?
2. *Measurable.* You will need progress markers along the way to see that you are moving on.
3. *Realistic.* There is no point in aiming for the Olympics if you're only going to ride once a week.
4. *With a time limit.* Without a deadline, you can take forever.
5. *Important to you.* You have to want to achieve your goal, and not just be doing it because your best friend is.
Therefore take 30 minutes to identify your current equestrian goal, and work out a time plan to achieve it.

Taking stock of where you and your horse are today

Now take a good look at your abilities and those of your horse. As your horse becomes fitter you will need to be able to keep up with him, so your personal fitness is an issue, too. Do you need to think about diet or general fitness training? If you haven't already done so, plan your own fitness development needs into your long-term equestrian goal plan.

How fit is your horse? As a general guide a horse in light competitive work should be able to complete a two-hour hack and come back with a spring in his step. Is he going to need any special training to become the horse of your dreams? Is he up to it? Schedule his requirements into your long-term plan, too. What about his health? Before embarking on any fitness programme be sure to check on the following:

- Is he sound?
- Are his vaccinations up to date?
- When was he last wormed, and do you have a worming programme in place?
- When did he last see the dentist?
- When is his next farrier's appointment?

⇧ *Depending on his condition to begin with, it takes between 8 and 12 weeks to bring a horse into fitness.*

If you are competing seriously rather than for pleasure, and aim to get your horse to peak fitness, it would also be a good idea to ask your vet to take a blood test now. You should then have another test taken at the end of the first stage of your fitness training to secure an accurate profile of his health.

How much time can you put in?

Before drawing up a day-by-day fitness programme, you need to decide on how much time you have, realistically, to spend with your horse. This is your target. There will be occasions when you will not be able to meet that target for one reason or another, but these should be the exception rather than the rule. Your relationship with your horse will benefit from your ability to see and work with him regularly.

In theory, your horse should be exercised for an hour a day, six days a week. However, many of us work and have to fit riding into our working and home lives. Work out what your optimum available time is, ask yourself whether it's adequate to get your horse fit enough for your requirement – and if not, what outside help you are going to need, and how you are going to secure it.

If you can't manage six days a week, try to space out the days on which you cannot get to the yard so that your horse has two days off, for example.

If your goals require your horse to be very fit, you must look at where you keep him in order that his training programme can be carried on by the yard manager and staff; and you must seriously question your fitness and ability to match his. Take 30 minutes to combine your fitness plan, any health checks your horse needs, plus his long-term routine health appointments, with your long-term goal plan.

⇧ *If you have the opportunity to make use of a horse-walker, take it, incorporating 10 to 15 minutes into your training programme – but don't leave your horse on the walker for hours, as this will do him no good at all.*

Getting down to work

Once you have decided how long you can spend with your horse each day, it's time to organize a varied training programme to match the time you have available. The traditional fitness programme was designed for horses that were turned away after a heavy season of competing or hunting. However, these days very few professional riders give their horses any long periods of time off (eventers, hunters and racing horses seem to be the exceptions). For the recreational rider or pleasure competitor the only time that a horse is likely to be out of work is when he is on box rest. Bringing a horse into work after a period of rest should take about eight weeks. If you already work your horse regularly, you can either begin at week one (see page 90), or decide where you are in the training programme and pick up from there – but there is no substitute for the benefits of initial roadwork on the horse's legs and muscles.

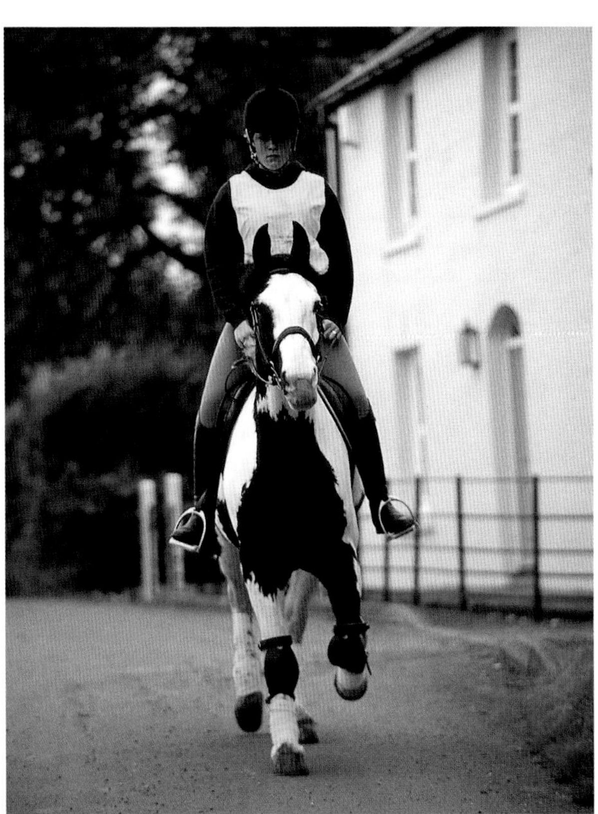

⇨ *When you introduce trotting on the roads, ensure that your horse's legs are properly booted and bandaged.*

SUGGESTED WEEKLY TRAINING FORMULA FOR A FIT HORSE

Remember to vary your training schedule to keep your horse interested in his work. He should always finish willing and able to do a little more.

MONDAY	Day off
TUESDAY	Light hack
WEDNESDAY	Lesson
THURSDAY	Light hack
FRIDAY	Groundwork
SATURDAY	Schooling
SUNDAY	Competition

Weeks 1–3: Roadwork in walk beginning at 20 minutes a day and increasing to 60 minutes.
Week 4: Introduce hacking for 60–90 minutes to your programme, with short bursts of trot work on suitable surfaces. Always begin and end in walk.
Week 5: Lungeing can now be introduced for up to 20 minutes. Begin to school your horse for not longer than 20 minutes, on alternate days to his hacking. Keep the schooling in walk and trot at this stage. Hacking should now increase to 2 hours, with some uphill work when possible.
Week 6: Cantering uphill can now be introduced to your hacking and controlled canter to your schooling, which can now last about 30–45 minutes.
Week 7: The length and speed of your canters can now be increased, and schooling sessions can last up to an hour (including warm-up and cool-down time). Easy circling and lateral work can be introduced into the schooling, and gymnastic jumping over small grids can begin.
Week 8: You will now be into your own personal training programme, and the directions in which you focus your attentions will depend on your ambitions and the needs of your horse.

⇧ *A good controlled blast on a hack gives your horse the opportunity to let off some steam.*

THE NECESSARY FUEL

Don't forget that your horse's feed requirements will change as his fitness increases. Here's a guide to the forage-to-concentrates ratio, from light work to hard work; for more detailed information, see '30 Minutes Analysing Your Horse's Diet', page 12.

Workload	% Forage	% Concentrate
At rest/light work (quiet hacking, light schooling)	75	25
Moderate work (hacking 1–2 hours, 30–60 minutes schooling, riding club activities)	50–60	50–40
Hard work (intensive schooling, regular competing)	40	60

ESTIMATED DAILY FOOD REQUIREMENTS ACCORDING TO WORKLOAD

Girth (cm)	Height (hh)	Approximate bodyweight (kg)	Total daily requirements (kg)	In light work (kg)		In moderate work (kg)		In hard work (kg)	
				Concentrate	Forage	Concentrate	Forage	Concentrate	Forage
128	12–12.2	182	3.6	0.9	2.7	1.8	1.8	2.2	1.4
140	12.2–13	227	4.5	1.1	3.4	2.3	2.3	2.7	1.8
148	13–13.2	273	5.5	1.4	4.1	2.8	2.8	3.3	2.2
156	13.2–14	318	6.4	1.6	4.8	3.2	3.2	3.8	2.6
164	14–14.2	364	7.3	1.8	5.5	3.7	3.7	4.4	2.9
171	14.2–15	409	8.2	2.0	6.2	4.1	4.1	4.9	3.3
178	15–15.2	455	9	2.2	6.8	4.5	4.5	5.4	3.6
185	15.2–16	500	10	2.5	7.5	5.0	5.0	6.0	6.0
192	16+	545	11	2.8	8.2	5.5	5.5	6.6	4.4
197	16+	591	11.8	3.0	8.8	5.9	5.9	7.1	4.7

Charts by courtesy of Baileys Horse Feeds.

30 minutes to Workout Your Horse

Even if you've only 30 minutes to spare, it is still possible to give your horse a great workout.

On almost every occasion that you and your horse go into the school it should be with the aim of working on a specific area of his training. However, there will be days when you don't have enough time, or you're just not focused enough to concentrate on what you are trying to achieve. In these circumstances, there are many other things you can do, as you will have discovered from reading this book. One possibility is to go into your schooling area, whether it's a proper arena or a designated part of a field, and give your horse a suppling nose-to-tail workout.

The workout

This is a progressive workout. Begin at the beginning, work as directed until you are totally satisfied with the way your horse is going, and then move on. If you find that initially you don't proceed much further than the first phase, don't worry. As long as you remain consistent in your aids and patient with your horse, he's probably going to work out what it is you're asking, and respond. If you really find you're not moving on, seek professional help. Remember to work equally on both reins – and don't forget to leave 5–10 minutes at the end of your session for you both to relax.

Phase 1: Warm up

- Begin in walk on a long rein. Whilst your horse is stretching his neck and back, check your own position to ensure you are in balance. If you are a tense rider, take a few minutes to work on relaxing into your position, perhaps using breathing exercises (see Develop a strategic breathing technique, page 142) or working through some stretching exercises yourself. Focus on what you are about to ask of your horse.
- Bring your horse on to a 20m (65ft) circle, still in walk. Although you are on a long rein you should have a soft contact with the bit. Keeping your seat as supple as possible, try to feel the rhythm of your horse's walk. Begin to take up a contact. Once you are satisfied with the walk, test your horse's acceptance of the bit with lateral and direct flexion.

• Lateral flexion: as you walk on your 20m circle, sponge with your fingers from one rein to the other in an encouraging way. Your aim is for your horse to chew on the bit and begin to flex in the direction in which you are encouraging him. You want him to create saliva and feel content in what he is doing. This should not be a battle.

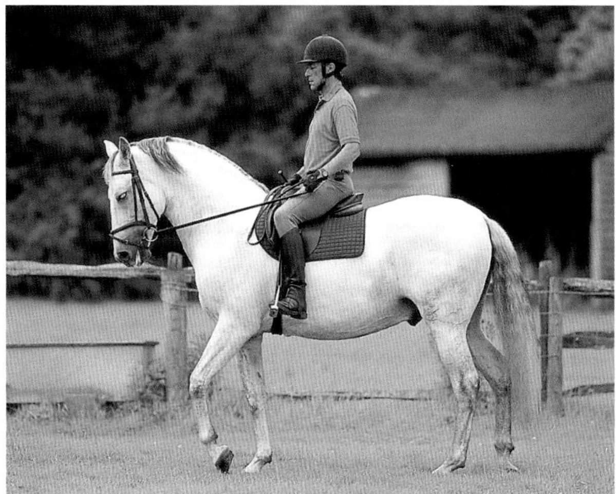

• Direct flexion: when your horse is flexing gently in each direction, ride him into a halt, using your seat. To do this, brace your back, sink your weight into the saddle, and gently feel, with both hands, on the rein. If your horse is accepting the bit and understanding your aids, he should come to a halt.

LEARN TO HALT FROM YOUR SEAT

One of the main purposes of schooling is to educate your horse to take his weight off his forehand and to carry himself more on his haunches. If you block him at the front end with your hands and the bit, you are encouraging him to rest on your hands, which will make him lean on you, and not carry himself.

TIP

If your horse isn't accepting direct flexion, do extra work on lateral flexion and check whether he is stiffer on one rein than the other. You may need to use a little more strength with your aids on the stiffer side, but proceed cautiously.

THE IMPORTANCE OF WALK

The work that can be done in walk is so often underestimated, especially in the early stages of ridden work when both horse and rider are enthusiastic to move on. But without a good walk, you will never achieve a good trot, and without a good trot you will never progress to a good canter. When summing up a horse's gaits for the first time, the way he goes in walk will tell you a great deal about his attitude and paces.

• Now while you are in halt, ask for some lateral flexion to each side, encouraging your horse to drop his poll and look in the appropriate direction. Don't forget to make a fuss of him when he does as you ask.

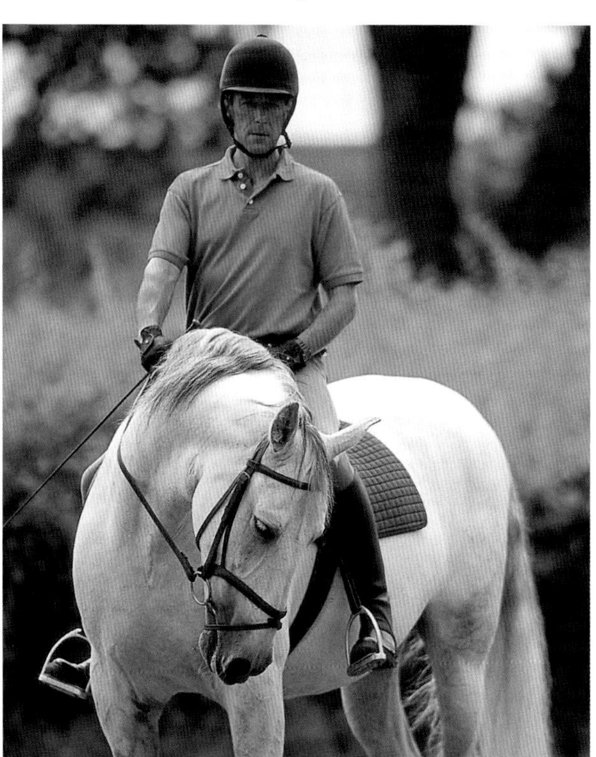

• Ride a 20m (65ft) circle on both reins in walk, and then a 15m (49ft) circle. Repeat in trot, continuing until your horse feels even and balanced on both circles.

Phase 2: Acceptance of your aids and impulsion

WHAT WORKS FOR YOUR HORSE?

Whilst making your transitions, nothing should feel solid or blocked in your hands. If you feel your horse is not really listening to your fingers and playing with his bit, you may have to be a little firmer, or change the speed, either slower or faster. It's up to you to find out what works for your horse. If you do have to be firmer, remember that as soon as your horse accepts your aid, you must respond by using a lighter aid once again. He will soon work out which is more comfortable.

To work on acceptance of your aids and impulsion, introduce transitions.

- Ride walk-to-halt transitions, lengthening the amount of time you spend in halt. Once your horse is standing square and waiting for your next aid, move on to walk-to-trot and trot-to-walk transitions.

Try to use your seat and legs, rather than your hands, to make the transitions. Initially it may take your horse two or three strides to make both downward and upward transitions, but your aim is to reduce the number of strides it takes your horse to make the transition, and to teach him to respond sharply to your leg aids. Don't forget to reward him with periods of stretching.

Phase 3: Bending through the body

To begin to supple your horse through his body, work on shallow loops and figures of eight.

- Ride deep into the corner of the school in walk, then ride a shallow loop down the long side with its apex at the halfway marker. Use a block or cone to mark the deepest point of your loop. Remember to sit square to the front of the horse, with your inside leg deep into the stirrup and keeping contact with the outside rein.

As you progress, move the cone further away from the halfway marker; the deeper the loop, the more difficult it becomes for the horse. Ride in walk and trot.

- Now progress to two shallow loops down the long side, and repeat in walk and trot.
- In walk, ride a figure of eight from the A or C marker. Take care to ride accurately, using the letters of the school to ensure you remain on course. Ride a straight

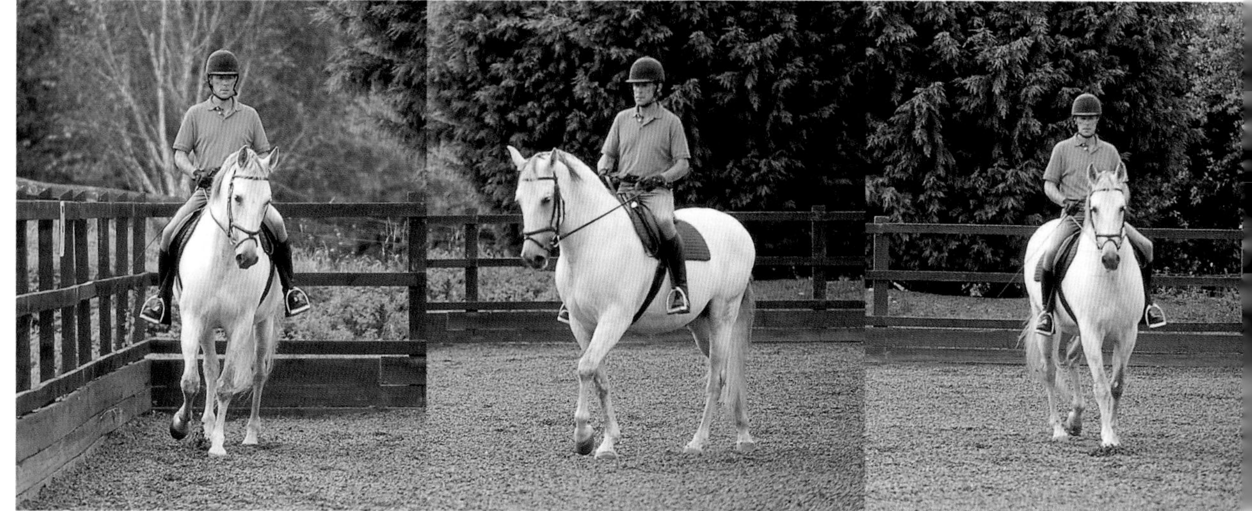

diagonal line across the middle of the school, connected by segments of circles at each end. Focus on your horse's way of going on each rein. When you are happy with his bending, incorporate transitions at X, and once this is successful, at the beginning of each of the diagonals. Ride this exercise in walk and trot.

USE BOTH REINS

Most riders tend to favour one rein or the other. Figures of eight are a useful exercise as they oblige you to work equally on each rein with their constant changes of direction.

Phase 4: Begin some lateral work

The simplest introduction to lateral work is to spiral in and out of a circle, then progress to leg-yielding.

- Begin on a 20m (65ft) circle and spiral in to a 10m (33ft) circle and then out again. This is a good test of your horse's obedience, as well as a suppling exercise.

Remember to remain straight and square in the saddle. Work in walk and trot on both reins.

- Begin on a 20m circle and in walk, spiral in to a 10m circle, then leg-yield back to the 20m circle. This exercise is best ridden with minimum bend in order to avoid your horse becoming unbalanced and putting excessive weight on his inside foreleg. The rider's 'asking' leg should only be placed a little behind the girth – any more would place the horse's hindquarters crooked. When the horse has to cross his limbs this is a good way of engaging the hindquarters. Repeat on the other rein.

Phase 5: Finish with a canter

Cantering on a circle is preferable to cantering large (around the school) because you have more control.

- Put your horse on to a 20m (65ft) circle, and ask for a transition to canter; whether you ask for canter from trot, or canter from walk, depends on your horse's ability. You could try first asking for a transition from trot to canter: if your horse runs into canter and you cannot gather him or collect him by half-halting and slowing the trot down, then ask for a walk-to-canter transition.

In order to obtain the correct canter lead, it is vital to have your horse bending correctly in the direction you wish him to canter. Invite him to canter using the normal canter aids, including raising your hand on the side of the leading leg (if you are going to canter right, raise the right hand). Repeat until you have a snappy transition and a controlled, even-paced canter. Then repeat on the opposite rein.

TIP

Remember every schooling session must begin with a period of warming up, the length of time of which will depend on the abilities and temperament of your horse. It is better to warm up for 20 minutes, have 5 minutes good work, and spend 5 minutes cooling down, than to warm up for 5 minutes and spend the next 25 minutes fighting with your horse. Phases 1 and 2 of this workout can be used to begin every schooling session.

Phase 6: Cool down

Finally allow your horse to walk on a long rein, stretching through his back and neck once again.

30 minutes to Work on Focused Schooling

If you've only 30 minutes to school your horse, spend it focusing on one aspect of his performance that needs work, and you'll discover inspiring results. For your horse to work properly, his way of going must encompass the following qualities:

- Looseness
- Acceptance of the bit
- Rhythm
- Straightness
- Engagement of the hindquarters
- Impulsion

Once these are all in place your horse will work in collection and will allow you to use your aids properly – a state of working that many of us aspire to, but only on occasion achieve. However, while in training towards this goal, both you and your horse will learn much about the way in which a horse works, and about each other.

For example, if you know that his impulsion is lacking, then your schooling should focus on exercises that will improve it. Furthermore, at various times during your training you may find that different aspects of his performance need attention, in which case you should be flexible and prepared to review what you are working on. If, however, you are generally satisfied with the way your horse is going, then you simply need to refine his skills and abilities in the areas that could be improved, and introduce lateral work.

All of these exercises can be ridden wherever you school your horse, be it a field or an arena. Begin in walk and with the simplest exercise. Once you are satisfied with your horse's progress (a helper on the ground will be useful to watch how you are both doing), move on to the next stage. Take your time: don't be tempted to rush, or become concerned if you do not progress far on the first or second attempts.

Begin your schooling session with Phases 1 and 2 of our workout routine (see pages 92–5); these cover looseness and acceptance of the bit.

Rhythm

In each gait, your horse's strides should be of the same length, and they should be maintained through transitions and turns as well as on straight lines. For this reason we work on loops, serpentines and circles.

Exercise 1: Shallow loops

Begin by riding a single loop down the long side of the school. Use a block to mark out the apex of your loop, which should be level with the halfway marker. Begin with your loop about 2.4m (8ft) deep, and work it up to a loop of 5m (16ft) deep: the deeper the loop, the more difficult it is for the horse. There should be no straight lines in this exercise. Flexion and bend need to be changed after each turn. Keep your shoulders and elbows square to your horse's shoulders, and your inside leg deep into the stirrup. Listen to the rhythm of your horse's strides, and try to feel this rhythm through your seat. Work in walk, and then in trot. When you are satisfied with your horse's progress, introduce a second loop down the long side of the school.

Exercise 2: Three-loop serpentine

As well as working on your horse's rhythm, the serpentine also works on the rider's looseness and accuracy. In this exercise begin your serpentine at A or C, and ride three

loops, making sure you are straight when you cross the school on your way to the next loop. Remember that your loops are half circles, and your horse will need to be straightened at the end of each loop, and then bent the other way to commence the next. Your loops should be absolutely equal in shape and size, and your rhythm absolutely even and level throughout the exercise. Your horse will almost certainly find it easier to bend and turn on one rein rather than the other, and you must be sure that you are changing your whole position to make the changes in bend, and are not just moving your hands. Master this exercise in walk before proceeding to trot.

Exercise 3: Canter on the circle

Ride on a 20m (65ft) circle, and ask for a transition to canter either from walk or trot according to your horse's capabilities. You may find it helpful to use four blocks or cones to mark out the quarter points on your circle, as this will help with direction and enable you to concentrate on rhythm. Once again the rhythm should be even throughout the circle. Practise this exercise on both reins.

Improving straightness

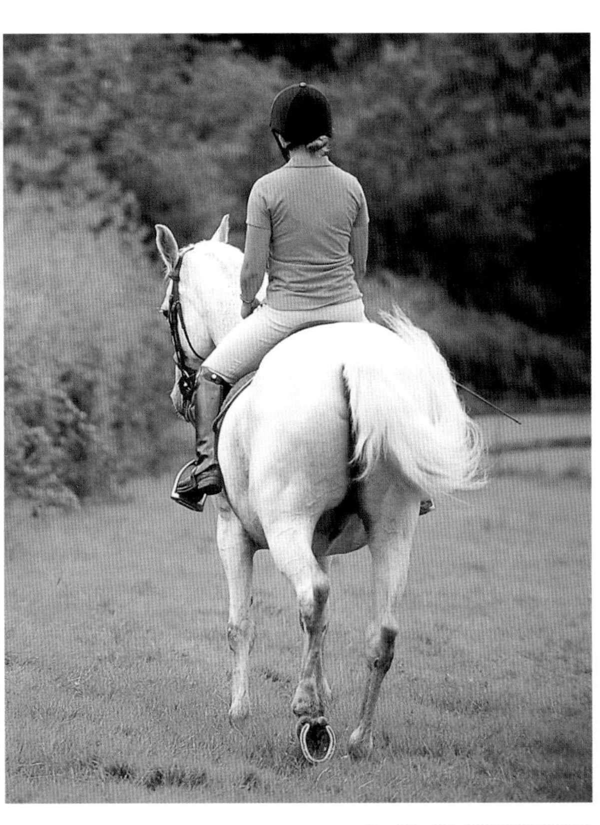

Straightness in the horse means the ability of the hind legs to move under the horse's body, and the hind hooves to be placed into the imprints made by the front hooves – otherwise known as 'tracking up'. Like most humans, most horses are naturally crooked and tend to carry their quarters to one side or the other.

The best group of exercises to improve straightness is based on the shoulder-in, and especially counter shoulder-in. Shoulder-in shifts the forehand and improves the horse's bend.

Exercise 1: Counter shoulder-in

Use the edge of your school, field or fence, as it will tend to give your horse stability. You are basically looking towards the boundary with a left bend if you are on your right rein and vice versa. On the right rein, keep your left leg on the girth supporting the quarters, your right leg behind. Your hands should go sideways towards the boundary, feeling softly down the rein. Your left hand will ask for flexion, your right rein will close against your

horse's neck. Turn your waist and shoulders towards the boundary. Repeat on the opposite rein. Once your horse has grasped what you are asking of him in walk, move on to trot. Initially this exercise is ridden 'on three tracks' with the outside hind falling into the imprint left by the inside fore (see photograph bottom page 97); for the more advanced horse this can be ridden on four tracks (see photograph above).

Exercise 2: Shoulder-in

Think of shoulder-in as a section of a circle. For this exercise you remain on the track, looking away from the boundary and into the school, with a right bend on the right rein and vice versa. On the right rein, your right leg remains on the girth, your left leg behind the girth. Your hands move to the right, with the right hand helping with the bend, and the left rein against the horse's neck, holding the contact. Turn your waist and shoulders to the right, ensuring you are still sitting square to the shoulders of your horse. Repeat on the opposite rein, and progress to trot. Once again, this exercise can be ridden on four tracks for the more advanced horse.

Exercise 3: Alternating counter shoulder-in/shoulder-in

Now combine the two previous exercises, riding along the side of your school.

Exercise 4: Shoulder-in on a circle

Shoulder-in on the circle is more demanding of the horse. In walk, ride on a 20m (65ft) circle, using the aids for shoulder-in as above. You will need a little more inside leg to hold your horse's quarters around the circle. Repeat in trot, and advance to performing the movement on four tracks.

Exercise 5: Alternate shoulder-in/counter shoulder-in on the circle

Repeat the aids as before. Ride in walk initially, and then in trot, finally advancing to four tracks

Engaging the hindquarters

For a horse to work effectively, the hindquarters need to be 'engaged': that is, they need to work under the horse to help support the weight of the rider and to power the horse's movements. As a consequence of this, the forehand lightens; hence we talk about getting a horse 'off his forehand'. Transitions, and in particular canter transitions, are good for this.

Exercise 1: Trot-to-canter transitions

Before you begin this exercise, mark out the quarter points of a large circle with blocks or cones. Working on a circle in trot, make a transition to canter at one of the markers, and canter a full circle. As you pass that marker for the second time, make a transition back down to trot. At the next marker ask for a transition to canter, and a transition back down to trot at the opposite marker on

the circle. Once your horse is settled in these transitions, ask for a transition up or down, through trot and canter, at each marker. Repeat on both reins. You are looking for a snappy transition from your leg aids.

Exercise 2: Walk-to-canter transitions

Repeat the above exercise, making walk-to-canter transitions. To get a good canter transition, the walk has to be rhythmic, with impulsion. In order to prepare your horse for the transition, make a half-halt just before you ask for the change of gait.

THE AIDS FOR HALF-HALT

Think 'activate and check'. Sit in the correct upright position. Close your lower leg on the girth, gently squeezing the horse into a restraining, but allowing hand. Lighten your seat. Close your legs on the girth again, and as your horse responds, allow him to go forwards. Apply the aids for the next movement.

Exercise 3: Spiralling out of a circle using leg-yield

Begin on a 20m (65ft) circle in walk, spiral in to a 10m (33ft) circle, and then leg-yield back to the 20m circle. As your horse crosses his hind legs, his quarters will engage. Repeat on both reins and in trot.

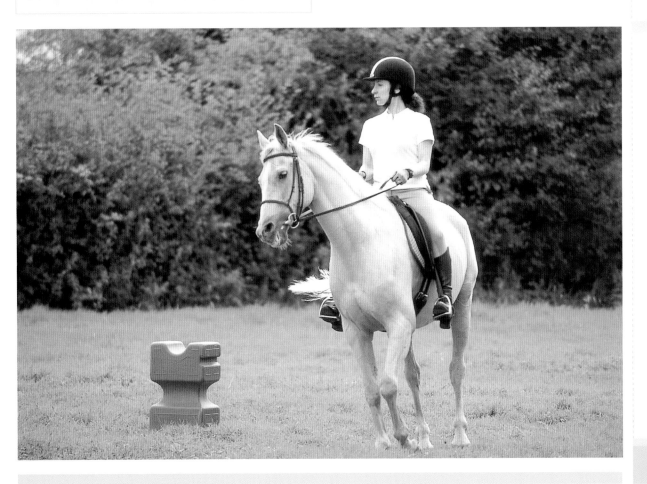

Improving impulsion

A horse is described as having impulsion when he works with suppleness, and the power generated by his hindquarters is expressed in the gait in which he is working. Impulsion only occurs in trot and canter as there needs to be a moment of suspension in the gait for impulsion to occur. The horse will swing through his back and the rider needs to be able to go with this movement.

Exercise 1: Transitions down the long side of the school

Begin by making one transition down the long side from trot to canter. On the opposite long side, make a downward transition from canter to trot. On the next long side, make two transitions up and down through trot and canter, and repeat on the opposite side. Finally make three transitions on each side. Repeat on both reins.

Exercise 2: Lengthening and shortening the strides

Establish a rhythmic trot around the arena. On the next long side, lengthen your horse's strides and then shorten them on the short side. Repeat around the arena. Take care not to chase your horse into the lengthened strides as you will lose your rhythm. Repeat this exercise on both reins and in canter. Try lengthening and shortening between specific markers along the long side of the school.

Exercise 3: Ride a 15m circle on the centre line

In trot, ride a 15m (49ft) circle on the centre line of the school, collecting and checking your horse two or three times. Rejoin the centre line, asking for a transition to canter as you do so. Repeat on the opposite rein.

Exercise 4: Lateral strides into trot

From the quarter line, ride two to three sideways strides of leg-yield, and then trot immediately forwards. Repeat on both reins.

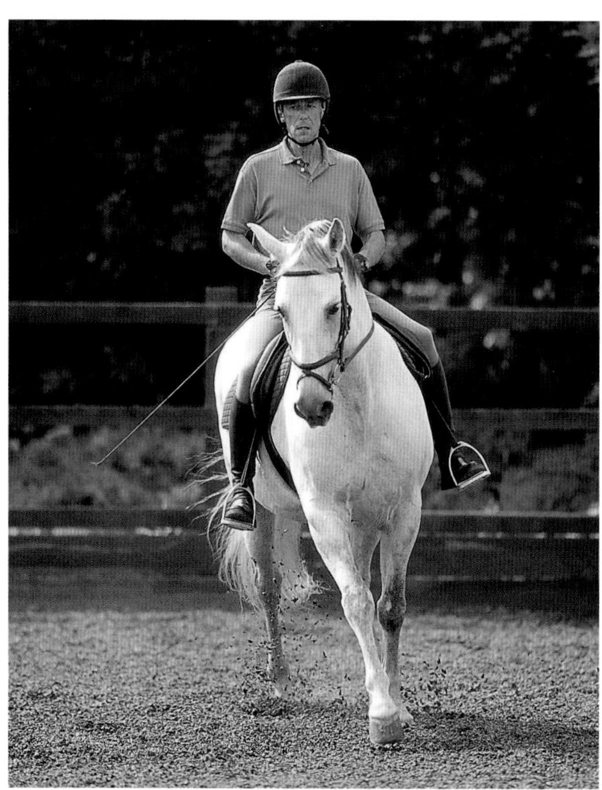

Lateral work

Leg-yielding is the first exercise in lateral work, and is good for suppleness and for teaching the rider to co-ordinate his or her aids. There should be no bend through the body when leg-yielding, although the horse's head and neck is slightly flexed in the opposite direction to the movement, which is a sideways/forward movement.

Exercise 1: Spiralling on the circle in and out

Begin on a 20m (65ft) circle, and in walk, spiral in to a 10m (33ft) circle, then leg-yield out back to the 20m circle. This exercise is best ridden with minimum bend in order to avoid your horse becoming unbalanced and putting excessive weight on his inside foreleg. Your asking leg should only come a little behind the girth, as any more would risk moving the horse's hindquarters over too much, so that he becomes crooked. When the horse has to cross his limbs, this is a good way of engaging the hindquarters. Repeat on the other rein.

OUR THANKS TO...

Julian Marczak, Chairman of the Association of British Riding Schools, for his expertise, and to his pupils Suzanne Dewdney and Flora Franklin for their help with these pictures.

Exercise 2: Leg-yielding line to line

In walk, ride leg-yield from the three-quarter line to the track. Your horse's body should remain parallel to the line/track. The hindquarters must not lead the forehand. Ride one straight stride on reaching the track, and then leg-yield back to the three-quarter line.

Exercise 3: Leg-yielding along the track

Collect your horse through the corner of the school, bring his forehand to the inside, and ride a leg-yield along the long side of the school. Keep him straight through his body with his hind feet on the track and just a slight flexion in his neck to the inside. His rhythm should remain consistent throughout the exercise. Repeat on the opposite rein.

30 minutes to Spend on a Rider Workout

If you don't feel fit when you're riding or working with your horse, you won't enjoy the experience nearly as much as you could. And it's hardly fair to expect your horse to improve his fitness and then find that you can't keep up with him and maximize his potential. There are different types of physical fitness that are important to the rider:

- aerobic
- postural fitness and balance
- suppleness and co-ordination

and most riders would benefit from taking part in some form of complimentary exercise such as walking, swimming or cycling, that improves all-round fitness, especially during the winter months when it is sometimes not as easy to ride regularly.

Balance is the key to a secure riding position, and if you are able to support your upper body in the saddle by using the muscles of your upper torso, you will find it less necessary to stabilize your position with your legs and your hands.

The important thing about any fitness regime is that it works with your lifestyle and becomes part of it, rather than something that is almost a punishment. The following exercises work through the muscles that are essential to a rider. Initially it should take you about 30 minutes to complete this routine, but if you have time to spare, go back to the beginning and work through it once again. Your aim is to go through the exercises, with the exception of the warm-up squats, as a circuit. However, as you improve and become more efficient in your movement and co-ordination, you should be able to increase the number of repeats that you perform for each exercise. You should always be pushing yourself just a little further – but never go beyond your capabilities.

1. Warm-up squats

Muscles working: Quadriceps (front thighs), hamstrings (back thighs), gluteals (bottom) and spinal errectus (lower back)

- Stand with your feet pointing forwards and hip-width apart. Your heels must remain on the ground. Hold your arms out in front of you, parallel to the floor. Keep your chin up and your eyes looking up to the sky-line.
- Now bend gently from the knees, keeping your arms straight ahead and dropping your bottom down towards your ankles. Keep your knees in line with your feet. You will need to tilt forwards slightly to maintain your balance.
- Gently see how low you can go without feeling discomfort or lifting your heels off the ground.

Practise five sets of 10 squats with a 20-second rest between each.

The squat is a compound exercise that works several groups of muscles and is therefore great as a warm-up. You will find that you improve rapidly as both the depth of your squats and the control you have increase. This is due to the fact that the muscles you are working in the squat (the agonists) will cause your supporting muscles (the antagonists) to relax. After 4–6 weeks your brain will begin to select the optimal muscle fibres for the purpose, and you will become neuromuscularly aware of the movement and will increase the number of muscle fibres used. This applies to all exercises.

2. Partial dead lift with dumb-bells

Muscles working: Spinal errectus, hamstrings, gluteals, quadriceps

You will need: Two weights, such as dumb-bells, of approximately 2.5kg (6lb) each

- Stand with a weight in each hand and your feet hip-width apart, your knees over your feet. Look up to a point where the wall meets the ceiling, imaginary or real.

- Now bend at the knees, keeping your bottom tucked in, your heels on the ground and your back as straight as possible. Keep your knees over your toes and don't allow them to turn in or out.

Repeat the exercise 10 times.

You could practise this exercise on the yard, using your buckets instead of the dumb-bells.

3. The one-arm row

Muscles working: Latissimus dorsi (upper back and trunk muscles)

You will need: A dumb-bell, or a weight of approximately 2.5kg (6lb)

• From a standing position, and with your weight in your right hand, lunge forwards with your left leg and rest your left forearm on your upper thigh, taking your weight onto your leg. Flatten your back as much as possible, and don't twist through the hips. Take a deep breath into this position.

Allow your right arm, with the weight, to drop parallel to your left lower leg.

• Now lift the weight, using your upper arm and your back muscles. Keep your elbow tucked in to your waist.

Repeat this exercise 10 times on each side.

This is an isolated exercise (that is, an exercise that focuses on a particular group of muscles), and a most gentle but effective back exercise. It will help you to use your arms independently, and maintain a secure position through your upper body whilst in the saddle.

4. Standing band row

Muscles working: Obliques (stomach), intercostals (stomach muscles holding the midriff stable and enabling the rotation of the trunk), abdominals, spinal errectus, and gluteals, latissimus dorsi and biceps

You will need: Exercise stretch band

• Pass your exercise band around a fixed bar of some form (see photograph). Now wrap the ends of the bands around both your hands.

• Stand with your feet hip-width apart. With the exercise band taut, bend your knees and tilt your pelvis in, allowing your bottom to tilt up and backwards. This will create an S-shape through your back, and it should be possible to draw a straight, vertical line from your shoulder blades to your bottom.

• Now increase the tension through the exercise band by pulling your elbows back, bringing your shoulder blades back and allowing them to relax. Repeat this exercise 10 times.

This is a compound exercise that will help to develop your back muscles through your trunk. If your top half can support itself, this will help to give you an independent seat, and do away with the necessity of balancing by gripping with your legs.

How not to do it: Don't allow your top half to be pulled forwards (think of a strong horse pulling you out of the saddle); your aim is to build a strong torso.

5. Walking the ball

Muscles working: Abdominals, obliques, spinal errectus, gluteals

You will need: Large inflated exercise ball available from most sport shops, department stores and catalogue stores

Practise sitting on the ball before trying this exercise.

• Begin by sitting on the ball with your feet hip-width apart and your hands resting on your knees.

• Keeping contact with the ball through your back, walk forwards slowly until your shoulders, neck and head are resting on the ball. Keep your back straight and your legs as near to 90 degrees as possible. Squeeze the buttocks, and hold for 30 seconds.

Similar to the 'standing band row', but now working against gravity, this exercise will strengthen your position through your torso and help you to control your pelvic muscles.

6. Chest press and dumb-bell fly

Muscles working: Pectoralis major (chest), anterior deltoids (shoulders) and triceps (back of arms) plus abdominals, obliques, spinal errectus and gluteals

You will need: Exercise ball, plus 2.5kg (6lb) weights such as dumb-bells

• Start as for the previous exercise, but holding your weights in each hand.

• Once you are balanced with your shoulders, neck and head on the ball, raise the dumb-bells above your

head, turning them at an angle (see photograph above) and bringing them in towards each other to make a triangular shape.

Repeat 10 times.

• Now open your arms, keeping your elbows bent, and bring the weights out to the side (photo below), and then return to your starting position.

Repeat 10 times.

These exercises work on your control through your upper body. The chest press works on your back muscles, and the 'dumb-bell fly' balances out the work done on the back muscles.

7. Ball squat

Muscles working: Quadriceps and gluteals

You will need: Exercise ball as before

• Place your exercise ball between you and a wall. Walk forwards a pace so that your weight is against the ball (**a**).

• Now bend your knees so that you are 'sitting' against the ball. Keep your feet hip-width apart and in front of your knees, your back straight, and your bottom tucked in (**b**).

How not to do it: Don't push your bottom back or tuck your heels in (**c**).

Repeat 15 times.

This exercise will help to build up your lower leg strength and your control over the muscles in your bottom.

8. Calf raise

Muscles working: Gastrocnemius (calf muscle)

• Place your toe on a step or something raised, but steady and secure (see photograph above).

• Rest one foot behind the other. Tuck your bottom under and, keeping your supporting leg straight, raise yourself up on to your toes. Make sure your heel stretches down as much as possible.

Repeat 10 times on each leg.

This is an isolated exercise that is great for strengthening the calf muscles and encouraging your weight to drop to your heels.

9. Sideline induction and calf raise

Muscles working: Gluteals
You will need: Exercise mat or something similar

• Lie on your side, on your mat, with your head resting upon your outstretched arm, and the hand of the other arm resting on your hip, with your elbow and knees bent.

• Keeping your body and hips straight, raise your upper leg in a scissor action. Hold for 2 seconds.
• Return to your original position and repeat the exercise 10 times on each side.

• Now keeping your heels together, and without allowing your hips to roll forwards or backwards, raise the upper knee and hold for 2 seconds.
• Return to your original position, and repeat 10 times on each side.

Gripping with the knees is a fault that is common when a rider has a slightly unstable balance or is unseated for a moment. This exercise helps develop your leg muscles and will enable you to use your legs without gripping with your knees.

10. Hamstring curl

Muscles working: Hamstrings
You will need: Exercise mat and 2.5kg (6lb) weight as before

• Lie on your tummy on the floor with the weight held between your feet and your upper body supported on your elbows and forearms (see photograph).

• Now, bending at the knee and squeezing the muscles of your bottom together, lift the weight as shown. Repeat 10 times.

This is an isolated exercise that will help you become aware of the connection between your gluteals and hamstrings, and will improve your lower leg control and position.

11. Hamstring curl with ball
Muscles working: Hamstrings plus abdominals, obliques, spinal errectus and gluteals
You will need: Exercise mat and ball as before

• Lie on your back on your mat, with your arms out to your sides at a 45-degree angle, your feet on the exercise ball and your knees bent.

• Balancing on your arms, lift your bottom up, keeping it tucked underneath you. Your toes should point towards the ceiling.

• Now, bending your knees, roll the ball in towards your bottom, keeping your back straight, and then roll it back out again.

Aim for 10 repeats, though eight will be sufficient in the early stages.

This is a compound exercise, taking the 'hamstring curl' a step further, combining use of the hamstrings with control of the upper body.

12. Reverse curl with ball
Muscles working: Lower abdominals
You will need: Exercise mat and ball as before
• Lie on the floor as for the previous exercise, but bring the ball in close to your seat.

• Grip the ball with your legs, then pick it up and bring it in towards your stomach, and then return it to its original position.

Aim for 10 repeats if possible.

This exercise works on trunk and hip flexion, drawing your legs closer to your stomach as in a jumping position.

13. Plank
Muscles working: Spinal errectus, transverse abdominals (deep stabilizing muscles of the trunk)
You will need: Exercise mat as before

• Lie on your tummy on your mat.
• Now, taking your weight on your toes and your forearms, and keeping your body as straight as possible, lift your weight from the floor. Hold for 10 seconds.

Repeat twice.

14. Ab crunch
Muscles working: Upper abdominals
You will need: Exercise mat as before
• Lie on your back with your hands beneath your head, your knees bent and hip-width apart, and your feet flat on the floor.

• Keeping your elbows open, raise your head, shoulders and chest towards your knees. Keep your back on the floor, and lift from your abdomen and not your hands or shoulders. Relax.

Repeat 10 times.

Whereas the 'ball lifts' focus on bringing your legs to your chest, this exercise does the reverse, developing flexion and stability through the trunk – both of which count towards a more secure upper body position and control.

15. Squirm

Muscles working: Obliques
You will need: Exercise mat as before

• Lie on your back on your mat with your knees bent and hip-width apart and your feet on the floor.

• Keeping your back on the floor, with your right hand, reach down to your right ankle.

Repeat 10 times on both sides.

It is important for the rider to have flexion through the upper part of his or her body without affecting the position of the seat. This exercise helps to develop that flexion.

16. Superman

Muscles working: Spinal errectus, gluteals
You will need: Exercise mat as before

• Lie on your tummy on your mat with your arms stretched out above your head and your toes pointed.

• Raise your arms and your toes, and hold for a count of 10.

Repeat twice.

• Return to the starting position. Now raise your right arm and your left leg and hold for a count of 10. Then repeat with your left arm and your right leg.

Repeat twice.

17. Serratus press

Muscles working: Serratus anterior (the muscle that keeps your shoulder blades against your back) and spinal errectus
You will need: Exercise mat as before

• Kneel on your mat with your knees and hands shoulder-width apart, and your knees at an angle of 90 degrees. Allow your head to drop forwards.

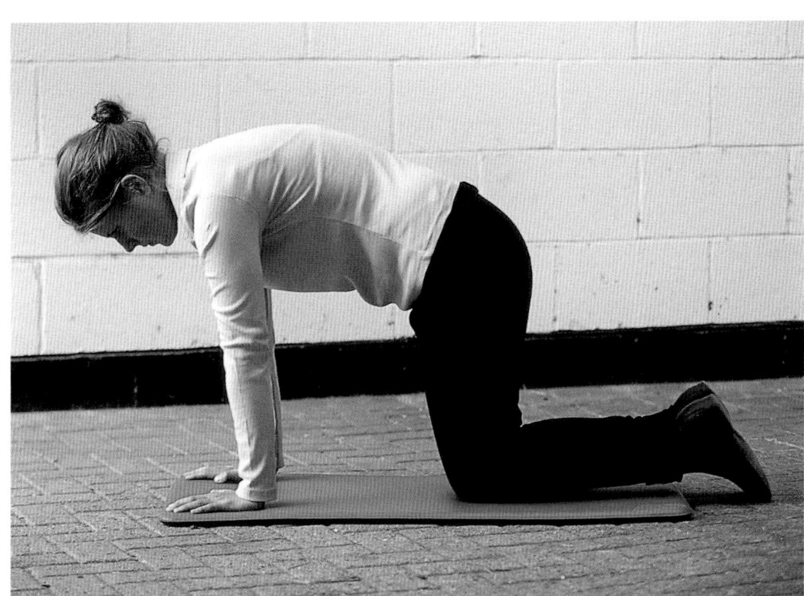

• Allowing your back to arch, draw your tummy and abdomen and chest up into your ribcage. Be sure that your head and neck are relaxed. Now draw your tummy, abdomen and chest up just a little bit further. Hold for 10 seconds.

Repeat twice.

Exercise workout devised by Jason Crow Bsc (Hons) Sport Science, CSCs. Jason Crow is a personal training and exercise coach based in Kent, working in corporate and private arenas.

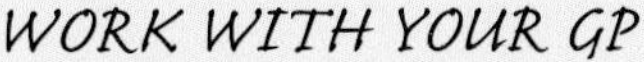

If you are in any doubt about whether you should embark on an exercise programme, check with your GP. He may recommend that you have a health check, and if you are exercising to a competitive level (ie training hard and possibly professionally), then a regular health check is always a good idea.

If you have any form of injury do not embark on an exercise routine without first clearing it with your GP.

5 30 MINUTES TO BETTER JUMPING

- 30 minutes to understand jumping theory
- 30 minutes of polework
- 30 minutes from ground pole to upright
- 30 minutes to confident jumping
- 30 minutes a week to tackle scary fences

Horses jump naturally; sadly, most humans don't! However, the feeling of 'flying' through the air on the back of a horse is liberating, and something that many riders become addicted to.

Jumping is a mix of technique, ability and flair, and dedicating 30 minutes to understanding the theory is your first step.

Whilst some riders refuse to 'leave the ground', few will turn a hair at training over ground poles – yet 30 minutes spent working over poles will prepare you and your horse for jumping. In this chapter, one horse-and-rider combination that has never jumped together before proves the point, progressing from ground pole to upright in just 30 minutes.

Once individual jumps have been mastered, the next step is to put them together as simple courses. The 30-minute courses given here are intended to be versatile so that, accuracy willing, you won't have to mount and dismount too often.

There will always be certain fences that 'test' the confidence of the rider and the skill of the horse. Spending hours working away at these can be counter-productive: better a 30-minute 'blitz' once a week, until you've mastered your scary fence!

30 minutes to Understand Jumping Theory

If seeing a horse clearing a jump gives you the biggest equestrian thrill and your ambitions lie in this direction, whilst practice may make perfect, understanding the theory is also important. Work on the principles at home and take your learning into the saddle when you train with your horse.

Understand what you are trying to achieve

Before you tackle your first fence, you need have:
• Good balance
• Harmony with your horse
• Security in the saddle

⇧ *Whether your heart is in clearing fences across country or in the show-jumping arena, there are certain skills you need to master.*

THE CROSS-COUNTRY AND SHOW-JUMPING SEATS

The only real difference between a show-jumping position and a cross-country position is that for the latter, your stirrups should be a couple of holes shorter. This brings the centre of balance closer to the horse, and gives better stability when jumping drop fences.

Good balance

Every rider knows that balance is crucial to good riding practice, and all your early exercises in the saddle are with the aim of improving your balance. If you are in control of your weight and hence your balance, your horse will be able to move more effectively beneath you: you will not be a burden, but part of 'the team'. The development of this skill continues throughout your riding career as you are confronted by different challenges.

When you jump you need to be as still as possible to enable your horse to make the most of his athleticism. If your weight is in the saddle this makes it more difficult for the horse, and this is one of the reasons why the jumping seat has evolved. Another is that your centre of gravity needs to be in line with that of your horse, and if you remain in the saddle this will not happen. Your weight should be taken through your legs down to your heels.

If you were to remain sitting upright your position would be very unsafe because it would not be in balance. Therefore the show jumper will close the angle of his or her hip and knee joints going over the fence to bring their centre of gravity closer to that of the horse. Shortening your stirrups makes it easier to maintain this position.

⇧ *Your centre of gravity needs to be in line with that of the horse, and for stability, as close to his as possible.*

Harmony with your horse

Once you have control of your balance you will be able to ride in harmony with your horse. Although your seat is mostly out of the saddle, it is still possible to go with the horse's movement. You will know if you have it wrong because you will bump along against your horse. This needs to be worked on until it is perfect; ridden lessons on the lunge line are a great help.

Equally important is your ability to go with the movement of your horse's head, so you do not jab him in the mouth. With jumping, the aim is to be able to slide your hands along your horse's neck – to 'give with the reins'. In the early stages of jump training it is best for the rider to give the reins entirely, and if necessary, to hold on to the mane if their balance is not absolutely secure. As balance improves it should become possible to slide the reins along the horse's neck without holding on to anything for support. However, with training a light contact to the mouth should be maintained throughout the jump to avoid what is described as 'knitting the reins' as the rider recovers contact on the other side.

Between jumps it is essential that your horse listens to your aids – if your basic schooling is not in place, communication between you and your horse will be lacking. Don't neglect this side of your equestrian training.

⇧ *It is important to be able to go with the movement of your horse's head.*

Security in the saddle

Your security in the saddle will come from a developed sense of balance and the ability to go with your horse's movement. This is really an area in which practical work achieves the best results, and your trainer will be able to work with you to develop the security of your seat. Once again, ridden lungework will help; you could also try the following exercise: practise remaining in the jumping position for as many circuits of your schooling training area as you can, first in trot and then in canter. Work on increasing the number of circuits.

The stages of a jump

There are five stages to a jump, for both horse and rider:

- the approach
- the take-off
- the flight
- the descent
- the landing

The five stages of a jump for the rider

The approach

Your weight should be through your lower leg rather than in the saddle. Your seat should be in light contact with the saddle. You should have soft rein contact and not be restricting the movement of your horse's head.

The take-off

Keep your weight through your lower leg, open your hip and knee joints, and fold your body over your horse's centre of gravity. Allow your hands to move along your horse's neck and ensure that you are not holding onto his mouth. Hold onto his mane if you feel insecure. Look ahead to the next jump.

The flight

Your weight remains through your lower leg, which should still be perpendicular to the ground. Close your hip and knee joints as necessary to maintain your balance in line with your horse's balance. Look ahead.

The descent

Now it is important to keep your lower leg straight, as your inclination may be to slide it forwards. Open your hip and knee joints and begin to resume your normal upper body position.

The landing

Readjust your balance, collect your reins, and ride forwards.

Understand how the horse moves

To complete a course of jumps your horse must:
- accept the bit and your aids;
- be going forwards with impulsion;
- be straight.

If any of these are lacking, get them right in your flatwork first. Most horses enjoy jumping, but an inconsiderate rider, a bad experience, physical shortcomings and being over-faced can ruin this enjoyment.

To show jump successfully your horse must accept the bit, listen to your aids, go forwards with impulsion, and be straight.

The five stages of a jump for the horse

The approach

The horse's approach to the fence should be calm and straight, with the horse listening to his rider's aids. As he begins his final stride before the fence he will bring his hind legs underneath him to provide the necessary power. Upon completion of this stride he will use his forelegs like a vaulting pole to lift his forehand off the ground. His head will begin to rise at this point.

The take-off

His hind legs will come together to provide the spring needed to take off; he will appear almost to sit back on his hind legs slightly. This is where a horse that is not sufficiently fit will have difficulty; it is also where an unbalanced rider or a rider who is not in harmony with the horse, can negatively affect the horse's performance. The hock and stifle joints will stretch open and then close to tuck the hind legs beneath the quarters. The horse will stretch his head and neck forwards.

The flight

The horse should form a curve (or bascule) over the fence, keeping all four legs tucked up beneath him as he does so. Both hocks and knees should be aligned. His shoulder will move forwards, and this brings the forelegs forwards too. The knee should now be higher than the line of the under belly. He will begin to lower his head.

The descent

As the horse begins to curve down past the jump he will open his hind-leg joints and stretch out his back legs to follow the arc he has just described. He will begin to raise his head to restore his balance. He will land on one foreleg, the other foreleg being the lead leg of the canter stride to follow; the lead leg lands just in front of the other, and takes the horse's weight. His fetlock joints act as shock absorbers, often touching the ground.

The landing

The outside hind leg will land first, followed by the inside hind. This follows a moment of suspension when the forelegs take off for the next stride. The horse will use his head, neck and back to regain his balance.

> **ANALYSING VIDEOS**
>
> Spend 30 minutes watching videos of horse-and-rider combinations, analysing how both rider and horse perform over a jump. Select one jump and imagine you and your horse tackling it. Take in every aspect of the scene – the crowd, the colours, the noise, the sound of your horse's hoofbeats and breathing, how you feel inside – and go over it again and again until you have taken the jump perfectly. Allow your body to assume the appropriate body position, and feel the balance.

Watch various combinations to see how they tackle competition situations, and learn from their experiences.

Seeing a stride

This term is used to describe the ability to see the right point at which your horse should take off for a jump. However, the theoretically 'correct' point changes according to the type of jump (see box, right). Riders worry endlessly about the ability to see a stride, and discussion ranges between whether it is a natural gift, to whether it can be taught and learnt. To work on seeing a stride your instructor should pursue the following:

- a good, well balanced canter;
- the ability to shorten and lengthen your horse's strides;
- gridwork.

If you have a good, even, forward-going canter and an experienced horse, there will be quite a bit of scope for variation in take-off point. However, to be able to see where the horse is going to take off does enable you to be prepared to go with him.

WATCH VIDEOS

Once again, 30 minutes spent watching videos and focusing on the take-off points of various horse-and-rider combinations at different types of jump will help to develop your sense of a stride.

TAKE-OFF POINTS

1. Uprights and parallels
You should take off and land at a safe distance from the fence. For instance, if a fence is 1m (3ft 3in) high, you should take off 1m in front of the fence and land 1m behind.

2. Parallels
The take-off point for a parallel should be the height + half the width before the fence.

3. Triple bar or ascending oxer
The lower the front pole, the closer the take-off point may be. The apex of the arc of your jump should be over the back rail of the jump.

A good exercise that you can work on alone to help develop this skill is to place a ground pole between two jump wings as a substitute for an upright fence. This way you can work on discovering your horse's stride. Remember that the apex of the arc over the fence should be directly above the fence and so you need to have your horse's canter stride centred over the ground pole.

Understanding distances

- A double is two fences with one or two strides between.
- A combination (or treble) is the same, but with an extra fence.
- A related distance is two fences with a certain number of strides between them, usually between three and ten.

The generally accepted length of a stride is 3.6m (12ft), but this can vary according to the level of the competition and the course builder, and it is important that you are aware of the accurate length of your stride.

When riders walk the distance between two jumps they tend to pace them out in slightly longer human strides of between 90cm (3ft) to 1m (3ft 3in). A generally accepted equation is that four human strides equal one horse's stride. However, when calculating the distance between two fences, you must remember to allow for your horse to land (two human strides) and take off (two human strides). As a rule of thumb:

- 16 human strides = three horse strides between fences
- 20 human strides = four horse strides between fences
- 24 human strides = five horse strides between fences

What you will normally find with a related distance fence is that it is either a little shorter or longer than a set number of strides, and you therefore have to shorten or lengthen your horse accordingly.

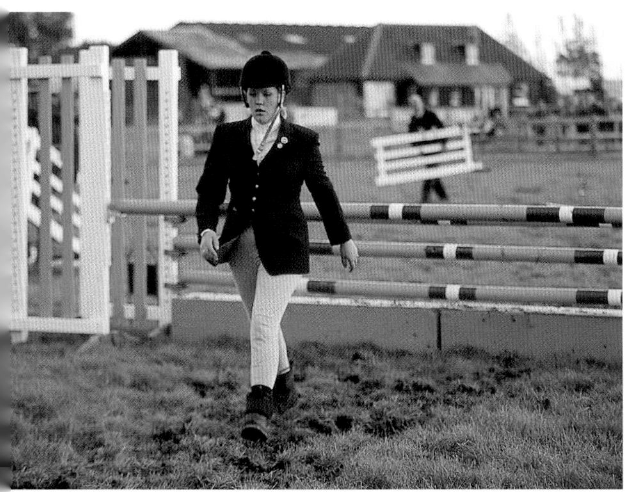

It is important to know the length of your horse's stride to enable you to judge distances between competition fences.

30 minutes of Polework

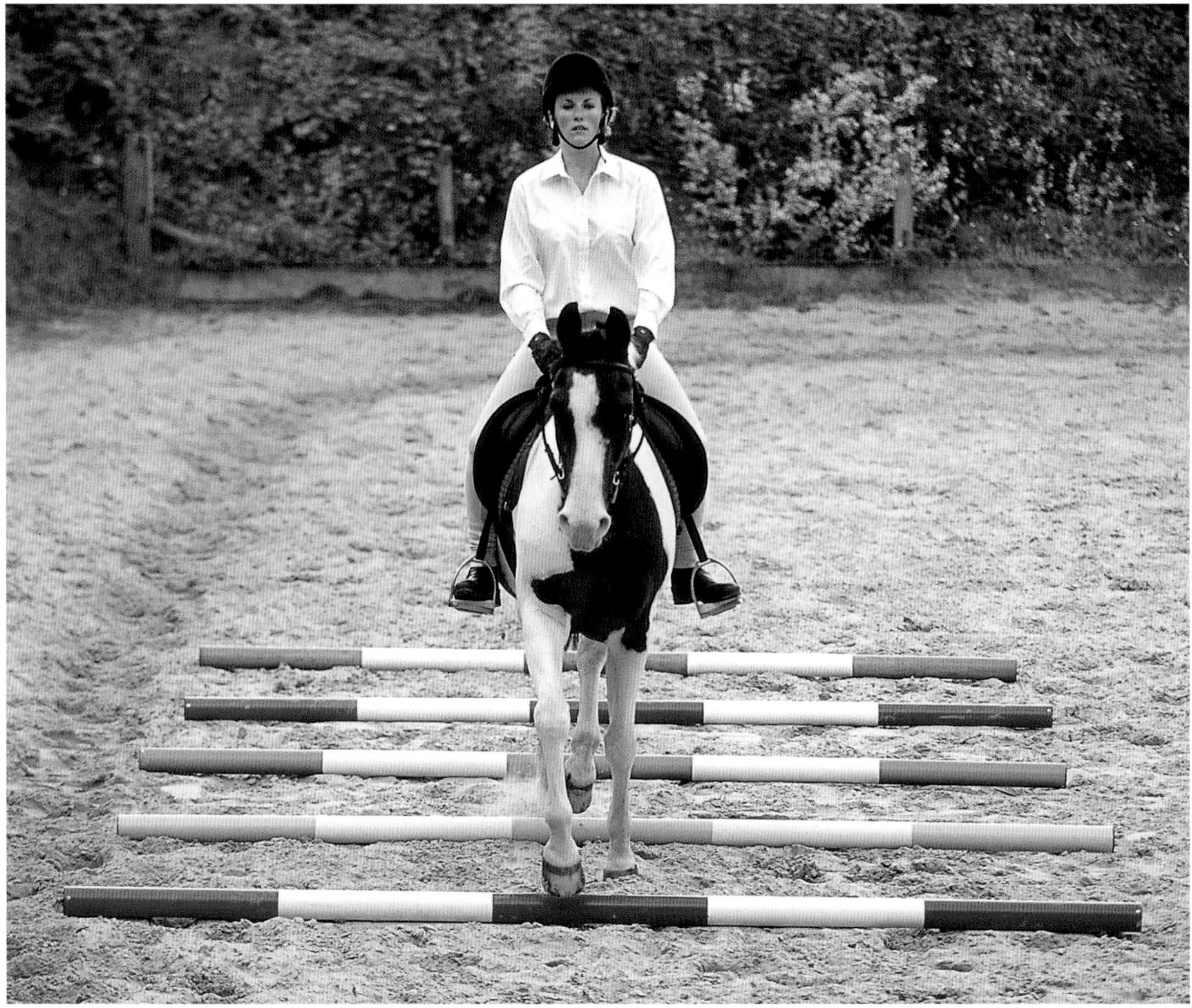

Riding over poles is the first step in learning to jump, and it will play an increasingly diverse role in training for jumping as you become more experienced. Most riders tend to underestimate what polework can achieve. This is a mistake. Incorporate one polework session into your training programme each week, and you and your horse will benefit in many ways.

Advantages to the horse:

Work over poles correctly and your horse will

- stretch his neck and back muscles;
- flex the joints in his legs;
- learn to use his hindquarters;
- establish a rhythm to his paces;
- stop rushing.

Advantages to the rider:

- Learning to judge the distances between poles on the ground will contribute towards an eye for judging the distance between jumps.
- You will develop the skill of giving the reins without throwing them away.
- You will establish an independent seat…
- …and will learn to feel extension and collection of the paces.

Setting up poles

The most important thing when setting up poles is to pay attention to your horse's stride, because the distance between the poles must suit his length of stride (see box). For this reason it is very useful to have a helper on the ground to adjust the poles if they are not correct.

Use either one, or three to eight poles, and preferably brightly coloured ones, as these stand out best in most schools. Do not use two poles, unless they are at quite a distance apart, as your horse may try to jump them. Do not use more than eight poles, as polework is quite tiring for your horse and he will find eight poles enough of a challenge. For the same reason make frequent changes of rein, take plenty of breaks, and allow your horse to stretch and relax.

Riding over poles

Don't forget the basic principles of rhythm, balance and forward movement as you school over your poles. It is likely that you will feel an increased activity as your horse crosses the poles – be prepared for this, and do not lose your balance or pull him in his mouth. Do most of your polework in rising trot, as this will increase your horse's ability to use his back. Maintain your rein contact, but be prepared to allow with the reins if your horse looks down (it is a good thing if he does this, as long as he isn't falling on to his forehand), and don't interfere with his head carriage.

⇧ *Whilst it is acceptable for your horse to lower his head to look where he is going, be sure that he is not just falling on to his forehand.*

For a 30-minute session, work on one of the exercises on pages 116–17 at a time. Each has many variations that you can use to fill your 30 minutes if all is going well. Remember to warm up first for about 10 minutes (see page 92), and be sure to give your horse time to cool down at the end of the session (page 95).

GETTING THE DISTANCE RIGHT

It is essential that the distance between the poles suits your horse's length of stride, and it is up to you to find this out. If he stands on a pole or trips, it can knock his confidence and discourage his enthusiasm for polework.

Distances vary according to the height and stride of your horse and the gait in which you are working. They can also be used to lengthen or shorten your horse's stride. In the initial stages your horse should not have to struggle over the poles: his feet should land mid-way between one pole and the next. Too far towards the next pole and the distance between the poles is too small; too close to the pole behind and the distance is too large.

Standard distances for walking or trotting are 1.2–1.5m (4–5ft), and for cantering 2.7–3.6m (9–12ft); any changes to a set distance should be made in no more or less than 7.5cm (3in) increments. This apparently small alteration is all it takes to make quite a difference to your horse's stride.

EXERCISE 1

The first exercise involves just a single pole placed in the middle of the school.

a. Begin by walking, trotting and cantering over this pole. Make sure you cross it in the middle.

⇧ *Even just a single pole in the middle of the school has many uses.*

b. Now find how much your horse is listening to your aids by crossing the pole in different places. For example, if you are using a striped pole, use each of the sections as a marker, and cross at the centre of that section. This can be done in all three paces.

c. Cross the pole at an angle of 45 degrees. This is quite difficult, as you will need to keep your horse straight. It encourages your horse to use a lengthened stride, and to use his hindquarters, as he has to push harder from behind. This exercise should be ridden in walk and trot.

⇧ *Your horse may find riding across the pole on a diagonal quite difficult at first, as it requires increased effort from his hindquarters.*

d. In walk and trot, ride circles over each end of the pole, incorporating half the pole, and then develop these circles into figures of eight. Start with 20m (65ft) circles, and then try 15m (49ft) circles. This exercise will help you and your horse to be more accurate, and will help you to feel when you need to change the bend.

e. Move up a pace to canter. 'Stretch' the figure of eight to the entire length of the school so that you are crossing the pole on a diagonal angle. Ask for trot several strides before the pole; don't leave it too late. Establish your rhythm in the trot, and ask for canter as you ride away and before the next bend. As your work improves, shorten the number of strides in trot both before and after the pole.

⇧ *Riding a line of ground poles is a good multi-purpose exercise for your horse.*

EXERCISE 2

Set out five or six ground poles at the appropriate distance apart for your horse.

a. Ride straight down the centre of the line in walk and then trot.

b. Now ride diagonally down the line starting on the left of the first pole and finishing on the right of the final pole. This is a great exercise for testing your leg aids.

c. Ask your horse to ride a serpentine between the poles. Pass between poles 2 and 3 for the first loop, poles 4 and 5 for the second loop, and maintain a third loop either with or without the help of the sixth pole. This will require accurate riding and will help to keep your horse straight between the poles.

d. Riding through every other gap between the poles, ask your horse for a few strides of extension between the poles, then collect him up to make the turns.

RAISING THE CHALLENGE

Once your horse is tackling poles with confidence and you are happy with his balance and rhythm, try raising certain poles to form small jumps.

Use purpose-made blocks, or home-made blocks with a central groove to support the pole. In the first instance raise the poles by about 10cm (4in).

- Raise the pole across the school centre, and you can repeat Exercise 1.
- Raise the ends of alternate poles in Exercise 2, and trot straight down the middle line. This is great for your horse's hock and shoulder action.
- Raise the final pole in Exercise 2 or 3, and then gradually increase the number of raised poles.
- Place two poles on opposite sides of a circle, as you would if they were jumps. Raise one but keep the other as a ground pole. Then raise both. With both poles raised this is a good exercise for working on lengthening and shortening your horse's strides.

EXERCISE 3

Set out five ground poles at a distance of about 2.7–3.6m (9–12ft) apart.

a. Begin this exercise on the centre line of the poles. When your horse has crossed the first pole, ask him to ride a circle to the left, which will take him over the end of the next pole. Make the size of the circle one that he is initially comfortable with, but concentrate on keeping it a perfect circle and his rhythm consistent. As you recross the pole on which you began your circle, straighten up, ride down the centre line over the next pole, and on the following pole turn right and begin another circle on the opposite rein. Finish by riding straight over the last pole.

Now repeat the exercise, beginning on the opposite rein to the one you began with initially. If your horse is managing this with ease, you could try reducing the size of your circles.

b. Now ride a figure of eight over each pole.

c. Ride a serpentine between the poles.

A line of poles at canter distance apart is also great for serpentines and circle work.

30 minutes from Ground Pole to Upright

Great leaps in progress can be made in 30 minutes when horse and rider are well trained and working together. Just to show how much can be achieved with care and the presence of an instructor, we challenged rider Tracey Tapsell to see if she felt confident enough to tackle a cross-pole.

Although Tracey had jumped before, it hadn't been for many years, and then on her 14.2hh pony. Her new horse, Disney, is a 10-year-old, 17.1hh, Percheron X Dutch Warmblood gelding; Tracey knew he had jumped, but that it certainly hadn't been in the previous five years.

From this....

...to this in 30 minutes

It is important that you know your horse's character and use it to your advantage when schooling. Disney takes a lot of winding up and peaks early, so a goal such as this in 30 minutes suits his training strengths.

Under instructor Helen's watchful eye, Tracey spent the first 10 minutes working Disney in. 'This is a hugely important phase,' said Helen. 'The horse must be going forwards, he must be balanced, and he must maintain an active rhythm.'

Once the pair were warmed up and going forwards, having worked on turns, circles and figures of eight during their warm-up, Helen asked Tracey to turn through the wing stands to ensure Disney was not going to spook at them, and to prepare him for the next phase. Throughout this lesson, Helen asked Tracey and Disney to ride each step several times and on both reins.

⇧ *Work on riding straight and through the middle of the wings. Even though a pole or jump is not present, ride as though it were, and keep your eyes up and looking where you are going.*

The next step was to put a pole on the ground, between the wings. Horse and rider must trot over this in both directions until they are doing it with ease. This was no problem for this intrepid pair!

⇧ *The presence of a pole on the ground between the wings should not cause your horse any concern. However, if he does try to run out, or veers to the left or the right, lay additional poles in a 'v'-shaped formation, peaking at the centre of the pole, but allowing him plenty of room to trot through, to encourage him to cross it at the correct point.*

A second pole was then placed on the ground 2.7–3m (9–10ft) in front of the first. There should be one trot stride between the poles, but this will certainly vary from one horse to the next, and the distance needs to be gradually adjusted until it suits the horse you are riding. Once Disney was going over both poles comfortably and on both reins, he and Tracey moved on to the next step.

⇧ *Adjust the distance between the ground poles to suit the stride of your horse. Eventually ground poles can be used to help shorten or lengthen your horse's stride, but at this point keeping an even, natural rhythm is the priority.*

Helen replaced the pole between the wings with a small cross-pole. Initially it was too small to have much effect on Disney, but once Tracey was confident of not having a run-out, Helen increased the height and Disney had to make more of a jump over it (see photographs below). On his second attempt at the increased height, Disney landed, albeit not beautifully, in canter.

NINE-POINT ABILITY CHECK

For a rider to attempt this exercise, first and foremost we would recommend that a professional instructor is present. Furthermore, the rider must be of a reasonable standard with an understanding of the importance of balance, flexibility and obedience: you should check the following nine points to establish whether you are ready to jump, because it would be better not to tackle a jump until you can tell the difference between the following:

1. Is the horse going forwards, as opposed to running on?
2. Is he lowering his neck for balance to look where he is going, as opposed to dropping on to the forehand?
3. Is he 'in the hand', as compared to being 'against the hand'?
4. Is he pushing from behind or pulling himself along from in front?

And ask yourself the following:

5. Can you remain in the basic jumping position for at least two circuits of the school both in trot and canter?
6. Are you secure in your trot, not falling into the saddle, and not balancing on the reins?
7. Do you have a secure leg position? Are you able to drop your weight through to your heel and ride without drawing your heels up? Can you use your legs effectively without flapping or sliding backwards unintentionally?
8. Do you balance on your hands? Are you able to give with the reins promptly and to shorten them when necessary without a fuss?
9. In canter can you feel which lead leg you are riding on, and in trot which diagonal you are on?

Don't forget: As Disney started to work at the jumps he became more enthusiastic and easier to ride. However, don't make the mistake of overworking your horse if this happens: he should be allowed to rest after three or four fences, especially if he is not used to jumping.

TIPS FOR TACKLING YOUR FIRST JUMP

- Do not attempt to jump until you are sure your horse is working in an even rhythm, initially in trot, but eventually also in canter.
- Your horse must be active before you tackle the jump. If necessary make use of any natural advantages at your disposal, such as a downhill incline, jumping towards the gate, or even taking a lead from another horse.
- If your horse lowers his neck, this is fine if he is looking where he is going, as he will consequently also relax through his back. However, it is important that you are able to recognize when your horse is stretching through his back and looking where he is going, as opposed to falling on the forehand.
- If your horse makes a longer or shorter stride, this is fine as long as his rhythm is not affected.
- Don't worry about which leg to land on at this stage; focus on balance.
- Remember, if your horse lands in trot he has probably lost his active rhythm coming into the jump.

⇧ *Some horses will find a higher jump easier than a lower one. This is because it encourages them to bascule (curve) over the jump. However, you should only raise a jump in increments of 10cm (4in) at any one time.*

Our thanks to Tracey Tapsell and Helen Anderson and, of course, to Disney.

⇩ Finally the cross-pole was replaced with an upright. The first attempt wasn't beautiful, but second time around Disney and Tracey performed their best jump of the day, clearing it with ease and just within the 30 minutes' deadline! Tracey was obviously delighted (see right), and at this point confessed she hadn't thought they would be able to do it when they began!

30 minutes to Confident Jumping

Once you've started jumping you will need instruction and practice to help you develop by working on your technical skills and building up your experience. Practising what you have learnt at home is part of the confidence-building process. It is quite possible to work on various aspects of your jumping in 30 minutes, remembering to allow your horse 10 minutes to warm up, but you will need the help of a friend to set up and adjust the jumps, and to watch your performance from the ground. Progress slowly. It is important that you do not knock your own confidence or that of your horse. Do not try to do any of these exercises if you feel they may overstretch your abilities.

HOW HIGH?

To begin with, set the height of your jumps according to your ability and confidence. If you are just learning to jump, begin with ground poles between the wings, and build up to an upright via a cross-pole (unless your instructor suggests something else). Begin with a 60cm (2ft) upright. At this height your horse should not be encouraged to rush at the jump. Increase the height gradually, and by never more than 10cm (4in) at a time; furthermore, note your horse's length of stride and adjust the distance between your jumps accordingly as you increase height. Aim for a regular 3.6m (12ft) stride, as that is what most competition courses are based upon.

Don't forget: If possible, always put some form of groundline (either a pole or filler) beneath any upright. (Remember that although it is possible to put a groundline just in front of a jump, many of the options here are tackled from both reins.)

When time is at a premium you don't want to spend too much of it setting up jumps, grids and courses. The following are suggestions for potential combinations of jump that will give you several possibilities for schooling practice, without having to spend time dismounting and remounting and making lots of changes. Select just one for each 30-minute session, and work on it until you have mastered it. If this only takes 10 minutes, that's great, but if you discover you are going to need some professional assistance, finish by replacing the jumps either with a confidence-inspiring jump that you have used before, or with ground poles to ensure you finish on a positive note.

Remember: Give your horse a breather after three or four jumps.

1. Two fences on a circle

The joy of this arrangement is that you can use it to build up confidence, practise related distances, perfect your canter leads, and work on tight turns.

Set up two fences at opposite points on a circle, with the centre of the circle at X (or the very middle point of your training area). Leave the outer track clear. Your aim is to put these fences on a 20m (65ft) circle, but if this feels too tight a turn for you and your horse, you can begin with as large a circle as your training area will allow. If you have just begun to jump, begin with a small cross-pole and an upright at a height you feel comfortable with. Begin in trot and progress to canter.

a. Using the whole school, build up your confidence over the cross-pole (or fence A), jumping from both reins.

b. When you are ready, and still using the whole school, incorporate the upright (or fence B). Work on both reins.

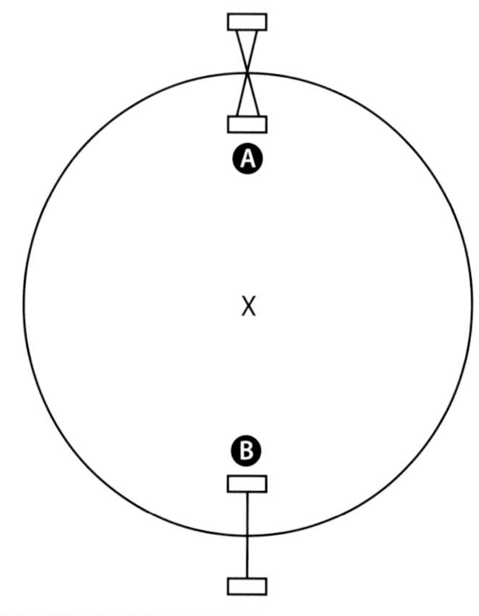

c. Using the length of the school, jump fence A on one rein, make a change of rein across the diagonal, and take fence B on the other rein.
d. When you can do this happily on both reins, finish by jumping fence A on the same rein as fence B, creating a small three-jump course!
e. Now ride a 20m circle over the two jumps on both reins.
You get the idea! As you progress you can add fences at the remaining quarter markers on the circle.

Don't forget: Always look where you are going. Concentrate throughout this exercise on rhythm, on maintaining the curve of the arc of your circles, and on keeping your horse straight on your straight lines. Be prepared for your horse to cut in or fall out, and help him accordingly.

2. Figure of eight over two uprights

On the three-quarter line of your school, set up two uprights ideally about 75–90cm (2ft 6in–3ft) high (but as high as you feel comfortable with initially) and about 14.6m (48ft) apart.
a. Ride a 20m (65ft) circle round the first jump, then turn on to the three-quarter line and jump both fences in a straight line; do this from both ends of the school.
b. Once you have done this several times and are feeling confident, jump both fences once again but after landing over the second jump, turn right and jump the first fence from the opposite side and at an angle.
c. When you land, turn left and jump the second fence, also at an angle.
d. Finish the exercise by riding another 20m circle around the second element. You can also ride this exercise beginning from the opposite end of the school, and in trot and canter.

This appears to be a very simple exercise, but it requires concentration from both you and your horse, and ensures he is listening to your directions. As you come out of the first circle and ride towards the third jump (the first vertical taken at an angle), lengthen your stride, then you will need to shorten it to turn the corner and balance the horse to get over the next jump. Riding directly between the two verticals will help you work on related distances. Riding the turns at each end will help with dog-leg turns.

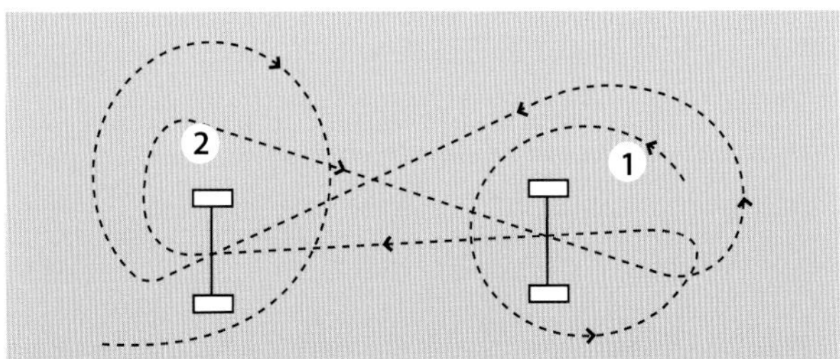

3. Circle and an oxer

This exercise will help you to work on the strength of your horse's canter and your ability to see a stride. Set your jumps up as shown in the diagram.
a. Begin by working on the circle at fence A, if necessary with the fence as a ground pole building up to a small upright 60cm (2ft) high. Working on your horse's rhythm and consistent length of stride, practise this fence in trot and then canter.
b. When you are happy with your horse's canter, on the right rein incorporate fence B. As you approach the fence on the long side of the school, ask your horse for increased power in his canter – though remember that you still want to maintain the same rhythm.
c. If your horse jumps this fence well, tackle the fence from the left rein. To build up the strength in canter, put in an extra circle around fence A before tackling fence B.
d. When you are happy with your horse's performance on both reins, add another parallel at the opposite side of the arena to fence B, and incorporate this in the exercise.

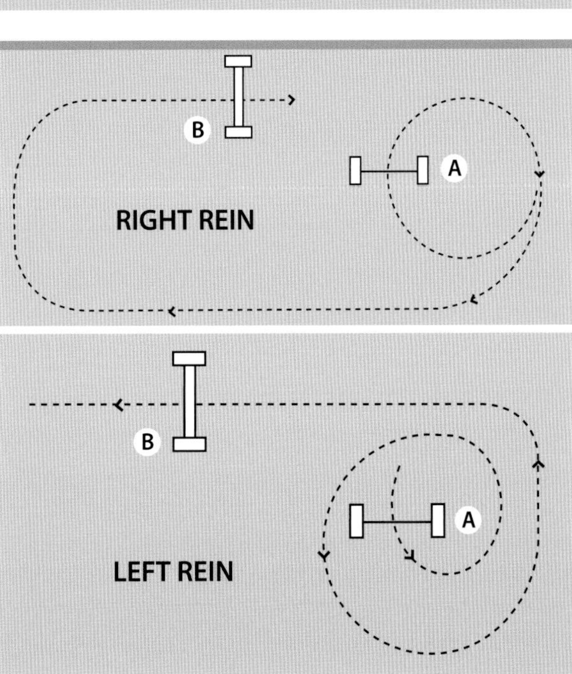

4. Three fences – lots of options

Set up your three upright fences as shown. There should be 14.6m (48ft) between fence 1 and fences 2 and 3, and 11m (36ft) between fences 2 and 3. There are all sorts of routes that you can ride around these fences, but here are three examples:

a. Begin by jumping fence 1, 2 and then 3. Concentrate on your approach from fence 2 to fence 3, and your rhythm throughout the course (diagram A).

b. From one long side of the school, begin by jumping fence 3, circle left to fence 2, making good use of your corners. From fence 2 ride to the opposite long side of the school, circle round and take fence 1 from the short end of the school. Finish by riding straight down the centre line (diagram B).

c. This route will test your turns and your correct canter leads. Begin with fence 1, ride straight down the centre of the school, turn right and jump fence 3: working on rhythm and balance, begin with a comfortable turn to fence 3 and each time you take the course, practise tightening up that turn. After fence 3, circle around fence 1 and, approaching diagonally across the school, jump fence 2. Now circle back around to fence 3. After jumping fence 3, ride diagonally across the school to the opposite side, circle back around behind fence 1, and jump it from the short end of the school (diagram C).

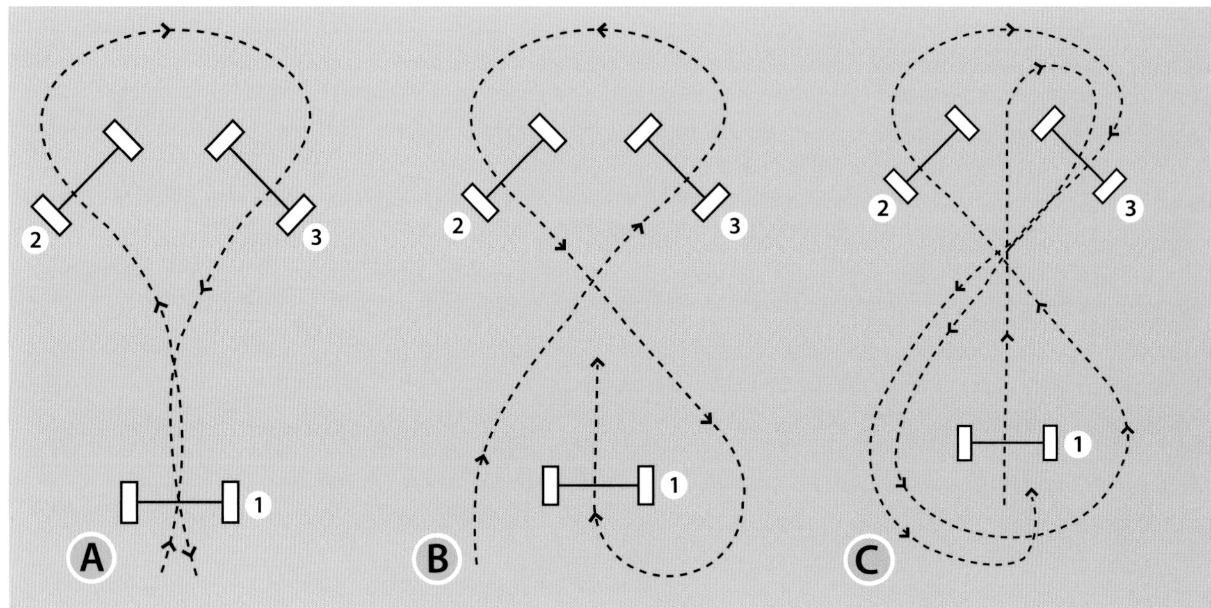

5. Using a grid

Grids are fantastic for developing the gymnastic prowess of your horse, and for establishing a constant rhythm to his paces; and for the rider, they help to develop a steady rein contact and stable position. However, you need to build up to them gradually, and not frighten your horse by over-facing him.

Set up your wings with a ground pole between them before you begin, and have any additional poles needed close at hand. Your helper can then put these into place without too much trouble.

a. Begin by riding over three ground poles, placed 1–1.2m (3ft 3in–4ft) apart, in walk and in trot (check the distances between the poles to ensure they suit your horse's stride).

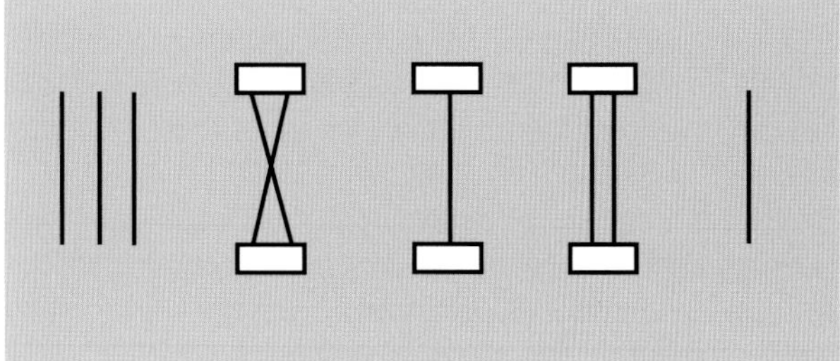

b. When you have an even rhythm and balanced approach to and over the ground poles, introduce a small cross-pole 2.4–2.9m (8ft–9ft 6in) away from the trotting poles, and 50–70cm (1ft 8in–2ft 3in) high.

c. The next fence will be an upright. There should be 6m (20ft) between the cross-pole and the upright.
d. Add a small oxer at a distance of 10m (33ft) from the upright.
e. Finally place a ground pole 10m from the oxer if your school is long enough and allows you room to turn away at the end.

Your horse should land in canter after the cross-pole. Maintain this pace throughout, look forward to your next fence, and try not to make any changes to your horse's stride. The final pole will give you and your horse something to focus on at the end of the grid.

Once you are jumping this grid with ease and in balance with a consistent soft rein contact, try raising the height of the fences.

6. The trot and canter exercise

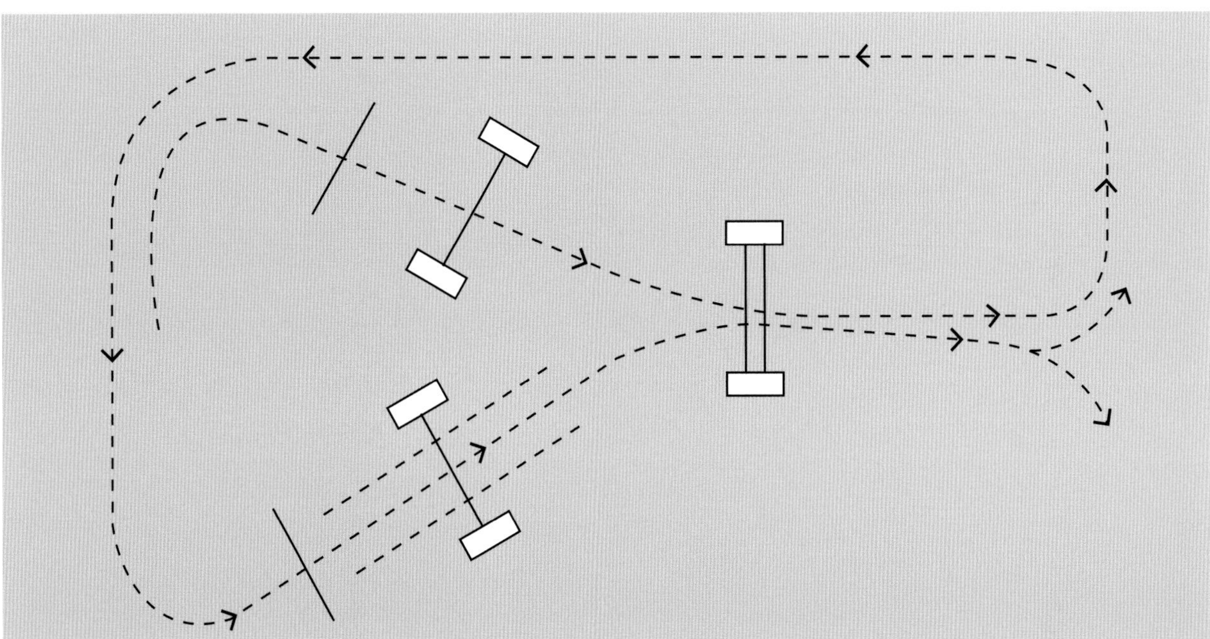

This exercise will test your concentration! It is ridden from trot on one side, and canter on the other, and can be used to work on lengthening and shortening the strides by crossing the first jump to the left, middle or right.

Arrange the jumps as shown in the diagram. On one side you will need 2.4m (8ft) between your ground pole and the first upright, and 5.5m (18ft) between the centre of the upright and the oxer for trotting. On the opposite side, allow 2.7m (9ft) between the ground pole and the first upright, and 6.4m (21ft) between the centre of the upright and the oxer for cantering.
a. Begin with the trot jumps on the right rein, riding a line over the centre of the poles.
b. Take the left rein at the top end of the school, come around the track and then take the canter jumps.
c. Now you can turn left or right to take either the canter or the trot arm of the jump. Once you are jumping this with confidence you can also try lengthening or shortening your stride, by taking a line to the left or the right of the poles (see diagram).
You must concentrate on an accurate approach line and a consistent rhythm. Use the trot jump to slow your horse down. Make sure you vary your choice of pace and approach line as your horse may start to anticipate where he is going.

30 minutes a Week to Tackle Scary Fences

Sounds almost too good to be true? Unfortunately there is no magic formula to help resolve any issues you may have with certain types of jump. That's the bad news. The good news is that dealing with scary fences can be a logical, progressive part of the everyday training of your horse, rather than crisis coaching the day after, or even – worse still – the day before a competition or day out.

There is no doubt that there are certain jumps that qualify for the title of 'bogey fences'. However, that label is a self-fulfilling prophecy, as most of us regard a bogey fence as something to be scared of. So the first step in dealing with difficult fences is to rethink your mental approach and regard them as a test of the skills you have developed with your horse.

And if you haven't developed the necessary skills with your horse, this is where the work needs to begin. Not so easy? Each one of us, if necessary with the help of a trainer, can break down our riding problems into bite-sized (or 30-minute!) pieces. By focusing on successfully mastering each of these training targets, if it is physically and psychologically possible for you and your horse to achieve your goal, it will happen. How much work you can fit into a 30-minute session will depend on you and your horse, but a few minutes of good work focused on one or two specific goals are far more beneficial than a couple of hours of battling to over-achieve.

FIRST QUESTIONS

- Am I in balance with my horse?
- Do I have a strong leg position?
- Can I maintain my upper-body position independently?

If you have progressively developed your jumping training from schooling to polework and through grids, you should be developing an independent seat, and your upper and lower body positions should be secure.

Try the following exercise: in trot, drop your weight down through your leg and into your heel. Now rise out of the saddle as you would in rising trot, and stay there for two or three strides. Don't stand on the stirrups and don't balance on your reins. How was your balance? In theory you should be able to ride around the entire arena, maintaining this position. If your balance or upper or lower body positions are insecure, this exercise will highlight the problem. The most effective solution is lungework, preferably with an instructor, ultimately without reins or stirrups and concentrating on sitting on your seatbones in balance with the horse. This work can be evolved to incorporate lungeing over small jumps.

⇧ *Are you in balance with your horse? Try our simple test to decide whether you need more schoolwork, and what you need to work on.*

Now let's take a look at those bogey fences. The best place to work on any jumping problems is in a secure arena or practice area, where you and your horse feel relaxed. You will probably need someone to help, both to move poles and as 'eyes-on-the-ground'.

Using our formula, break down the technique for tackling the fence that troubles you into steps (see the examples that follow), before you even put a saddle on your horse. And once in the arena, don't progress from one step to the next until the part you are working on has become almost boring; this may mean that it takes two, three, or even more 30-minute sessions to achieve your ultimate goal. But don't be impatient, because what you are building is a secure foundation that will last throughout your riding experiences with this particular horse, and probably longer.

Warming up

Take the first 10 minutes of a 30-minute session to warm up your horse (see page 92), and incorporate confidence-building exercises into your warm-up routine. Routine is an important word here, because within the familiarity of knowing what is to be asked of him, your horse's confidence and trust will develop. When tackling challenges, it is important that you and your horse have a mutual base of trust. One way to build trust is through a progressive training programme, much of which can be done at home.

If necessary, finish your warm-up by popping over a comfortable fence that you will both enjoy. Now tackle the first of your steps. If all goes well, move on to the next. Remember to reward your horse with a pat and/or an appropriate word each time he gets it right. Bear in mind that you probably want to spend about 15 minutes working on this jump, and 5 minutes settling down afterwards, and it is of utmost importance to end on a good note.

If you can move from the first step to the second or even the third within the 30-minute time frame, do so, but don't rush, and – and this can't be said enough – don't move on until you have mastered each stage. Remember that every horse is an individual, and as a rider it is up to you to assess the speed at which the horse you are riding is able to progress.

Don't move on from one step to the next until you are entirely satisfied with your progress. If you are having problems, seek professional help.

If you do find yourself running out of time at an awkward moment, go back a step to remind yourselves of that success, and finish off with your warm-up session's confidence-inspiring jump.

If things are going very wrong, don't imprint the bad experience on either your own or your horse's memory

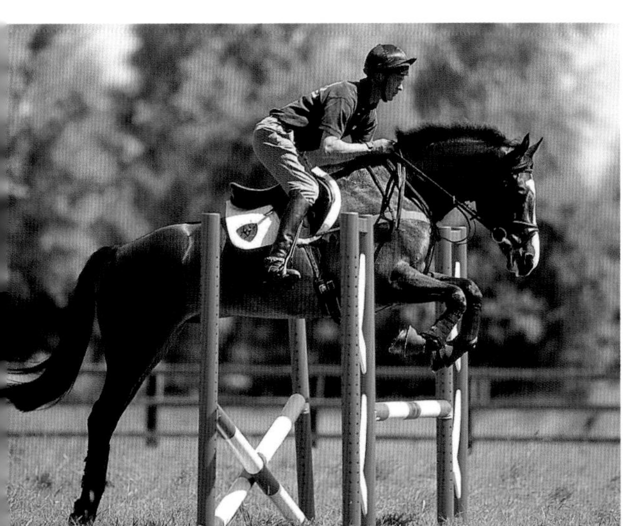

Make sure that you end every training session in a positive fashion.

by continually repeating it. If you can't see any chance for progress, no matter how small, make the positive decision to seek professional help, work through your warm-up routine again, and call it a day. There are always situations in which we need assistance. If there weren't, we'd all be fighting for places on our national teams!

THE FORMULA

- Warm up
- Build up confidence
- Break the problem fence down into three (or more, if necessary) steps
- Practise each step until it becomes almost boring
- Finish on a good note

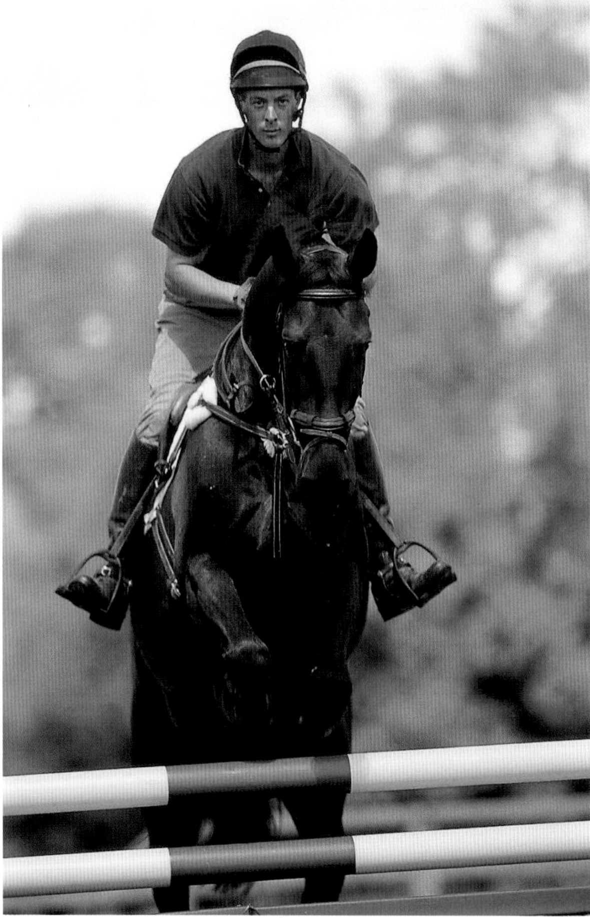

⇧ *With the help of event rider, Chris King, we've broken down the five most common scary fences into achievable steps.*

Tackling those difficult fences

What is your 'bogey' fence? The favourite contenders are:

- Coloured fillers
- Oxers
- Ditches
- Water jumps
- Arrowheads or narrow jumps

Don't forget: Warm your horse up, and before you begin, pop over a fence that you both feel comfortable with.

Coloured fillers

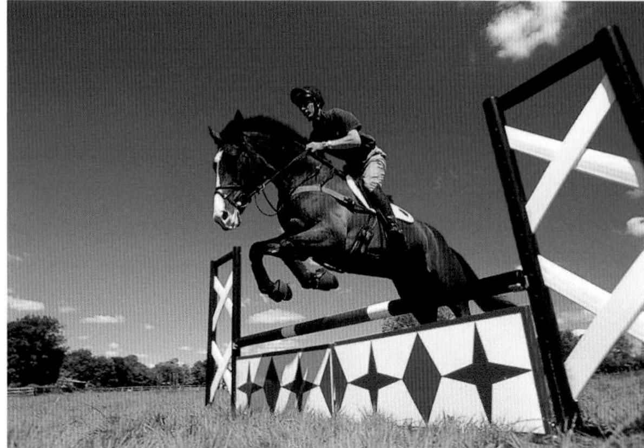

⇧ *This type of fence is usually more of a problem for the rider than the horse!*

***1** Use a confidence-inspiring cross-pole to begin with. Set up your jump in such a way that you can approach it on both reins.*

2 Introduce your coloured fillers by placing them one on each side of the jump, at an angle, at the sides of your cross-poles. Place them as far out as necessary to begin with. As you approach, make sure that you are in line with the centre of the jump. As soon as you have established your line, look up. If necessary either have your helper stand, at a safe distance, in front of you, or select a point on which to concentrate. Ensure that you have a firm leg position and an even rein contact. Ride away positively on the other side of the fence and make much of your horse if he has been a good boy. Jump this fence as many times as is necessary to ensure it is not a problem to either you or your horse.

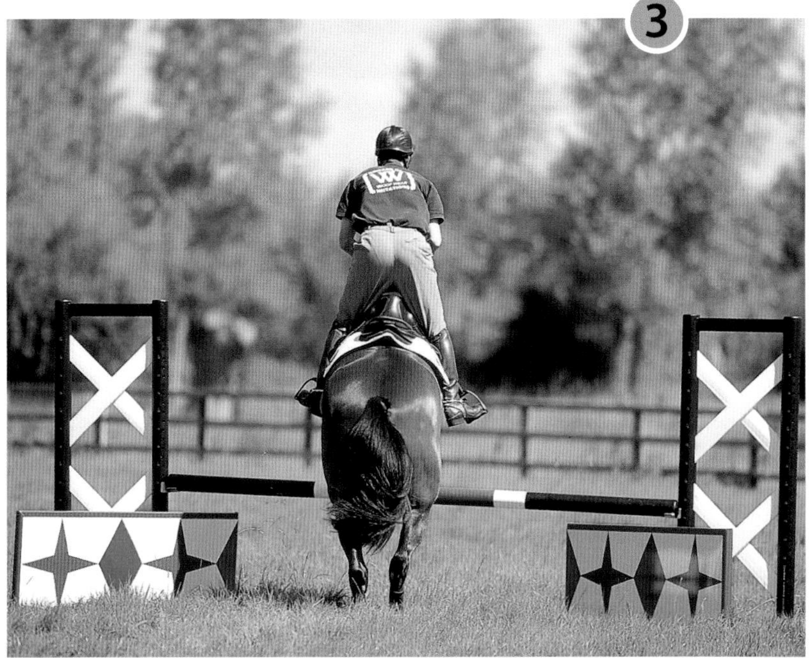

3 Gradually move the fillers in towards the centre of your jump, opening out the angle as you do. Depending on how your horse is reacting, this could take several steps. Don't rush him. If at any point he refuses and runs out, go back a step or two and try again – but don't forget to reward him when he does as you ask.

4 Your aim is for the fillers to finally end up in their correct position, and for your horse to pop over the fence with no problems.

Don't forget: If you run out of time and have to stop before achieving your final goal, be sure to end on a positive note, either jumping the fence comfortably with the fillers halfway in, or returning to the cross-pole. When you start your next 30-minute session, repeat the warm-up and initial steps. They should not take as long this time. If you find that you are really up against a block and your horse will not go forwards over the fence, seek professional help, as the problem may be more deeply rooted in your horse, or your position may need work.

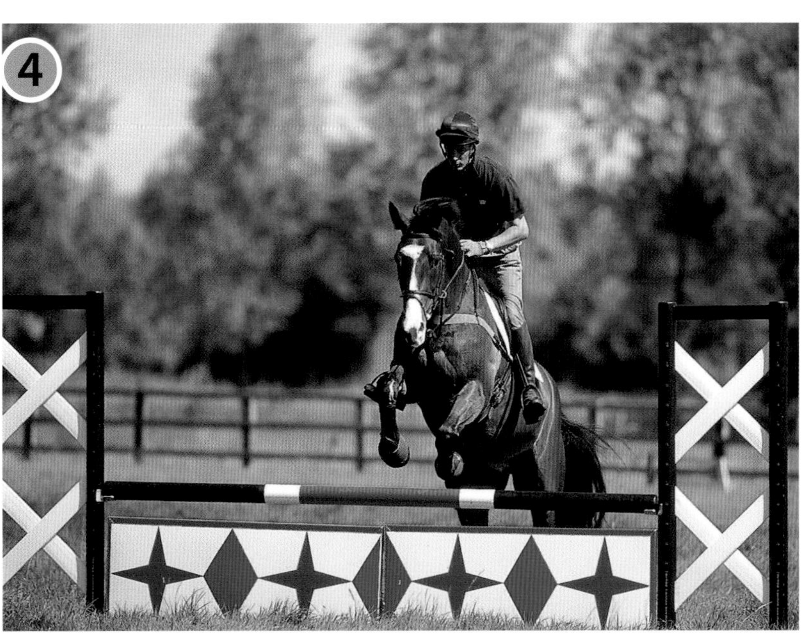

Tackling an oxer

No matter what level you compete at or what height of jump you feel happy with, gridwork is fundamental to schooling a horse over jumps, and a great way of building up confidence and introducing new challenges.

⇧⇩ *If either of these fences looks daunting, a grid is the answer to introducing them to your horse in a calm and confidence-inspiring manner.*

BUILDING A GRID

A grid normally consists of three or four jumps and can begin with something as reassuring as a ground pole and end in an oxer or even a triple bar. Begin in trot and allow approximately 6m (20ft) between each element (this is a guide for a 16hh horse and may need to be adjusted according to the length of your horse's stride). This will allow for one complete trot stride between each jump, plus landing and take-off. In canter the distance will have to be increased to around 6.8m (22ft 4in).

ELEMENT	DISTANCE
Ground poles in walk	80cm–1m (2ft 9in–3ft 3in)
Ground poles in trot	1.2–1.45m (4ft–4ft 9in)
Ground poles in canter	3–4.3m (10–14ft)
Trotting pole to cross-pole	2.4–2.9m (8ft–9ft 6in)
Cross-pole to upright in one stride	5.8–6.4m (19–21ft)
Upright to oxer in one stride	6–6.7m (20–22ft)
Upright to oxer in two strides	9.8–10.4m (32–34ft)

Don't forget: If your horse has never jumped a grid before, this could be enough of an achievement for your first 30-minute session.

⇨ *Set up your grid with one trot stride between each element. Begin with a trotting pole and end with a simple jump that your horse is confident with. Establish a balanced, rhythmical trot and approach the grid so you are taking the poles down the centre; take your horse through the three elements several times until he is confident with the format.*

Gradually, and possibly one element at a time, increase the challenge presented by each of the elements, though be careful not to over-face your horse. For example, increase the trotting pole to a small cross-pole, the middle element to an upright of similar height, and the final element to a cross-pole a couple of inches higher. Your target is to finally add a small spread consisting of a cross-pole and upright as your final element.

Don't forget: Each increase in the challenge must continue to build your horse's confidence. Don't be impatient.

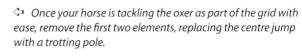

Once your horse is tackling the oxer as part of the grid with ease, remove the first two elements, replacing the centre jump with a trotting pole.

Don't forget: You have cleared this jump many times before as part of the grid. It is no higher or wider now!

If you have worked through this exercise carefully and with confidence, you and your horse should now be able to tackle an oxer whenever it is presented to you.

This same method can be used to increase the height of jump your horse will tackle, and you can gradually raise the height right through the grid along with his abilities and your courage!

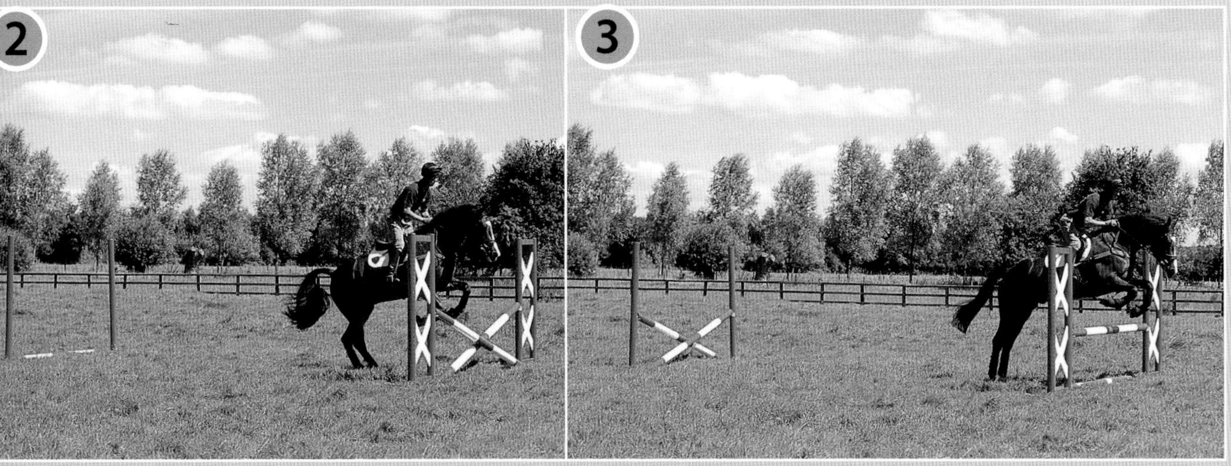

Ditches

Whilst few of us are lucky enough to have a ditch at home on which to practise, constructive work can be done using a false ditch made from sheets of black or blue plastic attached to a board. Another idea is to paint the reverse side of solid fillers black or blue and use them on the ground as your imaginary ditch. Allow your horse time to work out that your ditch (or the ditch on a cross-country course) is not really anything to worry about. Otherwise, if you push him on and make him do too much, too quickly, you could scare him permanently.

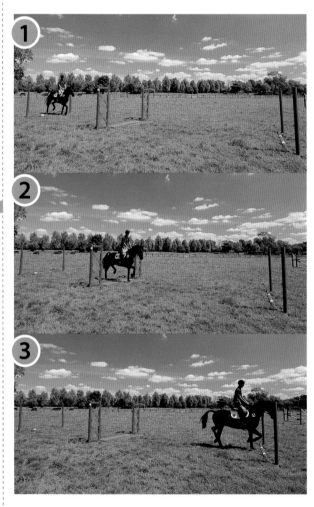

⇧ Position your 'ditch' as the middle element of a three jump grid, with trotting poles at the beginning and the end. Focus your attention on the furthest element. Ride forwards positively in a good rhythm, sit up and keep your leg on, your hands relaxed. Remember not to get ahead of your horse when you are tackling a new jump because if anything goes wrong, you will have difficulty remaining in the saddle. If you feel a run-out may be possible, use wings or poles at an angle to the ditch to guide you through.

Don't forget: If your horse tries to run out, or you suspect that he may, introduce wings or ground poles placed at an angle to the ditch to guide him in.

⇧ You may even find it easier to put in a small cross-pole as the third element for you both to focus on. If you do have problems getting over the ditch, consider the possibility of a lead from another, more confident horse.

Combination: Try a cross-pole before and after the ditch (above), or a cross-pole with a small upright as the final element. You can also place a jump over the ditch, which is more like the type of challenge you may face in a more advanced jumping competition.

Open ditches: Remove the first trotting pole, and then the final element of the grid, leaving just the ditch with supporting wings. Once you are tackling this with ease, remove the supporting wings (photographs below).

⇩ Once your horse is confident with the ditch as part of the grid, you can move forwards in several ways, depending on whether your scary fence is an open ditch or a ditch as part of a combination.

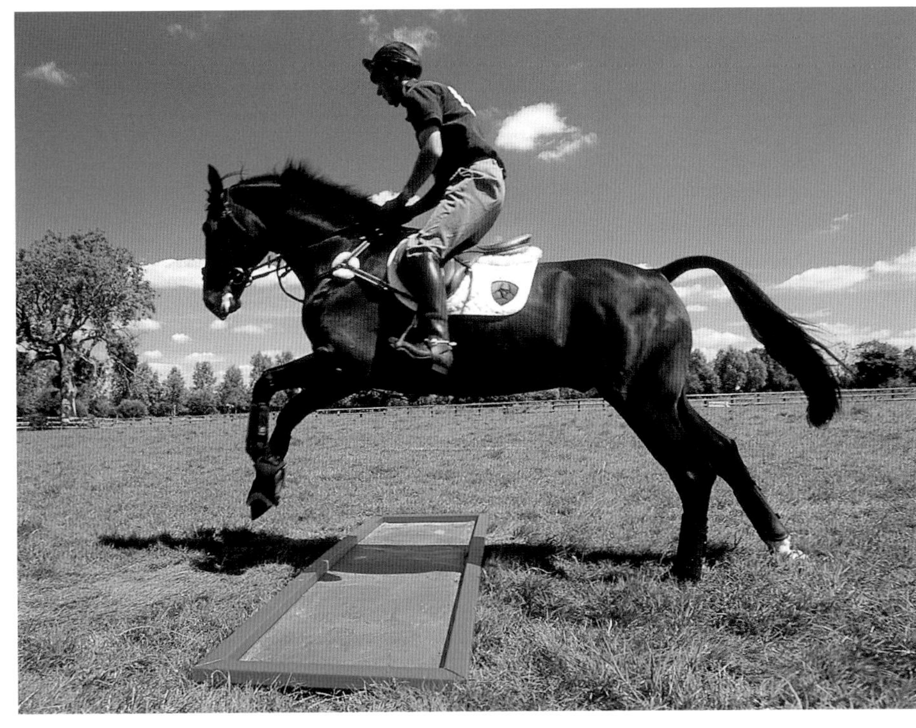

What was all the fuss about?!

Don't forget: Don't look down into your ditch.

NATURAL DITCHES

When you come to tackle an open ditch in the countryside or on a cross-country course, remember that in principle you have done this before. If either you or your horse have any doubts, approach the ditch in walk and give your horse time to take a look: the more slowly you come in, the more control you are going to have. You must ride forward positively, but not bully him across the ditch. Be ready to give with the reins a little to allow him to lower his head and take a look, but don't look down yourself.

Jumping into water

First find your water! Some of you will be lucky enough to have some form of water or water jump at home. However, if you are not in that position, you have two alternatives: either to find a natural situation that will be suitable, according to what stage of training you are at; or to hack or transport your horse to a cross-country course.

When out hacking, make use of any large puddles or streams to accustom your horse to the pull of the water on his feet and its splashing against his legs. Plan to set aside 30 minutes to focus on training your horse in the water. Take care that the ground below the water is safe and stable; a nasty experience with loss of balance could put your horse off water for life.

The alternative is to take your horse to a cross-country course. However, restricting yourself to a 30-minute training session is only appropriate if the prospect of tackling cross-country jumps makes you nervous, and you are trying to break down and tackle the source of your nerves. In such a situation, it is best not to attempt the more difficult fences and possibly to make use of the services of a professional instructor once you are there.

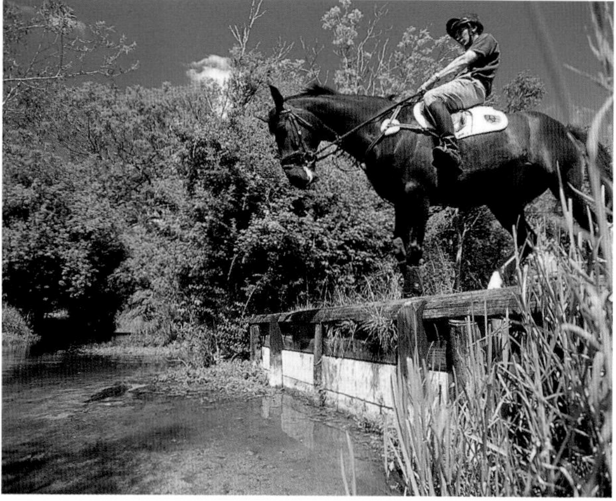

⇧ *Put in plenty of practice before you tackle a water jump at a competition, and with any luck you won't find yourself faced with a refusal.*

Don't forget: Many horses absolutely love water – watch out if they start to paw, as it is a sign that they intend to roll – but there are always exceptions.

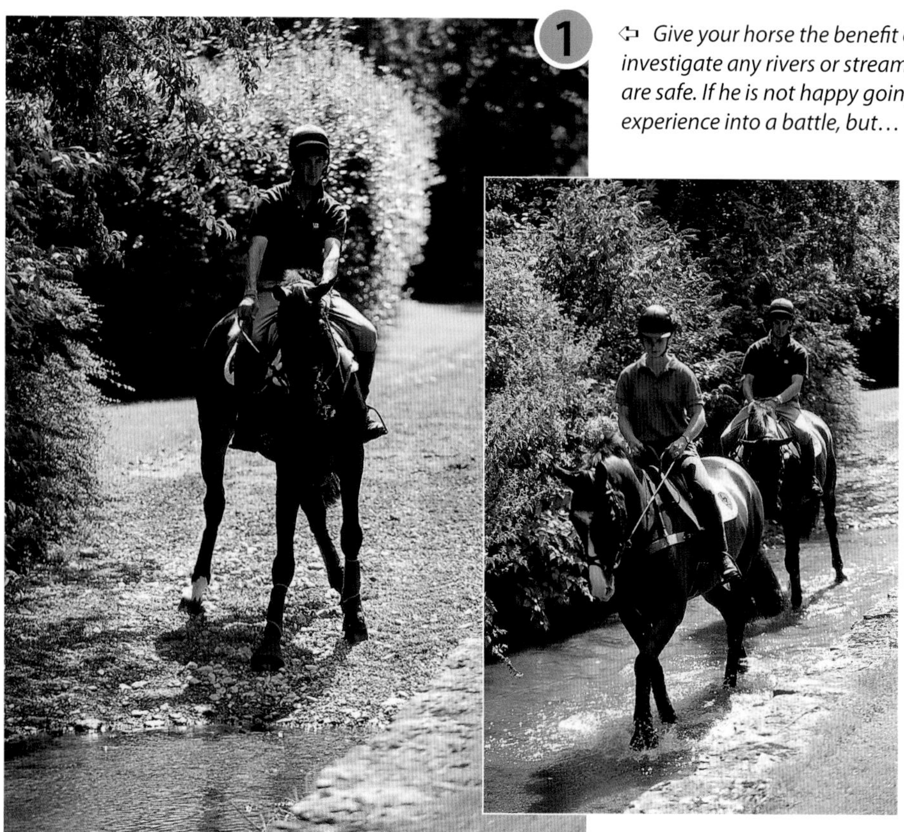

1

⇦ *Give your horse the benefit of the doubt, and let him investigate any rivers or streams in your area that you know are safe. If he is not happy going into water, don't turn his first experience into a battle, but…*

⇦ *…seek the help of another rider and a more confident horse to give you a lead. Walk into the water allowing your horse time to have a look. Sit up, be slightly behind the movement, and don't restrict him with your hands. When you have walked in and out of the water together several times and your horse is quite happy, ask him to walk into the water on his own. If he hesitates, be firm and encourage him forwards with your legs. Give with your hands when he obeys, and reward him with a pat. Once again, repeat this several times.*

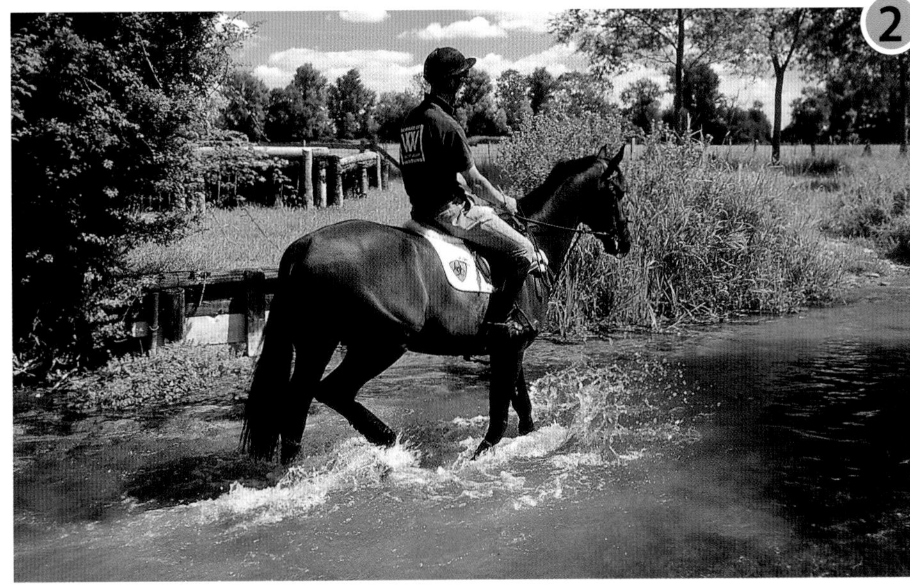

2

Once your horse is happy entering water alone, allow him to splash about for a bit to become accustomed to the feeling of water around his legs. Try trotting in the water if you know the bed is sound.

The next step is to introduce your horse to a drop into the water. Try to find a shallow slope or step for your initial attempts. Approach the drop in walk. Allow your lower leg to slide forwards, and be aware of opening your knee and hip joints. Sit well back, allowing the reins to slip through your hands. Be prepared for a bit of a stumble on the first attempts – by sitting back, you will help your horse to regain his balance more quickly. In the next stride, sit upright, regain your rein contact, and look in the direction you now wish to take.

3

4

When your horse is confident walking into water, try the exercise in trot.

JUMPING OUT OF WATER

If you cannot find a shallow enough bank from which to jump into water, it is sometimes a good idea to try jumping out of the water and up the bank first. You will also find that most cross-country courses give you the options of jumping out of the water or using a slope. On your first attempt to jump out of water, give your horse plenty of time to accustom himself to the feel and the pull of the water around his legs, and to find a good take-off point. You will need to maintain a secure leg position as your horse leaves the water – if necessary hold onto the mane for your first couple of tries.

Jumping a narrow jump

Arrowheads, stiles, logs: the challenge of a narrow fence can give many riders a problem, whether in the show-jumping ring or on a cross-country course. It can become the perfect opportunity for your horse to show that he can take control. Before you begin to work on your narrow fence, ask your horse to jump first to the left-hand side, and then to the right-hand side of a small upright to test whether he is listening to you, and not simply jumping the centre of the fence through habit. Working on his obedience to your directions could be your first step! However, on the assumption that your horse naturally does whatever you ask of him, move on to the next step!

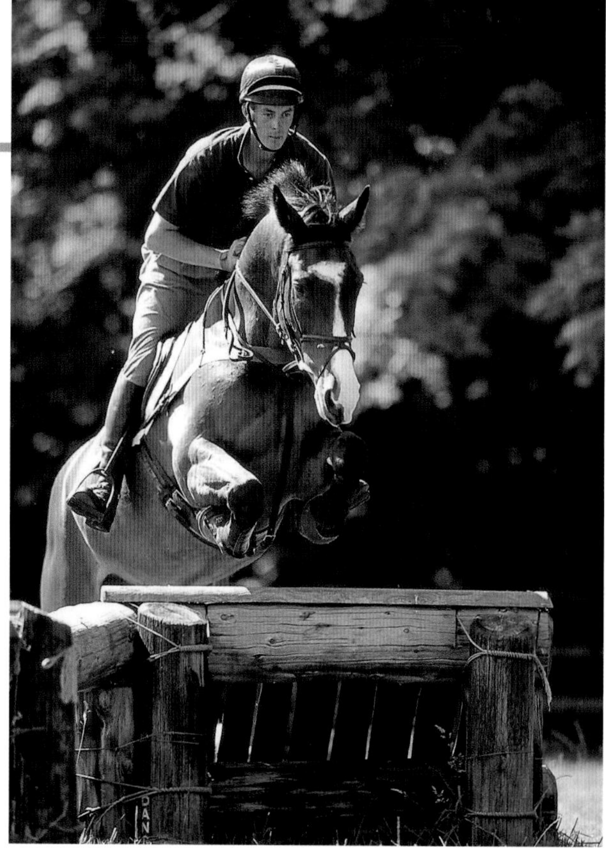

⇧ *A straight approach is the key to success over this type of jump.*

⇩ *Using either barrels on their side and held in place by ground poles, or fillers from your show jumps, create a small fence of normal width without wings and with two poles placed at an angle on either side. Once your horse is jumping this comfortably, remove one filler or barrel, and move the poles in closer: they will direct your horse to the centre of what is now a narrow fence. Allow him to take a good look at the obstacle before tackling it as a jump. Ride him forwards with a consistent hand and leg contact.*

⇧ *Once your horse is jumping the narrow fence with ease, remove first one, and then the second angled pole. If you know your horse is likely to run out, according to whether it is to the left or the right, remove the opposite angled pole first.*

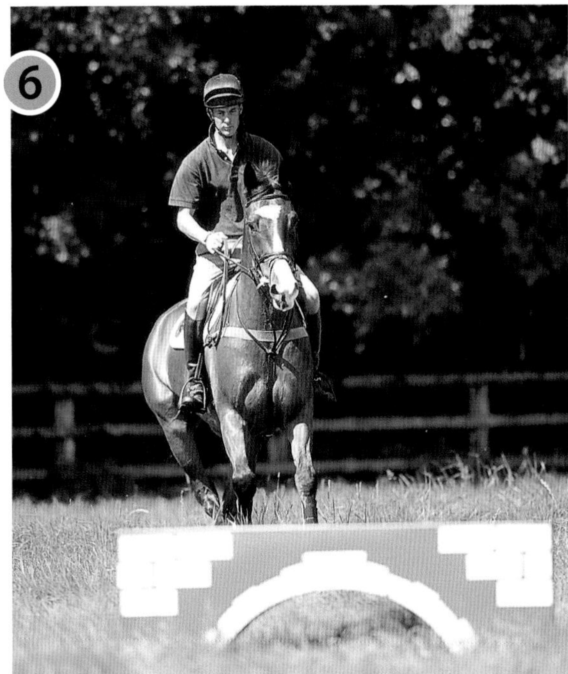

⇧ *With both angled poles removed, practise this jump on both reins until your horse is totally untroubled by it. You may now wish to increase the height, if possible, or the width.*

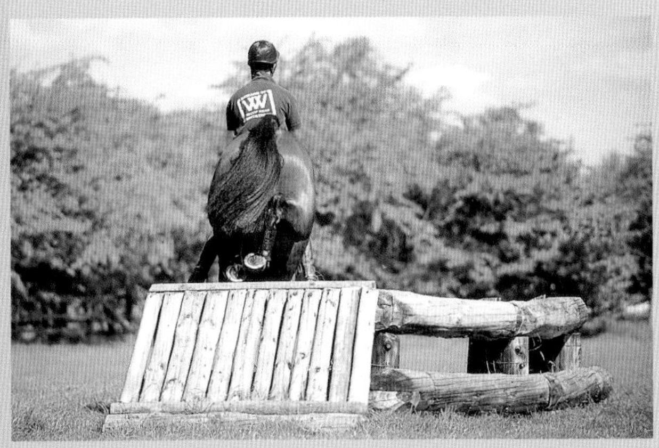

⇦ *Practise narrow fences whenever you have the opportunity, and never allow your horse to run to one side, as he will learn that in this way he can evade jumping it. Be sure to reward him for jumping correctly.*

EXPERT TIPS ON TACKLING SCARY FENCES

- Try to maintain a steady, balanced pace on your approach to, over, and away from a fence. Your horse will learn to establish a rhythm and maintain it once he has cleared the jump.
- Whenever possible, if tackling scary fences, school with another, more experienced horse that can give yours a lead over the more challenging jumps.
- Always begin with an inviting fence.
- When you are tackling new and complex fences, it is most important not to get ahead of the movement or you will find yourself 'out of the side door' (falling off sideways). Keep your horse in front of your leg.
- Remember the three Cs: calm, committed and confident.
- Work on maintaining a strong lower leg in case of run-outs, cat leaps or stops.
- Your horse must develop his own balance, so don't hang onto his mouth or lean to one side. It is important that he learns to develop a 'fifth leg' to help you both out of trouble when necessary.
- Relax, enjoy what you are doing – and if you don't, go home and practise.
- If you are leaning too far forwards and the horse decides to stop or run out at the last minute, you are powerless to do anything.
- Once your horse has taken off over a fence, don't relax and stop riding, because you'll get left behind. When you land you have to reorganize your balance immediately.
- Don't allow problems to fester: sort them out straightaway, with professional help, if necessary.
- Ask yourself why your horse is refusing: is it because he's naughty, or because of lack of confidence? If you're not sure, a professional trainer will be able to see what the problem is and help you work on it.
- Have a plan and stick to it. When you try to do too much, accidents happen.
- Tell yourself: 'I believe we can do this.'

6 30 MINUTES OF HAPPIER HACKING

- *30 minutes to build up your confidence*
- *30 minutes of interesting hacking*
- *30 minutes of three short schooling sessions*

Close your eyes and picture yourself having the time of your life on a horse: very probably your picture is going to be of you and the horse you are riding out on a hack. Sadly, however, for some people this picture becomes distorted by nerves, provoked either by imaginary events or by bad experiences – but these nerves can be overcome, and 30 minutes of focused work can be where new confidence begins.

Sometimes our hacking becomes routine, and we need fresh inspiration; by taking a good look around you, and bearing in mind what you are trying to achieve, you can pack a 30-minute hack full of training opportunities. And indeed, whilst hacks are intended to be fun, they should be work, too, and incorporating exercise routines into your riding out ensures that your horse remembers his job whilst he's having a good time.

30 minutes to Build Up Your Confidence

Riding out is one of the greatest pleasures in the long list of equestrian pastimes. It also presents a textbook of training opportunities. However, these can be viewed as such overwhelming challenges that they stop some riders from hacking out altogether.

The important thing is to focus on situations that you can control, rather than circumstances that you cannot anticipate and are beyond your control.

Before tacking up and venturing beyond the gates of your livery yard or paddock, ask yourself the following questions:

• Should I be hacking out at all: are my fundamental riding skills in place?
• Should I be hacking out now: are the weather, time and social conditions in my favour?
• Should I be hacking out on this particular horse: can I control him?

If the answer to any of these questions is no, then the likelihood is that some work needs to be put in to the relevant areas that you can control. However, if you answer 'yes' to every question, then what is to stop you venturing forth? The answer is nerves.

Nerves are part of our body's defence mechanism, and in 95 per cent of cases, they are not a bad thing. However, allowing nerves to take over can be debilitating – although the good news is that, like many components of fitness, you can train yourself to control your nerves.

Mental fitness

The next time someone returns to your yard from a hack, ask how it was. If it's been good, they'll say 'great' or 'I had a good canter' or 'she was a good girl'. If it was difficult, however, you'll hear every detail of what went wrong, or why it might have gone wrong. What all this is doing is building up a negative image in the subconscious of what happens on a hack.

Now there's nothing wrong with breaking down a bad riding experience and using what's been learnt as a springboard for future training. But that's exactly what it is – a tool for training, and not a sequence of events that will happen on every hack. Unfortunately, that's how most of us store and use the information.

⇧ *Try not to dwell on the scarier aspects of your hack, but think how well you dealt with the situation.*

If we treated a great ride in the same way – going over all the details, looking at how we could build on the experience, understanding how much work we've put in along the way, work that has put us in this great position – we'd be building up a positive picture. And let's be honest, most of us have more positive hacking experiences than negative ones.

The simple technique of positive imaging is just one of the tools used by sports psychologists to help athletes enhance their performance and overcome mental blocks to their training, and it's a technique that is just as useful to equestrians.

Begin a performance diary

Buy a diary and make a note in it of whether your last hack was good or bad. Give it a rating: this can be measured in terms of performance, training, enjoyment, or whatever is significant for you. For example, if hacking in wide open spaces is your challenge, how confident did you feel? Make detailed notes about the hack, your preparation, how you were feeling, how you and your horse performed, the weather, what you saw during your ride, any obstacles that were presented along the way, and so on. Go over this positive record several times until you have every detail lodged in your mind.

As well as building up a picture of your hacking experiences, you'll soon discover whether your rides tend to be mostly bad, in which case you'll need some professional help with your fundamental riding techniques, your horse and your ambitions – or mostly good, in which case you can build on your success.

Imagine your success

The following three strategies can help build up your confidence in your abilities.

Talk the talk

If you spend your time telling anyone who will listen that you are a nervous rider, that's what you will be. People will expect you to behave as a nervous rider, and will put you in the position of a nervous rider, and gradually you will assume that role. Now that's fine if you always want to be a nervous rider, but if you're not happy to be categorized as such, then you will have to think of another way of describing yourself that capitalizes on your strengths.

Find a positive way to discuss your equestrian experiences and ambitions, and in particular avoid any negative words.

Take 30 minutes to list your equestrian achievements

Begin at the beginning. How did you 'discover' horses? How far have you come from then? How do non-equestrian friends see you as a rider? How would your horse judge you? Are you considerate, sensitive, a sympathetic trainer? How much have you learned over the years that you've been riding? How successful have you been? You get the picture: list everything positive. Give some thought to anything negative that springs to your mind, and see if you can give it a positive spin. For example, if you think 'I'm a nervous rider, afraid to move out of my comfort zone', look a bit further, for instance into how much you have overcome to become a rider, and how much effort you have put into improving.

Once you've compiled your list, hone it down to three statements that you feel sum you up as a rider. Write them on a piece of paper or an index card, and pin it up somewhere where you will see it regularly – the fridge would be good! – then every time you pass it by, take five minutes to absorb just what you have achieved, rather than dwelling on your shortcomings.

Walk the walk

Have you ever noticed how some riders carry themselves beautifully, whereas others slop around? Which would you rather be, and which would inspire you more? Think of a rider that you admire, picture their posture, and their way of moving and riding, and emulate their style. As you work with your horse, imagine how your role model would appear in the same situation, and use them as inspiration. When, and if, you next encounter a confidence crisis, ask yourself how your role model might deal with it, and try to tackle the obstacle in that way.

Take 30 minutes to identify your equestrian hero
There is nothing wrong with hero worship, and many a top athlete has arrived at their destination by modelling themselves on someone else. Once you have identified the equestrian sportsman or woman whom you admire, and who could serve as an inspiration to you, think back to a situation that has challenged your confidence. Analyse how you dealt with that situation and what you learned from it, and then ask yourself how your role model might have faced the same challenge. If you don't feel able to answer the question at this point, spend some time watching the performances of that person either on video – many top trainers now produce educational videos, and many top events also have their records – or at competitions. Note any discrepancies in approach, and learn from them if this is appropriate.

Picture the picture

Use visualization to prepare yourself for any equestrian challenges. For example, walk a hack before you ride it. Imagine how you will deal with each section of the route, and picture you and your horse doing so. Note any areas that might present a challenge, and picture how you would deal with that challenge successfully. Go over this time and time again in your mind until you are familiar with every possible detail.

Take 30 minutes to go over every aspect of a forthcoming hack
Here are some tips to help you:
• Use your senses of sight, sound and smell to give substance to your visualization.
• Consider the time of day and the effect that light, and also traffic – both human and vehicular – might have on the location.

⇧ *If you are aware of challenges you might face on your ride – such as scary deer – picture in detail how you would deal with this successfully.*

THE PLEASURES OF HACKING OUT

Make a list of the positive aspects of riding out. Here's some inspiration:

- You can discover your local countryside.
- It gives you a great opportunity to get to know your horse in a more natural environment.
- It improves fitness for both of you.
- It's great fun.
- It's relaxing.

• If you don't really believe that everything will be perfectly all right, then don't pretend that it will be. Rather, consider the potential challenges in terms of worst possible scenario, best possible scenario, and most likely scenario. Give each one a likelihood score from 1 to 10, and then picture how you would deal with them on the same ratio.

Controlling your nerves

There are certain strategies you can employ if you feel your nerves are taking control at any time:

Develop a strategic breathing technique
If you feel your breathing becoming hollow, practise the following deep breathing technique to restore your breathing to normal:
• Take a deep breath through your nose: feel it pass through your chest and into the deepest cavities of your stomach. Feel your ribcage expand, your chest open, your spine straighten.
• Allow your chin to tuck in and your shoulders to relax. Think about your centre of gravity, just below and behind your tummy button.
• Allow the breath to leave your body slowly through your mouth. Mentally count how long it takes.
• Repeat this until your breathing feels regulated, your shoulders are relaxed, and you feel more focused on the task in hand.
Take 30 minutes to practise your breathing technique. You will be bordering on the fringes of meditation if you get this right.

Finding key words
When a situation is tense, focusing on it will only increase the tension both for you and your horse. Find a positive and uplifting word or phrase that encapsulates how you would like your attitude to be, such as 'We can do this', 'No sweat', or 'Go for it'. Use the chosen phrase repeatedly, and gradually you will find that it helps to pull you together and keep you calm.

Take 30 minutes to explore words and phrases that motivate, calm and influence you. Try to refine these to a personal motivation statement, such as: 'I am a sympathetic and conscientious rider, riding with nerves, who wants to progress to the peak of my abilities.' Look also for phrases and words that you can use at times of stress.

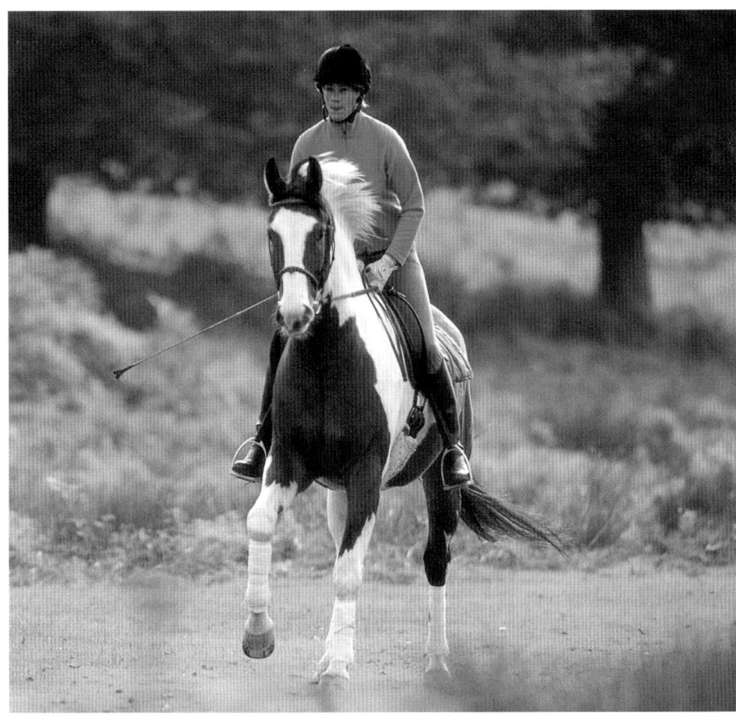

If you've had a bad experience

If your fears are based on a bad experience, it is important to keep the memories in context. If what happened was out of your control, or was bad luck, or due to unforeseeable circumstances, remind yourself of the number of times you have ridden out with success, compare it to this event, and appreciate the likelihood of it happening again. Don't let what has happened control your future.

If, however, you look back on the occasion and realize that there was something you could have done about it, then act upon what you have learnt. Would better planning, training, or a faster reaction on your part have helped? If this is the case you can use this information to improve your ability and competence as a rider.

The most important recovery step is to learn to be in control once again. Train your mind to focus on what you enjoy about hacking by putting aside any negative memories when they arise and telling yourself: 'That happened to me at such-and-such time and place, but it has made me a better prepared rider.'

This doesn't mean that you should ignore what can happen on a hack, but when planning your hack, focus on the possible events that might occur, and find some positive statement (see Finding key words, opposite) that will reiterate your ability to cope and to be in control, such as: 'That won't happen to me if I have a good contact'; or 'I can reduce the effect of my horse spooking by staying calm myself.'

Remember: anticipation can cause results!

TIPS FOR SAFE HACKING IN THE COUNTRYSIDE OR ON THE ROADS

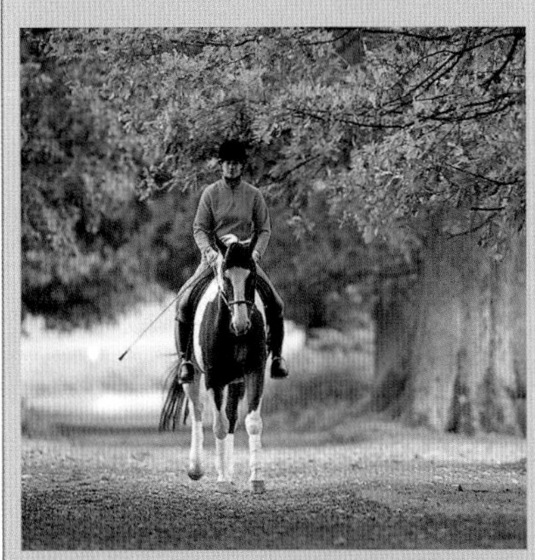

- Wear the necessary safety gear, and especially a hat that meets the current safety regulations.
- Carry a mobile phone.
- Plan your route. If necessary walk it before you ride it. This will enable you to visualize yourself riding the route. Use your senses to imagine how it will be. Picture yourself as the rider you want to be, riding with confidence and pleasure.
- Break your route down into manageable chunks (30-minute hacks!), and build up to the complete ride gradually.
- Make sure that you have done your homework with your horse. He should listen to and respect your aids. If there are any types of hazard, such as tractors, that you know he will worry about, work on them at home, familiarizing him to the challenge via desensitization (see 30 Minutes on Spookiness and Napping, page 82).
- Ride out with a sensible companion. Ensure you pick someone who can empathize with your concerns.
- If your horse is particularly lively, school or lunge him before your hack.
- Don't be a passenger. Ride your horse, but remember that this is meant to be fun as well as work for both of you.

30 minutes of Interesting Hacking

Wherever you keep your horse, you'll know the route of your 30-minute hack. However, you can do better than mount up and ride along in a dream when 30 minutes are all you have. Here are some ideas to enable you to use that precious time more constructively.

Sometimes, usually due to over-use of the school, a muddy horse or shorter evenings, all you have time for is a 30-minute hack, and perhaps you've been overcome by a sense of futility at the prospect and decided to put your horse back in his stable or field: but in these circumstances, think again, because 30 minutes of focused riding in a different environment is worth doing. The important thing is not to plod around your usual route in a vacant state of mind, but to look at the opportunities it presents, and at what you can bring to the situation, and to capitalize on them. On pages 149–50 you'll find three 10-minute exercise sessions that you can introduce into your hack, but in the meantime, here are some ideas to inspire you. For instance, you could practise your balance in a forward seat, ride in company, work on developing a feeling seat, try out different tack, swop horses, make use of natural obstacles: all these will give your ride a real purpose.

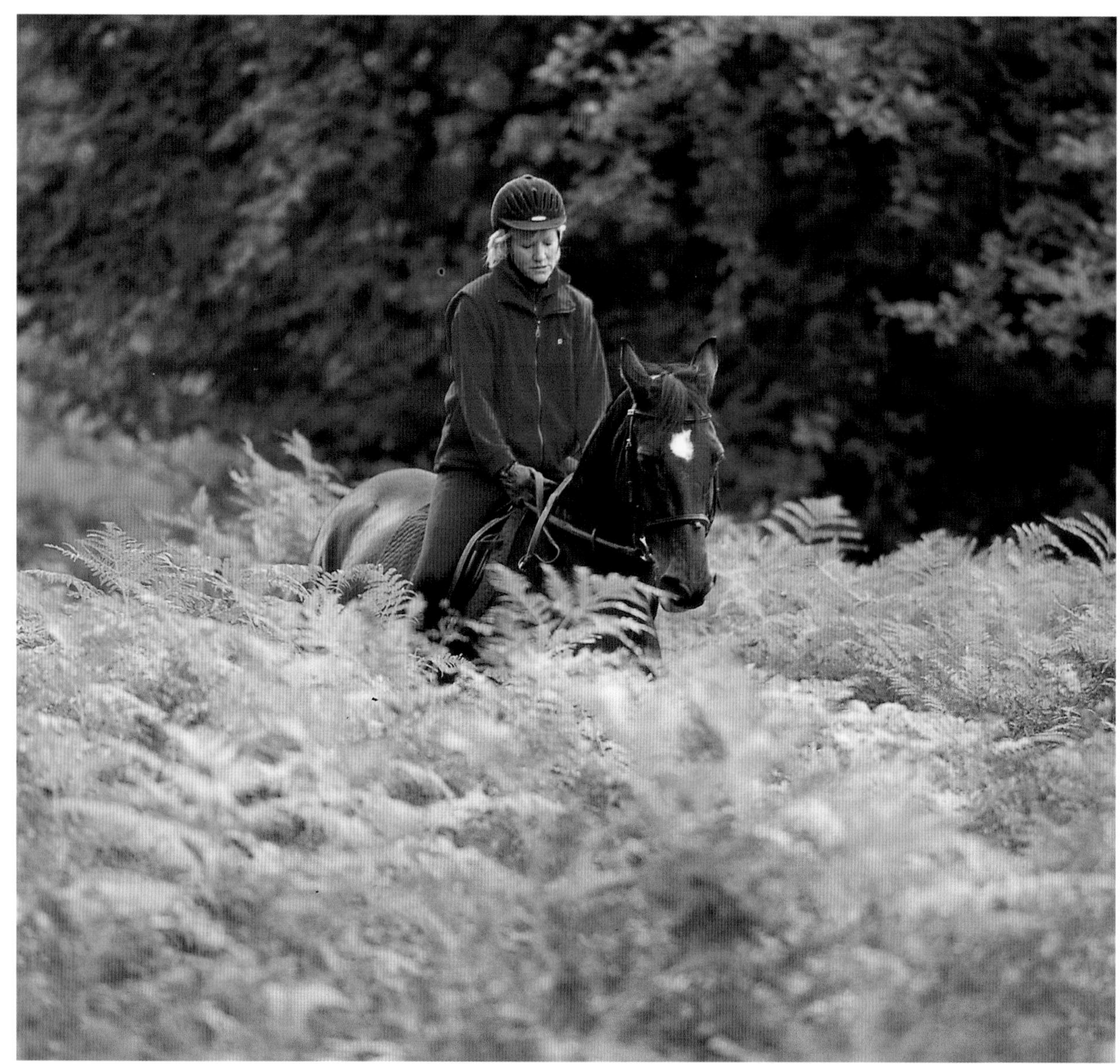

Practise your balance in a forward seat

⇦ *Practise your jumping seat riding up and down hills – though watch out that your horse doesn't take the signal of your weight out of the saddle as a command to go faster!*

Good balance is the key to successful jumping, and maintaining your balance in the jumping position takes considerable muscle control (see 30 Minutes to Spend on a Rider Workout, page 102) and is quite hard work.

Begin by practising in walk on any gentle slope or hill that presents itself. Take a forward jumping seat (see 30 Minutes to Understand Jumping Theory, page 110), and allow your weight to drop through your lower leg and into your heel; do not grip the horse's sides with your legs. This is hard work. You must be careful not to balance on your reins, as the reins should move along the horse's neck; initially you could hold on to the mane if necessary to help with your balance. Your lower leg must remain vertical both up and down hill. Going downhill, the angle of the joint at your knee will open, and your knee should remain in line with the ball of your foot. Concentrate on moving with your horse. When you can do this in walk, both up and down hill, try it in trot, and then in canter if possible.

If you can find a small step or bank, you can begin to practise your jumping. Riding up and down a step will break the 'jump' into two sections and give you time to reflect in between. Hold your jumping position and allow your horse a reasonably long rein so that he can use his head and neck without your interference. Practise from trot and also from canter, if there is enough room.

Ride in company

How often do you manage to ride out in the company of one or more horses? If the prospect of doing so makes you nervous, because it is based on the unknown or on past experience of your horse becoming overexcited, 30 minutes is a short enough period of time to summon up your courage and give it a try. As we know, horses are gregarious and like company, and your own horse may become braver and attempt things he would not even contemplate doing on his own. This is a good learning opportunity for a horse that is nappy.

If your 30-minute hack can include a field where there is enough space to canter, try riding in a slightly larger group. There are many exercises that can be worked on in a group of three or four. For example:

Work on riding in file: Halt the ride and bring the rear horse up to the front and continue, taking it in turns to ride either at the rear or the front. This training is good for those horses that 'only go' at the front or the back of the ride. If this goes well, try it in trot. Take your time and progress slowly, and be sure that everybody on the ride is prepared and willing.

Work on halt: Halt the entire ride for a count of five, and then proceed. Increase the count for as long as you all agree. Alternatively, halt the whole ride, and then ask the lead horse to go forwards for a measured distance (possibly 15m/49ft), as long as he is in sight; then bring the second horse up to join him, and so on throughout the group.

Now try halting the rear horse only for a count of three strides and then walk on. The rest of the ride must proceed in walk. This is more difficult, because your horse will not be at all sure about being left behind; if you find that he is unhappy with a count of three, reduce it to two or one. Make much of him when he listens to you and does as you ask. Slowly increase the number of strides you can hold your horse for within both your comfort zones. Do not approach the rear of the ride any faster than the pace at which it is proceeding.

Ride side by side: Many horses like to ride nose to tail, as they seem to think this relieves them of the responsibility of work! With the co-operation of another rider, practise riding side by side. Be watchful for any signs of aggression, and use your inside leg and outside rein to correct any misbehaviour; once you have achieved one or two 'relaxed' strides, make much of your horse and drop back again. Aim for an extra stride on the next hack.

Likewise, if your horse is impetuous or a bit of a plod on a hack, use this exercise to encourage him to stay with a better or more consistently schooled horse.

Improve your seat and develop better feel

Can you tell which diagonal your horse is on without looking? Practise trotting for six to ten strides, and then changing diagonals. Now ride for the same number of strides and try to feel which diagonal your horse is on. Once you are sure, take a look. Did you get it right?

When it's safe to do so, bring your horse to a halt. Don't look down, but ask yourself if he is standing square. And if not, which leg is trailing? It can help to be riding with a companion to develop a feeling for this. Continue to work in this way to build a connection between your seat and your horse's feet. Try to get the feeling of a square halt.

Remember those early lessons on the lunge when your instructor took away your stirrups? If you feel secure on your horse and are in a safe place, try riding for stretches without your stirrups. Push your weight into your heel, and feel and go with your horse's movement. Don't grip with your knees. When you feel secure in walk, try rising trot without stirrups to strengthen your leg control.

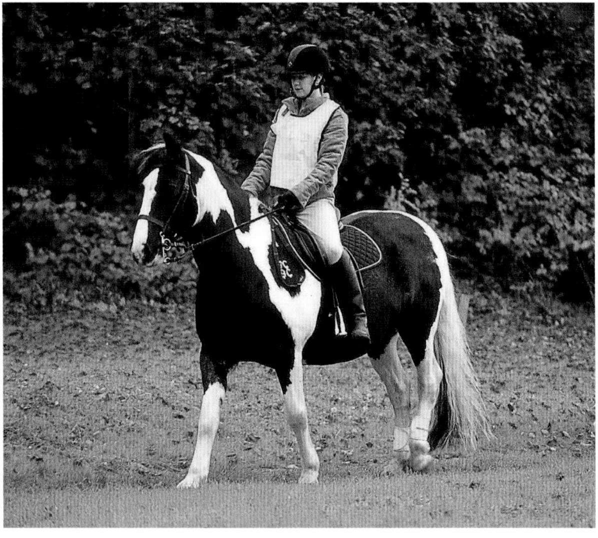

⇧ *When it is safe to do so, ride without stirrups to help lengthen your leg.*

Ride in reverse!

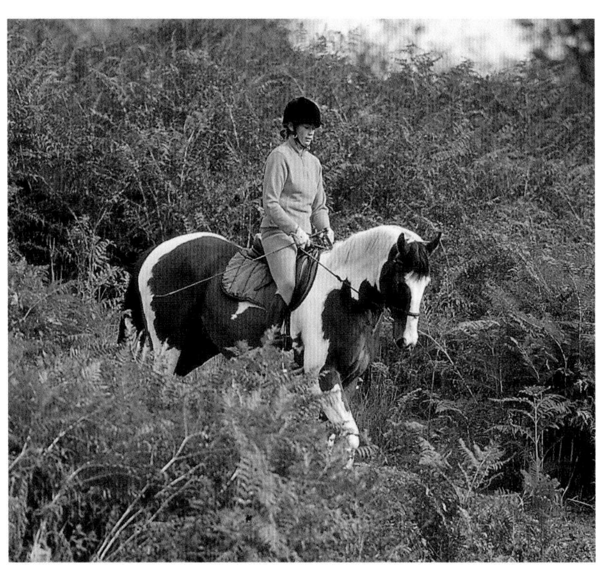

Not always, but all too often, we will take a hack in a certain direction. Sadly this is often to avoid challenges, but it is better to see these as an opportunity and a part of training and learning.

Try taking your usual 30-minute hack in the opposite direction – in company, if that will make you feel more secure.

⇦ *Do you always canter up the same hill? Try walking down it instead: this is much better balance practice for you and your horse.*

Try out different tack

If your horse is a safe hack and you are both confident in each other, a 30-minute ride is a good opportunity to try out some new tack. If there's a bit or a noseband you've wanted to try, this could be the perfect opportunity.

We also often become very reliant on our tack from a psychological point of view, and challenging this reliance is a good step in riding development. Do you really need to ride in long boots, for example? Perhaps you'd feel more flexible in jodhpur boots and half chaps – or have you always wanted to try full chaps?

Does your horse really need a drop noseband? Can you really not ride without spurs? The more flexible and effective a rider we can become, the more honed our skills will be.

Make use of those natural obstacles

Logs, ditches, hills and water can all be incorporated into your training on a 30-minute hack. If you've been avoiding them because you were nervous, tackle the challenge in two possible ways.

Firstly, go with a rider and horse combination in which you have total confidence, and ask them to tackle the obstacle first while you watch. If this gives you sufficient confidence, have a go yourself.

Secondly, break down your concerns into bite-sized pieces. For example, do you know of a log that you've always wanted to pop over but never had the confidence? The initial thing to do is to ensure that it is safe. If necessary, go and take a look on foot. The next time you hack out, ride up to the log in walk, ride all around it, and then go home. Set up a jump in your school that's the same height, preferably during a lesson with your instructor. Once you're clearing that jump (see 30 Minutes from Ground Pole to Upright, page 118) hack back to your log again. Now you know you can tackle the height, how's it looking? Do you need more practice? Could you do with a lead over the log?

If you're still not ready for it, ask yourself whether you really want to tackle it anyway, or are you being persuaded that's what you want to do? All too often our own riding ambitions become muddled up with those of other riders.

If your horse is afraid of water, splashing through the smallest of puddles is a step in the right direction. You may need a lead to do this, or several attempts, but even a foot in a puddle deserves praise.

Practise your gate-opening skills

⇧ *Make the most of every opportunity to practise opening and shutting gates.*

If your horse could do with some practice at gates, a short hack to the nearest challenge could provide the perfect opportunity.

To open a gate correctly you should position your horse parallel to the gate with his head at the same end as the latch. Put your reins and stick (if you are carrying one) into the opposite hand (ie if the fence is on your left, put them in your right hand). Use your inside leg behind the girth to move his hindquarters sideways, and your outside leg to ask him to move forwards, pushing the gate open as he does so. You should try to keep your hand on the gate, although this is not always possible. And, if you push the gate away, do so strongly enough to give your horse time to get through, as he will probably object to being struck by it closing on him.

If the gate opens towards you, this is more difficult because you have to ask your horse to rein back as he moves sideways. Both movements require co-ordination and practice.

SAFETY FIRST

- Common sense must be used at all times. Whilst riding on roads where there is, or may be, heavy traffic, your focus of attention must be on safety, for both you and your horse. Riding your horse properly, and not slopping along on a long rein thinking about supper, is therefore important.
- Always wear hi-viz clothing of some form when you are riding on the roads. It is also recommended to do so when riding in the countryside for the purposes of visibility, especially if you are in an area that is used for helicopter training, because pilots are now taught to look out for riders, and hi-viz clothing helps in their recognition.
- Always ensure that you are wearing a hat that meets the current safety standards.
- Whenever you hack out, take a mobile phone with you, and make sure that somebody knows where you are going.

30 minutes of Three Short Schooling Sessions

The school, whether yours is indoor, outdoor or an allocated section of a field, is not the only place where you can train your horse. The variety and challenges of riding out can be used to bring fun, inspiration and new ideas into your schooling routine. Even if you've only 30 minutes to spare, work one of the following 10-minute programmes into your exercising, or work through all three during the course of a longer ride, to ensure your horse has had a thorough workout.

Safety

The most important consideration when schooling on a ride is that of safety. Let's begin with the rider. It cannot be said often enough that your riding hat must conform to current safety standards, and you must be visible to other road users, preferably with you and your horse wearing some form of reflective clothing.

Secondly, consider the character and performance history of the horse you are riding. If you know he is spooky, choose your area for schooling with care, ensuring it is somewhere he feels secure. If he is a youngster, consider riding out with another rider, and working on these exercises together where suitable. If the horse is lethargic in the school, you may see an entirely different side to his character when you begin your work in a more natural environment.

Choose where you work in the course of your schooling programme with care: bridleways of appropriate width, fields, private roads on which it is permissible to ride and footpaths are the safest places. You do not want to be in a location where cars or farm vehicles are likely to be a problem.

Finally, be sure you are aware of the condition of the surface on which you are riding. Changes resulting from different weather conditions are part of the novelty of riding out, and can be used accordingly; but take no chances, and if in doubt, remain in walk.

Whilst it is recommended that you carry a riding crop or schooling whip, don't use this for the first time on an unknown horse in an unrestricted space, and always use it with discretion.

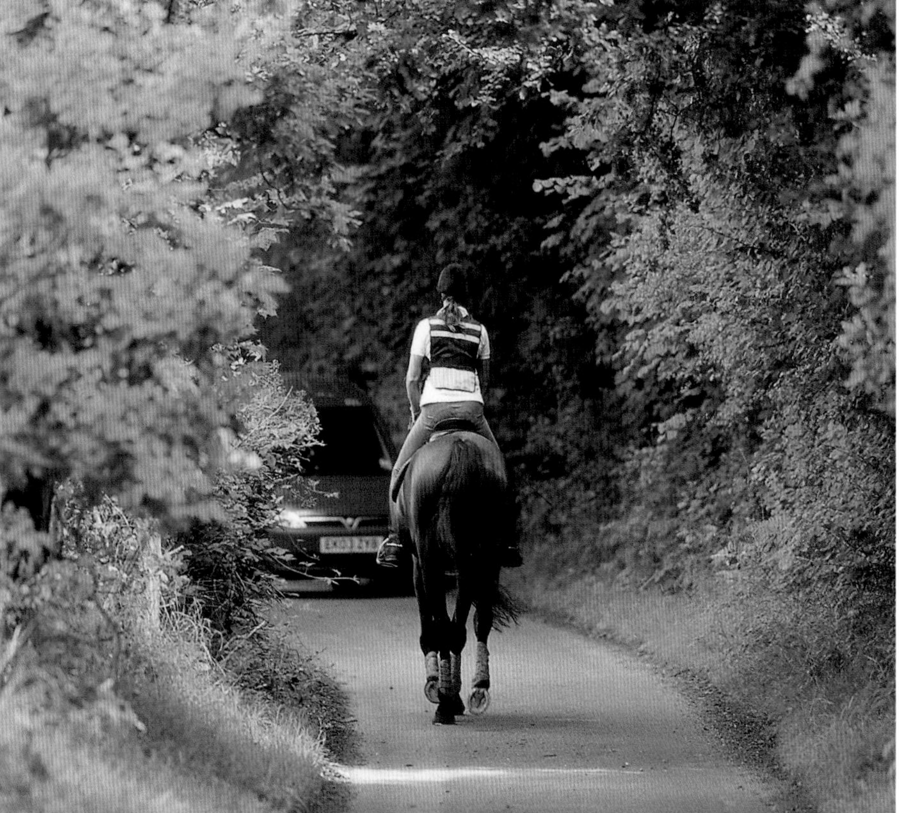

Ensure that you and your horse are wearing the appropriate safety gear when out riding, even if you are schooling on normally quiet roads.

Warming up

In the initial stages of your ride, allow your horse to walk forwards on a longer rein, stretching his neck (working long and low). If you have artificial lines along the roadside, use these to judge how straight your horse is going, and correct him accordingly. Introduce easy suppling exercises, flexing his neck gently to the left and to the right to loosen the neck muscles and the poll. When you feel he has loosened up and is relaxed, ask him to go forwards in a free-moving trot, still allowing him to carry his head long and low. Remember to change the diagonal regularly.

Once your horse has settled and is working forwards, relaxed and into your hands, try concentrating on your own balance for a bit. As you rise to the trot, allow your weight to drop down through your legs into your heels and remain 'standing' (although not standing on the stirrups) for as many strides as you can maintain a secure position. Try to gradually increase the number of strides that you can support your weight.

Now it's time to begin some work.

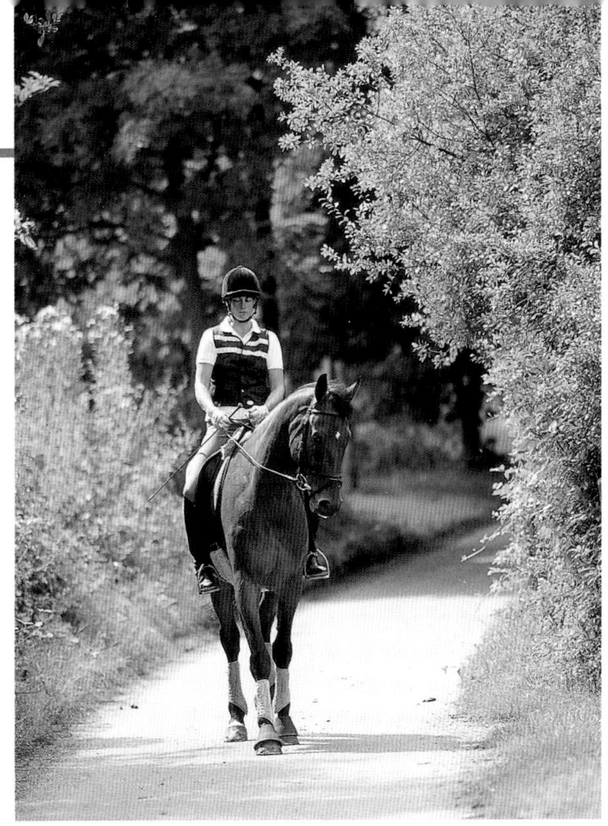

⇧ *Flex your horse gently to the left and to the right before you begin any more strenuous exercises.*

10 minutes work on impulsion

Focus on changes of pace to encourage your horse to become responsive to your leg aids, and use natural markers such as telegraph poles, fence posts or marks in the road to gauge distances. Begin by riding forwards into a halt. Make sure that it is square. Now ask your horse to walk forwards: you are looking for an immediate response to your leg aids, and if this is what your horse gives you, reward him with a pat. If not, bring him back to halt and then ask him again, using a slightly stronger leg aid. If this does not achieve the desired result, on the next attempt use your voice, and finally reinforce your aid with a tap of the schooling whip. If you do not achieve the response you are looking for, more work is needed but in an arena, and perhaps with the help of an instructor.

Once you have achieved a satisfactory walk to halt to walk transition, introduce trot, taking your horse up and down progressively through the paces. Vary the distance you travel in each pace: for example, from halt go forwards into walk. Walk for one gap between two telegraph poles, at the telegraph pole go forwards into trot for one gap between two poles, come back down to walk for the next gap, but then trot for two gaps the next time.

Next introduce changes within each pace by selecting two road or pathside markers and counting the number of strides your horse takes between them. Now come past them again and, squeezing your horse forwards whilst maintaining an allowing hand but not giving the reins away, try to reduce the number of strides between the markers. Finally, as an aid to collecting your horse, try to squeeze in an extra stride between the markers.

⇧ *Practise working on extension and collection by increasing or decreasing the number of strides your horse puts in between two given markers, such as a tree and a fence pole.*

10 minutes work on suppleness

Using the roadside, the grass verge, a hedge or similar as your guide, flexion exercises can help to increase your horse's suppleness. Choose your exercises according to your horse's abilities. Take it slowly and focus on establishing each step correctly before moving on to the next. If your horse masters a new movement in five minutes, leave it at that and move on to another exercise to give him time to absorb what he has learnt.

Once your horse has warmed up, flexing through his neck to left and right, begin by working on shoulder-fore, before progressing to shoulder-in.

If you can find a suitably safe track, work on both reins to ensure your horse does not begin to favour one rein. For the more advanced horse you could continue with work on renvers and travers.

When you are satisfied with your horse's performance, if you are working on a bridle path or track, and you have the space – 10–12m (33–40ft) is enough – use it to ride serpentines. Be sure to use your seat, leg and hand aids properly to ride your horse through the bends, and ride at least one straight stride before beginning the next bend. A suitable row of trees is another good place around which to practise serpentines.

Finish by leg-yielding from one side of the track to the other, then allow your horse to stretch long and low, and finally continue your ride.

Quiet lanes are perfect for practising shoulder-fore and shoulder-in.

Practise leg-yielding from one side of the track to the other.

CLARIFYING FOOT POSITION AND BEND

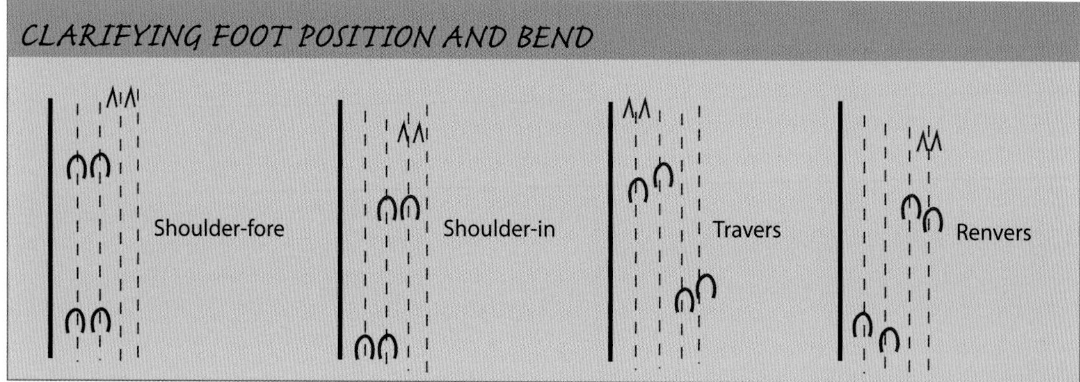

10 minutes to work on collection

The natural enthusiasm that most horses have when riding out can be harnessed to aid collection. Begin by riding forwards into a good, square halt, preferably using direct transitions from trot, or, for the more advanced horse and in a suitable place, from canter. Now ask your horse to make two or three strides of rein-back, but no more. Initially ask him to go forwards out of the rein-back in walk, then you could ask him to do it in trot.

Now find an appropriate marker such as a telegraph pole or tree and, using it as your guide, ride a turn on the haunches. If possible you can use the proximity of a fence or hedge to discourage your horse from stepping backwards.

Finally put all three movements together. Ride your horse forwards into halt; then ask him for a few strides of rein-back; ride forwards into trot, but then make a progressive transition back to walk; halt at the next marker, and ride turn on the haunches. Repeat on the opposite rein in the opposite direction if safety considerations allow.

HOW TO RIDE TURN ON THE HAUNCHES

Ride a transition to halt. With your weight on the inside seat bone, flex your horse in the direction you will be travelling. Position your inside leg close to the girth to encourage the horse forwards, and also to prevent the inside hind leg from stepping to the inside. Your outside leg also maintains impulsion and is used to create the bend and keep the hind leg stepping forwards under the horse's body. The inside rein leads the horse into the turn, the outside rein prevents too much bend, and gives to allow the horse to turn.

➪ *Use a telegraph pole or tree as a marker to practise turn on the haunches.*

Acknowledgments

I would like to thank the following people for the considerable help they have given me in completing this book.

Locations, models and horses!
Meryl Doran, the liveries and their horses at The Old Stables, Godden Green, Sevenoaks, Kent

For their help on photographic shoots:
Charlotte Mahoney and Jo Balsys

For their assistance with:

The 30-minute massage
Alison Nye of Equitherapy
Alison set up her company in 1998 having trained as a human sports therapist and with Mary Bromiley. She has since completed the Advanced Equine Body Worker programme.
To contact Alison telephone 07880 948562

The 30-minute mane and tail make-over; and 30-minutes to competition ready
Sam Gardener
Sam Gardner produces and trains at her yard in Kent, where, whilst mainly top class showing, she also has dressage and show jumping clients. Since she began national competition at the age of 10 she has won many country and county shows and major championships. She is also a panel show judge. She is passionate about the production of fit and healthy horses and to teaching others how to turnout their horses to their best advantage. Sam can be reached on 07793 820395

The 30-minute clip
Nancy Harker BHSAI, ABRS
Nancy has been clipping professionally for the last 20 years and clips on average 5 horses each day, five days a week in the south eastern regions of England. She can be contacted on 07984 413548.

30 minutes to solve your handling problems; and Spend 30 minutes long-lining
Richard Maxwell
Contact Max via his website www.richard-maxwell.com or Nicky on 01440 702327

Groundwork Games
Richard Marriott
National Equine Ethology Centre
P O Box 2233
Wrexham
LL11 0AY
(0)870 0781254
www.EquineEthology.com

The 30 minute workout and 30 minutes of better schooling
Julian Marczak
Julian is Chairman of the Association of British Riding Schools, a classical trainer and co-author of 'The Principles of Teaching Riding'. Previously co-proprietor of Suzannes' Riding School, Harrow. Julian now runs a training / livery yard in West Sussex and may be contacted on 07885 585814.

The 30-minute rider workout
Jason Crow BSc (Hons) Sport Science
Personal trainer and exercise coach based in Kent, working in corporate and private arenas. For more information visit www.advancedexercise.co.uk or telephone 01227 283791.

From Groundpole to upright in 30-minutes
Instructor, Helen Anderson and Tracey Tapsell

30-minutes to tackle scary fences
International 3-day eventer, Chris King

Index